About This Book

Why is this topic important?

The workplace learning and performance (WLP) profession continues to grow and change. Some mark the launch of the profession with the beginning of the American Society for Training and Development (ASTD) over sixty years ago. Throughout these sixty years, many people contributed to the foundation of the profession. These early trainers broke new ground and developed the underpinnings of the profession, leading the way for the rest of us; they explored new frontiers and challenged us to stretch; they provided us with a vision for the future. This book gathers the favorite activities from ninety of these master trainers in one place.

What can you achieve with this book?

This book offers you a selection of ninety of the best activities from ninety world-class trainers—trainers who are steeped in experience and expertise. Those of us in the training field are grateful for the generosity of these stellar trainers, names that you know: Bell, Bellman, Blanchard, Booher, Chang, Crum, de Bono, Brody, Herrmann-Nehdi, Kaye, Kirkpatrick, Kouzes, Masie, Nelson, O'Mara, Phillips, Pike, Robinson, Scannell, Silberman, Stolovitch, Thiagi, VanGundy, and Zenger are some of the talented trainers who have shared their best activities with you. Draw on their expertise and implement several of the activities to enhance your next training sessions. Your success is guaranteed.

How is this book organized?

The book is divided into two sections and sixteen chapters. Section One, "Training and Consulting Topics," includes twelve of the sixteen chapters. Each chapter represents a specific training topic: change management; coaching, mentoring, and feedback; communication; conflict and collaboration; creativity; customer service; diversity and differences; leadership; organizations and process improvement; self-management; solving problems and making decisions; and teamwork. In many instances the activities may be used for a variety of training topics, even though they are located in one specific chapter. The activities are presented as complete and ready-to-use designs for working with groups: facilitator instructions, lecturettes, handouts, and participant materials are included. Section Two, "Training Tools and Skill Development," represents two broad areas of interest to trainers, speakers, and others in the WLP field. Chapter Thirteen, "Trainer and Speaker Skills," presents three activities to assist WLP professionals enhance their presentation skills. Chapters Fourteen through Sixteen include a collection of twenty-seven generic training tools that can be adapted to any session, including icebreakers, closing activities, and transfer tools. All will enrich your training designs.

About Pfeiffer

Pfeiffer serves the professional development and hands-on resource needs of training and human resource practitioners and gives them products to do their jobs better. We deliver proven ideas and solutions from experts in HR development and HR management, and we offer effective and customizable tools to improve workplace performance. From novice to seasoned professional, Pfeiffer is the source you can trust to make yourself and your organization more successful.

Essential Knowledge   Pfeiffer produces insightful, practical, and comprehensive materials on topics that matter the most to training and HR professionals. Our Essential Knowledge resources translate the expertise of seasoned professionals into practical, how-to guidance on critical workplace issues and problems. These resources are supported by case studies, worksheets, and job aids and are frequently supplemented with CD-ROMs, websites, and other means of making the content easier to read, understand, and use.

Essential Tools   Pfeiffer's Essential Tools resources save time and expense by offering proven, ready-to-use materials—including exercises, activities, games, instruments, and assessments—for use during a training or team-learning event. These resources are frequently offered in looseleaf or CD-ROM format to facilitate copying and customization of the material.

Pfeiffer also recognizes the remarkable power of new technologies in expanding the reach and effectiveness of training. While e-hype has often created whizbang solutions in search of a problem, we are dedicated to bringing convenience and enhancements to proven training solutions. All our e-tools comply with rigorous functionality standards. The most appropriate technology wrapped around essential content yields the perfect solution for today's on-the-go trainers and human resource professionals.

Pfeiffer *Essential resources for training and HR professionals*
www.pfeiffer.com

90 World-Class Activities by 90 World-Class Trainers

Elaine Biech

Editor

BICENTENNIAL
1807
WILEY
2007
BICENTENNIAL

John Wiley & Sons, Inc.

Pfeiffer™

Published by Pfeiffer
A Wiley Imprint
989 Market Street, San Francisco, CA 94103-1741 www.pfeiffer.com

For additional copies/bulk purchases of this book in the U.S. please contact 800-274-4434.

Pfeiffer books and products are available through most bookstores. To contact Pfeiffer directly call our Customer Care Department within the U.S. at 800-274-4434, outside the U.S. at 317-572-3985, fax 317-572-4002, or visit www.pfeiffer.com.

Pfeiffer also publishes its books in a variety of electronic formats. Some content that appears in print may not be available in electronic books.

Library of Congress Cataloging-in-Publication Data

90 world-class activities by 90 world-class trainers / Elaine Biech, editor.
    p. cm.
  ISBN-13: 978-0-7879-8198-3 (pbk.)
  ISBN-10: 0-7879-8198-2 (pbk.)
  1. Employees—Training of. 2. Organizational change. I. Biech, Elaine. II. Title: Ninety world-class activities by ninety world-class trainers.
  HF5549.5.T7A15 2007
  658.3'124—dc22
                          2006026760

Acquiring Editor: Martin Delahoussaye
Director of Development: Kathleen Dolan Davies
Developmental Editor: Susan Rachmeler
Production Editor: Nina Kreiden

Editor: Michele D. Jones
Manufacturing Supervisor: Becky Carreño
Editorial Assistant: Julie Rodriguez

Printed in the United States of America

Printing   10 9 8 7 6 5 4 3 2 1

For Shane and Thad,
two world-class kids

—Elaine Biech

Contents

Section 2: Training Tools and Skill Development   283

Chapter 13: Trainer and Speaker Skills   285

Chapter 14: Tools for Trainers   299

Presenting . . .

90 World-Class Activities by 90 World-Class Trainers

Who's in This Book?

Ninety of the best trainers in the world have contributed to this collection. My primary objective for compiling these activities is to ensure that the best of the past is preserved for the future. I believe we have accomplished just that. This book presents ninety favorite activities from ninety world-class trainers.

Who is world class? World-class trainers are trainers who have not only experience but also expertise. How do you know if someone has expertise? Expertise is proficiency in a skill or knowledge in a particular field. Expertise is what you know as well as what you *do* with what you know. It is based on the contribution you make to a field and the respect you garner from the members of that field. Experts are asked for advice, they give advice, and they are paid for advice.

The National Speakers Association (NSA) has written a white paper titled "The Expertise Imperative." (This paper is free at the NSA website, www.nsaspeaker.org.) The research categorizes six levels of expertise. Ranked from lowest to highest, they are

- A perceived authority
- An educator and interpreter
- A contributor in the field
- Someone sought after by others
- A counsel and mentor
- Someone with longevity or consistency

So what do experts do? They write books—lots of books. They write articles for magazines and journals. They appear as expert witnesses and rate others' work. They serve as mentors and coaches. They consult. They conduct workshops, speak at conferences, serve on panels, and teach classes. They design coursework. They conduct research. They hold copyrights. The world-class trainers who have contributed to this book do all of that and more.

I am humbled by what these world-class trainers have accomplished. Read the short bio sketches after each of the activities, and you will be amazed at what these contributors have done—and, in most cases, are still doing.

The world-class trainers presented in this collection have written and edited almost eight hundred books—and still counting! They have written more than thirty-seven hundred articles and chapters. Several contributors are members of the HRD Hall of Fame. Eight contributors have been ASTD presidents and almost 75 percent have served on national professional boards such as ASTD, NSA, ISA, ISPI, and others. They have received hundreds of awards from many organizations. They have served as Malcolm Baldrige judges and have been honored by well-known magazines and journals; they advise some of the largest private and public organizations in the world. They have trained millions of participants, have presented at thousands of conferences, have designed thousands of courses, have taught thousands of classes, have led and continue to lead hundreds of successful businesses, and have had national as well as international best-sellers.

But read between the lines. World-class trainers *give*. They give back to their professions and their communities. They give to the profession by writing, speaking, mentoring, and coaching others. They give to the community by volunteering in the education system and supporting local volunteer organizations. They serve on environmental, historical, and alumni committees. They share their knowledge with youth, provide pro bono work for nonprofit organizations, create scholarship funds, and mentor new trainers and consultants in the field. Training is a profession that gives a great deal of satisfaction to its members; *world-class* trainers find ways to give back to both the profession and the world. I hope this inspires you to give to your profession and your community, too.

A world-class book would not be truly world class unless it contained contributions from all over the world. Contributions come from *every* continent—even though we needed to provide some warm-up assistance for Antarctica. (See Pole R. Bear's submission.) In addition to those from the United States, contributors come from Canada, Germany, India, Japan, New Zealand, Peru, Poland, Saudi Arabia, South Africa, Sweden, and the United Kingdom.

So who are these stellar trainers? Names you know. Names you rely on every day. Here's a tease—just a sample of names you will recognize:

- Geoff Bellman, wise and warm consultant and author
- Marjorie Blanchard, cofounder of the Ken Blanchard Companies
- Dianna Booher, world-renowned communication author and speaker
- Tom Crum, aikido master and conflict management guru
- Edward de Bono, prolific worldwide authority on creativity
- Beverly Kaye, international best-selling author of *Love 'Em or Lose 'Em*
- Don Kirkpatrick, creator of the Four Levels of Evaluation
- Jim Kouzes, best-selling international author of *The Leadership Challenge*
- Elliott Masie, internationally recognized futurist and e-learning guru
- Bob Nelson, the "guru of thank you" and author of *1001 Ways to Reward Employees*
- Bob Pike, trainer extraordinaire and model for most trainers—around the world
- Dana and Jim Robinson, performance consulting leaders
- Mel Silberman, scholar, authority, and author on active learning
- Thiagi, the master of games and simulations
- Jack Zenger, authority on organizational change and leadership development

The list goes on and on. To each of these ninety world-class trainers I say thank you for sharing your best with the rest of us.

What's in This Book?

Ninety activities that have been conducted by the best trainers in our profession are all gathered here. Most of the activities were developed by the trainers who submitted them; in some cases, trainers have given credit to colleagues or others from whom they acquired the idea. The activities are presented in two sections.

Section One: Training and Consulting Topics

The first section is a collection of sixty-one activities geared toward specific workshop or seminar topics. Within the section, activities are grouped by topic into chapters, which are arranged alphabetically. Within each chapter, the authors are listed alphabetically. Be aware, however, that many of the activities cross over to topics in other chapters. For example, the activities in the conflict and collaboration chapter may also meet your needs for a communication activity. Activities in the leadership chapter may be appropriate in a change management session you may be conducting.

The twelve chapters are "Change Management"; "Coaching, Mentoring, and Feedback"; "Communication"; "Conflict and Collaboration"; "Creativity"; "Customer Service"; "Diversity and Differences"; "Leadership"; "Organizations and Process Improvement"; "Self-Management: Time, Meetings, and Values"; "Solving Problems and Making Decisions"; and "Teamwork." A description of each of these topics precedes the activities.

Section Two: Training Tools and Skill Development

The second section represents two different areas. The chapter titled "Trainer and Speaker Skills" is aimed specifically at helping trainers and speakers improve their skills. These three activities could easily have appeared in Section One, but they have been placed in this section because of their audience: you.

The remaining three chapters, "Tools for Trainers," "Icebreakers and Energizers," and "Closure: Reviewing Content and Transferring Knowledge," are a collection of twenty-seven generic training tools that can be adapted to any session you may be conducting.

So what might you find in this book? Many oldies but goodies, all favorites of our stellar contributors. Here's a sample:

- Have you ever used Bingo as an icebreaker? Ed Scannell, the original creator of the Bingo icebreaker, presents a model.
- Wondering how to help your clients understand the importance of clarifying values? Jim Kouzes shares Credo Memo, one of his favorite activities for helping leaders identify their personal values.
- Need a tried-and-true process improvement activity? Richard Chang, a recognized guru on the topic, shares Process Improvement in Action, one that he uses in his workshops.
- Have you ever been a part of the Peter Block activity in which everyone takes part in arranging a conference room so that it is more conducive to learning? (Imagine five hundred people rearranging chairs in a convention center room!) Phil Grosnick has shared this activity as one of his favorites.

- Looking for a team-building activity that covers everything? Mary Wacker reached back a quarter of a century to submit an activity originally conducted by Geoff Bellman and Forest Belcher at a 1981 ASTD national conference. It's still as good as it was the day it was designed.
- Need something for a diversity workshop? Julie O'Mara has revised and updated her signature Diversity Crossword Puzzle.
- Have a client who needs to examine customer service? You won't want to miss Bill Rothwell's activity—lots of involvement, lots of learning.
- Want to read about an activity that looks like so much fun you want to force-fit it into anything you are doing? Try Arthur VanGundy's Tell Me Why. Although located in the creativity chapter, it could be used in other situations. For example, I will be using an adaptation as an afternoon energizer in an interview skills workshop.

The list goes on. You will find exciting yet practical activities every time you open this book. I hope that you enjoy using this book as much as I have enjoyed compiling it for you.

Elaine Biech
ebb associates inc

Expressions of Gratitude

Many world-class people helped make this book the best collection of our time.

First and foremost, the contributors to this book—the world-class trainers—all ninety of them, who took the time to share their favorite activity with me. You are all so busy with all that you do for your clients, your students, the profession, and the world in general. Thank you for seeing the value in this project. I am humbled by your generosity. Your activities will inspire all who follow you.

Martin Delahoussaye, editor, thank you for your ingenious idea for this book.

Cat Russo, ASTD, I am grateful for your willingness to share this publication with the members of a world-class society.

Lorraine Kohart, ebb associates inc, I am indebted to you for your diligence, deliberation, and decisiveness. Dan Greene, I am blessed to have your support.

Susan Rachmeler, developmental editor, my appreciation for your ability to simplify the difficult, correct the wrong, and create order from chaos. You are truly a world-class editor.

Nina Kreiden, production editor, one of the most caring editors in the world. I am delighted that we were able to work together again.

Section 1

Training and
Consulting Topics

## Chapter 1

Change Management

Change—the reason most of us are in business. Whether you are a consultant who assists organizations in implementing corporation-wide changes, a trainer who helps employees change how they are performing, a coach who guides individuals through personal growth changes, or one of a host of other change agents, the topic du jour is change.

Although the topics for this book have been listed in alphabetical order, I couldn't have planned for a better topic as the first chapter. The ability to change is the single most important element of successful organizations today. Planning for change, implementing change, having a positive attitude toward change, and understanding the reasons for change are actions that all of you are involved in every day.

Change management isn't easy. It is an all-encompassing task that requires you to understand all the forces affecting the decision for change. This includes external forces, such as customer expectations and competitor strategy; internal forces, such as employee involvement and leadership skill; and environmental and global impacts as well. Although the topic is huge, you can plan for and address all the forces that you know will position your clients and yourself for a better future.

A quick glance at the objectives of the first four activities of this book shows you how well they will meet your needs for addressing change.

As I mentioned in the second paragraph, I couldn't have planned for a better topic as the first chapter. Further, I couldn't have planned for a better activity to lead off this chapter and the book as a whole. Phil Grosnick shares an activity created by Peter Block that I have observed on several occasions. The activity forces participants to examine the personal choices they make and the results that accrue due to their choices. I've been a part of the discussion that follows. This activity may very well be one of the best ever designed. We are all fortunate that Phil chose to share it with us. What a way to begin this book!

Peggy Hutcheson shows us a practical way to increase stakeholders' awareness of what they have to gain from a change and how to surface and address resistance. Muralidhar Rao (India) takes us through a lively exercise that allows the participants to experience the impact of change and learn how to cope with it. Joanne Sujansky leads us to respond constructively to people's hot buttons. Doesn't this list of possibilities make you want to jump up and create some chaos so that you can address the change with one of these activities?!?

Managing change and, moreover, assisting others in managing change are daily challenges that bring with them powerful responsibility. They are neither easy nor often appreciated, and they are usually expensive. Unfortunately, the alternative—failing to recognize the need to change—is far more costly and is rarely an acceptable choice.

Choosing Structure to Fit Intentions

Submitted by Phil Grosnick

Objectives

- To demonstrate the influence of the physical space we occupy on how we operate within it.
- To place choice and accountability in the hands of those participating in a meeting.
- To provide an opportunity to deal with the tension between choices people make that is always part of any change effort.

Audience

Any size audience can participate, although very small groups (fewer than 6) may provide less creativity and fodder for discussion.

Time Required

45 minutes, including discussion, and it can be open-ended:

- 5 minutes to set the context and give the instructions.
- 5 minutes (or 10 if you prefer) to rearrange the room.
- 5 minutes for reflection.
- The remainder for discussion.

Materials and Equipment

- Flip charts may be helpful to present the questions for reflection and discussion, but are not required.

Area Setup

Until this activity is introduced, the room should remain set up in its default (initial) arrangement.

Process

1. Present the context for the activity. Say,

   What we do in this room is a metaphor for what we do in the "larger room" of our workplace. If there is no change in this room today, there will be no change in that room tomorrow. The design of a room is the visible expression of the kind of learning and community we plan to create. We are mostly unconscious of the influence of physical space on how we operate. The space we occupy has usually been designed by someone else. It is an example of what the default culture has passed on to us. In every change effort, we are asked to examine the legacy of the default culture to decide whether it suits our current intentions.

2. Provide instructions to the participants by saying, "Take the next 5 minutes to rearrange this room and your place in it to better fit your intentions." Allow about 5–10 minutes for this step.

3. Once the participants have completed the task, say, "Now take some time to reflect on how the room has changed and what meaning this has for you. Even if you are now in the exact same place as you were in the beginning, your choice to stay put has meaning. Take 5–10 minutes to reflect on these questions" (posted on a flip chart):

   - What did you do with the freedom handed to you?
   - How did you respond to the ambiguity of the assignment (especially in the moment of confusion or void as the exercise first began)?
   - What changed in the room?
   - Is the room any less structured now than it was before?
   - What was the impact/effect on

     - Energy?
     - Ownership?
     - Emotions?
     - Involvement?
     - Role of leadership?
     - Sense of community?
   - What was your intention?
   - How did the way you managed the exercise reflect the way you manage your life right now?

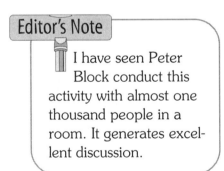

Editor's Note

I have seen Peter Block conduct this activity with almost one thousand people in a room. It generates excellent discussion.

4. After 5–10 minutes of reflection, collect thoughts and insights with open-ended questions to the participants.

5. Provide concluding remarks that transition to your next topic.

 nsider's Tips

- This is *not* a good first exercise. Let the group members get to know each other first. The early afternoon of day one or the morning of day two works well.
- Resist the urge as the facilitator to reduce confusion or provide more instruction. Let the group do its own thing.
- Even if the furniture is fixed and cannot be rearranged, people can rearrange themselves to better fit their intentions.

Source

This exercise was created by Peter Block and is an integral part of Designed Learning's workshop Building Accountability and Commitment. This exercise is also published in the participant manual for the Building Accountability and Commitment workshop.

Phil Grosnick is president of Designed Learning, Inc. His mastery of consulting skills has been central to the growth of Designed Learning. He has led Designed Learning in refining and adapting workshops to keep pace with the changing marketplace. Through his guidance and competence, Flawless Consulting, the well-known concept based on the book *Flawless Consulting,* by Peter Block (Pfeiffer, 1999), has reached all categories of organizations and all parts of the world. Phil's expertise is in successfully navigating the day-to-day problems facing staff groups making the transition to consulting units. In addition to leading Designed Learning's management team, Phil provides consulting and training for Designed Learning client companies to support their commitment to developing ownership and responsibility at every level. His work with clients affirms the belief that the person is central to the success of every organization. He is personally committed to living out the values he teaches, including authentic relationships, the confrontation of difficult issues, and the belief that courage and compassion are essential to optimum organizational performance.

Phil Grosnick
Designed Learning, Inc.
9949 Orchard Hills Road
Jacksonville, FL 32256
Phone: 904.519.5626
Email: info@designedlearning.com
Website: www.designedlearning.com

Benefits and Risks

Submitted by Peggy G. Hutcheson, Ph.D.

Objectives
- To increase awareness of what stakeholders have to gain from a change or a new program.
- To surface resistance so that it can be addressed (if appropriate).
- To provide participants with an opportunity to establish ways to maximize the benefits and minimize the risks of change efforts.

Audience
This works with groups up to about 30 and can be adapted for any size group. Participants work in teams of 5–6.

Time Required
45–60 minutes, depending on discussion time.

Materials and Equipment
- Flip chart and markers for each team of five to six people.
- Handout (or workbook page if part of a workshop) to capture key points.
- Instructions—either on the handout or on a slide.

Area Setup
Table groups with flip chart, stand, and markers for each.

Process
1. Prior to the session, identify the stakeholders. For example, if you use this activity for a mentoring program or a coaching training, the stakeholders are the person being mentored (or coached), the mentor (or coach), the manager of the person being mentored (or coached), and the organization.
2. If the group has fewer than twenty participants, assign one stakeholder group to each team to identify the benefits and the risks of the new initiative for that stakeholder group. For larger groups, you can assign benefits to one team and risks to another for each stakeholder group.

3. Tell the teams that they are to brainstorm as many potential benefits and risks as possible in the next 15 minutes. Tell them to write these on the flip charts as they identify them and to be prepared to report to the full group.
4. After the brainstorming period, have each team report out to the larger group.
5. Lead a discussion on how to maximize the benefits and minimize or mitigate the risks.

Insider's Tip

- Be careful to keep the discussion realistic. Avoid leading the group toward the conclusion that the benefits will eliminate the need to pay attention to potential risks. This isn't true, and participants should not leave the activity with this assumption.

Peggy G. Hutcheson, Ph.D., is president of the Odyssey Group, Inc. She works to help organizations manage and develop talent, with a focus on mentoring, coaching, and career and leadership development in business, government, and nonprofit organizations.

Peggy G. Hutcheson, Ph.D.
The Odyssey Group, Inc.
1708 Peachtree Street NW, Suite 525
Atlanta, GA 30309
Phone: 404.943.0313
Email: p_hutcheson@odysseygroupinc.com
Website: www.odysseygroupinc.com

Change—But Don't Drop the Customer

Submitted by Muralidhar Rao, B.Tech, PGDM,
with Max Rodrigues, M.Sc., LL.B, Dip Ind'l Mgt.

Objectives

- To experience the benefits of the team's adhering to a process.
- To experience the impact of change in the environment and to learn how to cope with it.

Audience

12–25 participants, divided into 2–4 teams with 6–10 team members on each team. Each team must have an equal number of team members.

Time Required

60–90 minutes, depending on the number of teams.

Materials and Equipment

- Six tennis balls or plastic balls of the same size for each team.
- One small plastic bucket to collect the balls for each team.
- One scoring sheet for each team.
- Flip charts or whiteboard with scoring sheet drawn.
- Markers.
- Six different-size balls or marbles for each team (optional).

Area Setup

Use the center of the training room if the seating arrangement is U-shaped. This activity can also be conducted outdoors if weather permits.

Process

1. Divide the group into teams and have them sit in a circle with the bucket off to one side. There should be an arm's-length distance between team members.
2. Brief the teams on the objective of the game and the rules. Explain that each team will play six periods and that each period lasts for 2 minutes. The goal is to have as many completed rounds as possible during each period. A completed round is defined as one ball passing through the hands of *every* team member and being placed in the plastic bucket by the last team member. The

rule of passing is that a member cannot pass the ball to either of his or her immediate neighbors. Every member has to receive the ball once and pass it within a round (except the last member, who places it in the bucket). Repetitions are not allowed. If the ball is dropped by any member, it is counted as a drop, and the ball is out of play.

3. Explain the scoreboard on the flip chart or whiteboard.
4. Invite the teams to practice the game with only one ball being used at a time.
5. Give the teams 3 minutes to set the target for the number of completed rounds of the ball in 2 minutes and also to estimate the maximum number of drops during the 2 minutes. Tell them they must work out the sequence of passing the ball to complete a round. (See the diagram for the correct sequence.)

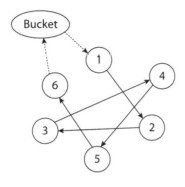

Even number of team members   Odd number of team members

6. On the flip chart, note the targets for the first period as given by the teams. Start the first period by handing the ball to the first person of each of the teams.
7. Call time at the end of 2 minutes. Record the scores of completed rounds and drops for the first period.
8. For the second period, add two more balls so that three balls are simultaneously in play. Repeat Steps 5 through 7.
9. For the third and fourth periods, add three more balls so that six balls are in play simultaneously. Repeat Steps 5 through 7. (Optional: play a fifth and sixth period with six additional dissimilar balls.)
10. Have the teams return to the large group and conduct the debriefing, asking these questions:
    - How was the target set?
    - Did you underestimate your potential? Why?
    - Did you overestimate your potential? Why?

- Did everyone understand the process? Was their understanding checked?
- Was the methodology for exceeding or achieving the target for the completed rounds discussed? (Or did the team jump into action without doing this?)
- Did the methodology include how to minimize or avoid drops?
- Did the team invest in time after a cycle to analyze performance and adherence to the methodology? Did the analysis lead to action and improvement in subsequent cycles?
- What was the team's reaction when I introduced additional balls (change in rules of the game)?
- Did the team recognize the need to modify the methodology? Was it effective?
- How are the balls analogous to customers in real life?
- What role does change play in this activity?
- What lessons do you take away from this activity?

 # Insider's Tips

- You may use metaphors and tell teams that each round is the equivalent of a year in the industry. Tell them that each ball is a customer. A team's dropping a ball is tantamount to the inability to deal with the customer. It is not only the number of customers handled that matters but also the retention of customers.
- Constantly challenge the teams to set higher targets than the performance recorded in the previous cycle.

Muralidhar Rao, B.Tech, PGDM, is the president of NIS Sparta Ltd, a performance enhancement solutions company. Muralidhar has been a trainer for twenty-two years and specializes in programs for senior management teams, focusing on leadership, change management, team working, and managerial effectiveness.

Max Rodrigues, M.Sc., LL.B, Dip Ind'l Mgt., is a master trainer with NIS Sparta Ltd.

Muralidhar Rao, B.Tech, PGDM
NIS Sparta Ltd
G Block, 2nd floor DAKC
Khopar Khairane, Navi Mumbai
India
Phone: 0932.3966072; 0932.4604712
Email: mdr@nissparta.com

Scoring Sheet

Period	Number of Balls in Play Simultaneously	Targeted Number of Completed Rounds in 2 Minutes	Estimated Drops in 2 Minutes	Actual Number of Completed Rounds in 2 Minutes	Actual Number of Drops in 2 Minutes
1	1				
2	3				
3	6				
4	6				
5	6 + 6 balls (different size and material)				
6	6 + 6 balls (different size and material)				

Hot Buttons

Submitted by Joanne G. Sujansky, Ph.D., CSP

Objective

- To practice responding constructively to people's "hot buttons" as a way of influencing their participation in a common goal or activity.

Audience

Unlimited number of small groups of 4–6.

Time Required

30–45 minutes.

Materials and Equipment

- A flip chart and markers for the facilitator.
- Paper and pencil or pen for each small group.
- A set of Hot Buttons cards (copy and cut from the master handout).

Area Setup

Small group breakout areas within a larger space, or a table for each small group.

Process

1. Discuss the concept of "hot buttons" with participants as follows: effective influencers analyze their listeners' point of view. Influencers attempt to determine what makes their listeners "tick." You are influencing your listeners by
   - Addressing their problems, opportunities, hopes, and fears.
   - Considering the benefits and disadvantages, *from their perspective,* of your proposal.
2. Ask group members to form small groups of four to six. Distribute one Hot Button card to each group.
3. Direct each group to take 10 minutes to list the "hot buttons" of the audience described on the assigned card. Remind the groups to identify (a) the problems and opportunities for their audience; (b) the hopes and fears of their audience; and (c) the benefits or disadvantages, from the audience's perspective, of what the group is proposing.

4. List these three categories on a flip chart.
5. Explain to the groups that they will be sharing the results of their list with the entire group. Ask them to appoint a scribe for recording answers.
6. At the end of 10 minutes, ask one member of each small group to read the audience description aloud to the entire group and then report the potential hot buttons that his or her group identified.
7. At the completion of the discussion, debrief the activity by asking why the skill of influence is important in getting others to work with you.
8. Remind them that, as leaders, they should be considering hot buttons when influencing others. Unless employees are given a sense of the vision—the ultimate goal of an initiative or need for change—and where they fit in, they are going to respond with fear, denial, resistance, stubbornness, anger, resentment, suspicion, ambivalence, and withdrawal. It's critically important that leaders share the vision with employees. Having a vision—and communicating it—can make the process easier.

   Explain that people don't see the value in changing if they feel the change has no value for them. When faced with a change, people can't help but ask the question, "What's in it for me?" If someone tells employees why a change has value to them, that might help them accept and, in fact, make the required change or participate constructively, whatever the initiative.
9. Ask what hot buttons participants anticipate facing. Ask how they will use what they learned in this activity to address these hot buttons.

 **Insider's Tip**

- My experience has shown that participants are better able to give attention to what the hot buttons might be when they are not actively focused on their current workplace issues. However, should you wish to add scenarios that are workplace focused, consider the following:
  - Persuading managers to cut their budget to sustain the business.
  - Persuading employees to take on new responsibilities for which they are not yet trained.
  - Persuading employees to work longer hours to meet identified customer demand.

Source

This activity was published in my book *Activities to Unlock Leadership Potential* (KEYGroup, 2005).

Joanne G. Sujansky, Ph.D., CSP (Certified Speaking Professional), has over twenty-five years of experience helping leaders increase organizational growth and profitability. A member of the National Speakers Association, she holds the organization's highest earned designation, Certified Speaking Professional. She is also past national president of ASTD and recipient of ASTD's honorable Gordon M. Bliss Memorial Award.

Joanne G. Sujansky, Ph.D., CSP
KEYGroup®
1800 Sainte Claire Plaza
1121 Boyce Road
Pittsburgh, PA 15241
Phone: 724.942.7900
Email: jsujansky@keygroupconsulting.com
Website: www.keygroupconsulting.com

Hot Button Cards

Persuading a budget committee to invest in new equipment or computer technology	Persuading members of a professional organization to get more involved in growing and expanding the organization
Persuading a group of potential investors to provide capital for your business venture	Persuading a group of concerned citizens to approve an environmental waste incinerator in their community
Persuading a group of elderly community residents that an increase in school taxes is essential	Persuading a group of business colleagues to volunteer their time for a community project
Persuading local corporations and business owners to give money to a charity	Persuading the school board to require high school students to volunteer 100 hours of public service before graduation
Persuading the human resource department to include a gym membership as a company benefit	Persuading city council members to prevent the destruction of a 100-year-old landmark

## Chapter 2

Coaching, Mentoring, and Feedback

Whether your participants are just starting their careers or have a great deal of experience, they will require advice and ideas for personal development. Coaching, mentoring, and feedback are each different processes: long term versus single opportunity; personal versus career; sage advice versus guidance; continual learning versus reaction. Each has its own twist, but all are focused on individual development.

"Imagine you have an opportunity to spend 30 minutes with the undivided attention of some person whom you have admired." Thus starts Beverly Kaye's activity in this section. So go ahead. Whom would you choose? Beverly, author of *Love 'Em or Lose 'Em*? Kevin Daley, founder and chairman of one of the most successful communication training companies in the world, Communispond? Stephen Merman, a successful coach? Or perhaps Bob Nelson, the "guru of thank you" and author of *1001 Ways to Reward Employees*? Well, you can spend time with each of these world-renowned experts who have coached, mentored, and provided feedback to thousands of people around the globe.

Kevin Daley's submission is the most compassionate activity, and I hope that it will inspire you to give to your own community in some way. Bev Kaye's activity helps participants understand the value of networking and how to go about it. Steve Merman shares an elegantly simple adaptation for providing 360-degree feedback. And Bob Nelson shares what he does best with an activity that encourages participants to discuss the last time they were appreciated.

Categorizing activities is never a clear-cut process, so there have been several instances where I have debated with myself about where to place an activity. Peggy Hutcheson's activity, currently located in the change management chapter, is one of those. Although it is first and foremost about surfacing resistance to change, she suggested that it could be used in a mentoring situation. Therefore I mention it here.

Lifelong learners know the value of having a coach or a mentor (or both), encouraging feedback, and being an avid networker.

How to Be Impressive When Meeting Someone New

Submitted by Kevin Daley

Objectives
- To look at a person, eye to eye.
- To smile while being introduced.
- To shake hands firmly.
- To pronounce the person's name clearly when introduced.

Audience
Ideally kids ages 14, 15, and 16. There can be up to 20 per group.

Time Required
90 minutes.

Materials and Equipment
- Video camera and playback unit.
- Flip chart and markers or chalkboard and chalk.

Area Setup
Theater-style.

> **Editor's Note**
>
> This activity requires someone to video-tape the action. Two facilitators are best; however, you may ask one of the students to volunteer to assist you.

Process
1. Write the objectives on the board and refer to them as "the four steps" before the session.
2. Ask for a show of hands: "How many of you would like to make a good first impression when you meet a new person, especially an adult?" All will raise hands. If someone doesn't, ask the individual why.
3. Ask participants why they would like to make a good impression. Get a lot of input. This is an important step because it is at this stage that they commit.
4. Tell them they get only one chance to make a good first impression. Someone in the room will probably come up with that idea before you do. Fine. Build on it. "That's what we are going to learn how to do."

5. Explain the four objectives (the four steps) you have written on the board.

6. Develop a baseline videotape. Have each participant come to the front. Explain that you will introduce yourself to each one and that they should respond however they usually would. Have the second facilitator, or the volunteer student, videotape them consecutively. The students won't do well with the introductions, but that's okay; you're just creating a baseline. Try not to cue them in any way. That is, don't offer to shake their hands or smile unless they do it first.

7. After everyone has had a chance, ask the biggest student in the class to come to the front. Demonstrate the process by completing each of the four steps yourself. Then introduce yourself to the student and have him follow the four steps. He will probably botch each of the steps. Encourage him, praise him, and stay with him until he does it well. Ask the class what they observed. They will make fun of one another, but that's okay.

8. Have the participants pair off and select one of the pair to introduce himself or herself to his or her partner. Ask for feedback from the partners on each of the four steps, one at a time. They will be brutal in their feedback. Have the same student do it again. Repeat it four times. Then switch so that the other partner is in the "hot seat." Again, repeat the process.

9. Videotape the students' progress. Have each student come to the front individually while the second facilitator, or the volunteer student, videotapes the process. Begin by saying, "Hello, Mary. My name is Kevin Daley [use your name]. Thank you for stopping by." Mary then looks the instructor in the eye, smiles, shakes the instructor's hand firmly, and says, "How do you do, Mr. Daley." It won't be perfect the first time. So repeat it two, three, or four times. Get it perfect or close to it.

10. Praise each student with specific observations. Praise anything and everything that's good.

11. Play the baseline, the "before" tape, to the group. It will be awful, and they'll know it. But they like seeing it, and it dramatizes how good they look in the next tape.

12. Play the "after" videotapes back to the whole group with ample use of the Pause button so that you can highlight the good things. Praise, praise, praise. End with a round of applause.

 **I**nsider's Tip

- The key to this activity for this age group is to provide lots of encouragement and praise all along the way.

Source

For the last three years, my daughter Laura (who is a top-notch trainer) and I have worked in a special program for inner-city kids ages fourteen, fifteen, and sixteen. They are selected on the basis that they probably have the capability to go to college, but no one in their family has ever attended, nor do they see college in their future.

The sixty-four kids from four high schools spend three weeks during the summer at Sacred Heart University in Westport, Connecticut. They sleep in the dorms, eat in the college cafeteria, and go to class in college classrooms.

There are seven instructors. Laura and I teach "public speaking." It focuses on confidence building, interviewing skills, how to meet and greet, telling a story, and so on. This activity comes from that program. It changes lives more than I would have dreamed possible. It really lifts the kids. They stand taller, smile more broadly, speak up, and walk like they are going somewhere. And the skills don't seem to be taught anywhere in our standard education system.

Kevin Daley founded Communispond, Inc., in 1969. At that time he was a vice president and management supervisor for the J. Walter Thompson Company (JWT), the world's largest advertising agency. Effective presentations were the lifeblood of the advertising business, and Kevin was intent on creating a program to improve the presentation skills of the officers of JWT in order to make them more effective, dynamic speakers in front of any audience. The program was so successful that it was offered to clients and then to the business community at large. Since then, Communispond has grown into the largest company of its kind, a broad-based communications skills company offering programs in all areas of oral communications. Over 450,000 executives worldwide have graduated from Communispond programs. Kevin has personally trained sixty-two board chairmen, 320 company presidents, and thirty-one hundred sales managers. He is also a sought-after speaker, a former navy jet pilot, Fordham University graduate, and president of the Instructional Systems Association (a training industry group comprising 130 of the best-known training companies). Kevin is also the author of several top-selling business books, including *The Full Force of Your Ideas: Mastering the Science of Persuasion* (Communispond, 2004).

Kevin Daley
Founder and Chairman
Communispond
52 Vanderbilt Avenue
New York, NY 10017
Phone: 212.972.3865
Email: kdaley@communispond.com
Website: www.communispond.com

Admiration/Fantasy Exercise

Submitted by Beverly Kaye, Ed.D.

Objectives
- To develop the essential skills of networking.
- To have more productive conversations.

Audience
Any size. If the group numbers 15–20 or more, then break into smaller groups or pairs.

Time Required
30–40 minutes.

Materials and Equipment
- Paper and pencil or pens.
- Flip chart, flip-chart paper, and markers.

Area Setup
Any that allows participants to take notes.

Process
1. Begin the exercise by explaining to participants,

   Imagine you have an opportunity to spend 30 minutes with the undivided attention of some person whom you have admired. This can be someone who is currently alive, someone from history, someone long since dead, famous people, not-so-famous people, people from any walk of life. This is your choice. If you had 30 minutes to talk to someone, whom would you choose? Now, before you start coming up with that "who," let me tell you the criteria. Think of this in a networking—in a connection—kind of context. If you had 30 minutes alone with someone, why would you choose that particular person? What would you ask that person in 30 minutes? Because the real question is: What do you want to learn from that person?

2. Have participants answer the following questions:
   - With whom would you talk?
   - Why would you pick this person?

- What would you ask?
- What would you like to learn?

Give them a few minutes to reflect and make notes.

3. If working with a small group, ask each person to say whom they have selected and what he or she would like to learn from this person. If the group is larger, poll the pairs or small groups on whom they agreed.

4. Sum up the exercise by explaining how important it is to think about what we want from others—otherwise our requests are vague and nebulous.

5. Ask the participants to brainstorm what they feel are the essential skills of networking. You might hear answers like these:
   - Self-confidence
   - Honesty
   - Creativity
   - Assertiveness
   - Diplomacy
   - Good communicator
   - Good listener

6. Compliment the group on its list, and if no one has already said this, sum up the discussion by explaining that the two central skills of networking are *talking* and *listening.*

7. Ask the participants to raise their hands if they feel they are better at talking than they are at listening.

8. Now ask the participants to raise their hands if they feel they are better at listening than they are at talking.

9. Explain that total communication means using both listening and talking. We are usually better at one or the other. We often overutilize one and underutilize the other. The key to good networking is to strive for a balance between the two in order to maximize our effectiveness at building relationships.

 nsider's Tip

- This is a very simple exercise that I use to introduce a module on mentoring. It could probably also be used in a communications session.

Source

I published this activity in *The Art of Networking* (Career Systems International, a BKA Company, 1999).

Beverly Kaye, Ed.D., is founder and CEO of Career Systems International in Scranton, Pennsylvania, and one of the nation's leading authorities on career issues in the workplace. She is a highly regarded writer and speaker on talent management issues and author of the classic career development book *Up Is Not the Only Way* (Davies-Black, 2002), and is also the coauthor of the international best-seller on retaining talent, *Love 'Em or Lose 'Em: Getting Good People to Stay* (Berrett-Koehler, 2005), as well as the workplace satisfaction sequel, *Love It, Don't Leave It: 26 Ways to Get What You Want from Work* (Berrett-Koehler, 2003).

Beverly Kaye, Ed.D.
Beverly Kaye & Associates, Inc.
3545 Alana Drive
Sherman Oaks, CA 91403
Phone: 800.577.6916
Fax: 818.995.0984
Email: Beverly.Kaye@csibka.com
Website: www.careersystemsintl.com

360 Feedback

Submitted by Stephen K. Merman, Ed.D., PCC, CPCC

Objectives
- To receive group feedback from direct reports using 360 data.
- To speak as one voice to communicate developmental areas to a manager or supervisor.

Audience
Designed for a supervisor or manager and 8–12 direct reports.

Time Required
90 minutes with break.

Materials and Equipment
- One pad of Post-its for each participant.
- Three flip-chart stands with paper.
- Sharpies and felt-tipped pens.

Area Setup
Tables and chairs should be set up in a U shape.

Process
1. The manager or supervisor introduces the process and turns it over to you to fill in the details. Tell participants that they will provide feedback on what the group would like the leader to "stop doing," "be cautious doing," and "start or continue doing." Tell them they will brainstorm ideas in these three categories and then group the ideas and be prepared to report back in an hour. The leader leaves the room and returns one hour later to receive feedback.
2. Have individuals brainstorm behaviors in the three categories: "stop doing," "be cautious doing," and "start or continue doing." Tell them to write each idea on a Post-it.
3. Label three flip charts with the three categories. Have participants report out individually and post their notes on the appropriate chart.

4. Ask the group to cluster ideas around central themes.
5. Have the group summarize themes and determine feedback statements.
6. When the group is ready, ask the leader to return to receive feedback from the group.
7. Have the leader thank the group for its honest, candid feedback.
8. Inform the group of next steps—for example, how and when the leader will respond to the suggestions.

Editor's Note

Coach the leader prior to the session to accept the feedback positively. Suggest that the leader bring paper and pen to write some of the ideas—this sometimes creates breathing room when being bombarded with suggestions.

Insider's Tips

- Stay focused on positives. Make this activity nonthreatening and constructive.
- Have a note keeper agree to type the results and give them to the leader.
- Although this activity is not very creative, I find that it works very well.

Source
Beau Rezundes shared this activity with me.

Stephen K. Merman, Ed.D., PCC, CPCC, is currently the managing principal of Organization Consulting Group. His background includes being a professor of counselor education at the University of Colorado, manager of HR planning and development for Amoco Production Company, and faculty member with Amoco's Management Learning Center. He is active in ASTD and served as the organization's president. Steve has coauthored many ASTD publications on career management systems and assessments. Currently he is a member of the International Coaching Federation (ICF) and holds the Professional Certified Coach (PCC) designation from ICF.

Stephen K. Merman, Ed.D., PCC, CPCC
Organization Consulting Group
59 Lookout Mountain Circle
Golden, CO 80401
Phone: 303.526.3041
Email: smerman@earthlink.net

The Last Time You Were Appreciated

Submitted by Bob Nelson, Ph.D.

Objectives
- To allow people to reflect on their own experiences regarding recognition.
- To provide real examples from the group that serve as a foundation on which to build learning on the topic.

Audience
Any size.

Time Required
5–10 minutes.

Materials and Equipment
- None.

Area Setup
Can be used in any setting.

Process
1. Begin by stating, "We know from adult learning theory that people learn best when they start with something they already know. Therefore, think of the last time that you felt appreciated. What was said or done, who was present, how did it make you feel?" Tell them to be as specific as possible.
2. Tell the participants, "Once you have something in mind, turn to the person next to you and share that instance, then listen to his or her example." Suggest that they build on what the other person says and help draw out the example. Allow about 5–6 minutes.
3. After a while, ask if a few people in the room would be willing to share with the entire group.
4. After three people have shared, say, "We already have some learnings: first, no one mentioned money. I've done this activity hundreds of times across the country, and no one ever mentions money. Second, few if any of the items

that were shared even require money. The conclusion is that feeling valued and appreciated is more a function of how you are treated by those you work with whom you hold in high regard than the number on your paycheck."

 ## Insider's Tips

- Have fun with this and with the group. Give them a copy of *1001 Ways to Reward Employees* to reward their participation!
- This activity always works, and I find it can be used with other topics as well— for example, "Think of a time you took initiative and were successful" or "Think of the best boss you ever had," in which case I'd use a flip chart to capture common themes from various respondents.

Source
I believe I created this activity!

Bob Nelson, Ph.D., "the guru of thank you," is president of Nelson Motivation Inc. in San Diego, California, and the best-selling author of *1001 Ways to Reward Employees* (Workman Publishing Company, 2005), now in its second edition with 1.5 million copies sold, and *The 1001 Rewards & Recognition Fieldbook: The Complete Guide* (Workman Publishing Co., 2002), among others.

Bob Nelson, Ph.D.
Nelson Motivation Inc.
12245 World Trade Drive, #C
San Diego, CA 92128
Phone: 858.673.0690
Email: bobrewards@aol.com
Website: www.nelson-motivation.com

Chapter 3

Communication

We've all been communicating since we were born. With all that practice, we should be good at it, right? Right. In fact, all of us could use some improvement in our communication skills. Communication continues to be the key to success, whether between employees and supervisors, customers and suppliers, parents and children, husbands and wives, or any of a dozen other relationships we have. Yet in survey after survey, communication continues to top the list as something that needs to be improved. The late, great Peter Drucker advised us that over 60 percent of all management problems result from faulty communications.

This section offers a star-studded lineup of individuals who share their favorite communication activities—ways to improve communication skills. You will find many places to use these eleven activities: build them into training sessions for any topic, use as quick activities when coaching a manager, use them as a part of a team-building intervention, or even try them out with your teenagers at home.

Leading the list of activities is one by Dianna Booher, author of over forty books—most of them about communication. She introduces a well-used standby. A variation of this activity was also submitted by Bob Pike, a trainer who is known around the world. Both submitted the activity that introduces three truths and a lie. If you are one of the few trainers who have not used this activity, try it soon; it always works. Marjorie Brody and Suzanne Adele Schmidt both share energizing activities related to communication styles. Debra Dinnocenzo shares an activity to help us understand the challenges of communicating with geographically dispersed team members. A picture is worth a thousand words, and Deborah Dumaine describes a brief yet practical activity that you can use to demonstrate the concept.

In case you would like to plan a little "quiet time" into your communication session, both Jaime Galvez (Peru) and Agnieszka Niziol-Kaplucha (Poland) submitted activities that require participants to remain silent during the activity. Both are high energy and lots of fun. Kristina Gow (Sweden) shares a role-play opportunity around the serious subject of dealing with domination by others. Delving into her expertise with the Herrmann Brain Dominance Instrument (HBDI), Ann Herrmann-Nehdi presents a way to introduce participants to the skill of using metaphors in communication. Elliott Masie's activity may look similar to those in the conflict and collaboration chapter of this book; however, read the nuances of this brief but powerful activity, and you will see that it is communication based.

Communication skills continue to be an integral part of almost any training, coaching, or consulting assignment. Whether you are looking for ideas to help others become better communicators or to improve your own communication skills, the combined expertise of the individuals in this chapter will most likely provide answers for you. Between them, the eleven have written almost one hundred books. Check them out.

The Truth Be Known

Submitted by Dianna Booher, CSP, CPAE

Objectives
- To introduce communication and interpersonal skills.
- To create an experiential foundation for discussing communication skills.
- To create an opportunity to get to know other participants.

Audience
Any size, divided into subgroups of 4.

Time Required
20–25 minutes for the small groups; 5–20 minutes to process—depending on your purpose.

Materials and Equipment
- Paper and pencil for each participant.

Area Setup
Whatever arrangement you have will work as long as each group of four can have a separate space.

Process
1. Ask each participant to write four facts about himself or herself, one of which is a lie. Tell them not to share with anyone.
2. Have participants form groups of four and find a location in the training room, but away from the other groups.
3. Ask one participant to begin by saying, "My name is _____, and four facts about me are . . ."
4. For the remainder of the first person's turn (about 2 minutes for each person), the small group asks questions about the facts that were stated. The group members' objective is to determine which of the "facts" is really a lie by asking questions of the participant. The participant's objective is to lie convincingly to prevent the group from discovering the false statement.

5. After 2 minutes, call time on the questioning and have the other three participants discuss the responses to their questions. Tell them to reach consensus
and make one guess from the group as to which is the lie. Have the first participant reveal whether or not they are correct.
6. Repeat this for each participant in each small group. Allow about 2 minutes to
question each participant and about 1–2 minutes for the group to "talk it
over" and reach consensus.
7. After all the small groups have completed four rounds, bring them together as
a large group. Use the following questions to debrief:
   - How many of you stumped your group?
   - If you could tell when someone was lying, why wasn't that person convincing with the lie?
   - How did you determine the lie?
   - How many groups found it easy to come to consensus?
   - What does this tell us about communication?
8. Transition by saying, "You as a team have just used most of the key skills in
communication: listening, questioning (using both open and closed questions),
gathering data, reading body language and vocal tone, drawing conclusions,
making assumptions, and being persuasive with your team. These are the
same skills that will make you an *effective communicator!*"

 nsider's Tip

- Allow the small groups to move to the corners of the room, as the activity can
become noisy.

Source

I'm sure this takeoff on *To Tell the Truth* gives away my age, but the activity is
energizing and helps participants get to know each other better, thus setting the
stage and building trust for future activities. We use this well-worn but always effective activity to introduce our communication/interpersonal skills course.

Dianna Booher, CSP, CPAE, is the author of more than forty books and has been published by Simon & Schuster/Pocket Books, Warner, McGraw-Hill, Prentice Hall, HarperCollins, and Thomas Nelson. Her latest books include *Speak with Confidence! Powerful Presentations That Inform, Inspire and Persuade* (McGraw-Hill, 2002); *E-WRITING: 21st-Century Tools for Effective Communication* (Pocket Books, 2001); *Communicate with Confidence!* (McGraw-Hill, 1994); and *Get a Life Without Sacrificing Your Career* (McGraw-Hill, 1996). Several have been major book club selections. Her work has been published in sixteen foreign editions and is also widely available on audio, video, and online courseware (WBT and CBT).

Dianna Booher, CSP, CPAE
Booher Consultants, Inc.
2051 Hughes Road
Grapevine, TX 76051
Phone: 817.868.1200
Fax: 817.318.6521
Email: dianna_booher@booher.com
Websites: www.booher.com
        www.howyouwrite.com
        www.booherdirect.com

Learn to Drive a Motorcycle—with *Style*

Submitted by Marjorie Brody, CSP, CMC, PCC

Objective
- To demonstrate that people with different behavioral styles want to be taught differently.

Audience
Any size, but the participants first need to have taken a behavioral style assessment.

Time Required
15 minutes.

Materials and Equipment
- None.

Area Setup
Any.

Process
1. Begin this activity after you have introduced the behavioral or social style instrument you used (for example, the DISC assessment).
2. Have all the individuals of a similar style move into one corner of the room. For example, if you are using the DISC, the D's would go to one corner, the I's to a second corner, and the S's and C's to the last two corners.
3. Give the assignment: "Pretend that someone is going to teach you how to drive a motorcycle. How would you like to be taught?"
4. Give them 3 minutes. If the groups are very large, tell them to have their discussion in groups of five.
5. Ask each group to share the way members want to be taught.
   - Typically the D group will respond, "Tell me how and let me do it myself."
   - The I group often doesn't complete the assignment because they are so busy talking. They do say that they don't need much detail: they want to get on the road and do it.

- The S group wants an explanation, wants someone sitting with them, and will want to practice in the parking lot.
- The C group wants to read the instruction manual. They want to understand how the gear shift works, and so on. They wouldn't think of driving on the road until they have a thorough understanding and have practiced in a parking lot.

6. After each group has commented, complete a debrief. Ask how their preference for learning affects how they manage people, mentor others, prefer to spend their time, and make decisions. Bring the discussion back to the purpose of the training program.

 nsider's Tips

- Make it fun. You can tease each group.
- Manage the time. People typically like to spend more time, and I don't know that it warrants more.
- Always come back to the purpose of the activity.

Marjorie Brody, CSP, CMC, PCC, an executive coach and professional speaker, is the author of more than eighteen books, including *Career MAGIC: A Woman's Guide to Reward & Recognition* (Career Skills Press, 2004). She was one of Pennsylvania's "Best 50 Women in Business" and is the only professional worldwide to obtain the combined CSP, CMC, and PCC titles. Marjorie has had the privilege of serving such diverse clients as Microsoft, Pfizer, New York Life Insurance Company, and Johnson & Johnson. She is the founder and fearless leader of Brody Communications Ltd.

Marjorie Brody, CSP, CMC, PCC
Brody Communications Ltd
815 Greenwood Avenue, Suite 8
Jenkintown, PA 19046
Phone: 215.886.1688
Email: mbrody@brodycommunications.com
Website: www.brodycommunications.com

Hello! Hello! Can You Hear Me Now?!

Submitted by Debra A. Dinnocenzo, M.A.

Objective

- To help learners understand the challenges of and solutions to communicating effectively with a team of geographically dispersed members.

Audience

A team that is typically geographically dispersed, but has been brought together for this session or activity.

Time Required

20–30 minutes.

Materials and Equipment

- None.

Area Setup

Space to move around and to work in pairs.

Process

1. Introduce the activity by explaining, "This brief activity will help you understand the challenges we face and some of the frustrations we experience in communicating with team members when people are in different geographical locations. We'll also identify some of the keys to successful communications that are essential to a distributed team's ability to work well from a distance."
2. Divide the group into pairs. Ask each pair to sit back-to-back and discuss a problem, issue, or opportunity currently facing the team. If a particular need or situation is being addressed by the team or as part of the meeting or training event, assign this topic for pair discussions. Otherwise, ask the pairs to identify a problem or issue for discussion.
3. To bring more structure to this simulated "distance" discussion, provide the following discussion guidelines for this interaction (you may wish to post these on a flip chart):

- Agree on purpose and importance.
- LISTEN!
- Avoid monologues.
- Summarize frequently.
- Confirm understanding.
- Agree on actions or follow-up.
- Limit discussions to 10 minutes.

4. After the pairs have completed their discussions, reconvene in the large group and discuss the learning that occurred from this activity. Focus this debrief on the importance of listening in the communication process, noting, for example, that without the listening component, what's communicated is not heard and communication is not accomplished. Tailor the learning points to the needs of the group, and use the following questions to prompt insights from the participants:

- Did you accomplish the objective of mutual understanding and agreement to action?
- How did you use the discussion guidelines to achieve the objective?
- What might have happened without a structured process for this discussion?
- What would have been different if you could have seen each other during the discussion?
- Did not seeing each other affect the outcome?
- How can you clearly indicate you're listening during a distance discussion?
- What are some of the obstacles presented by distance discussions, and how can you overcome them?

Variation

If you prefer, you can introduce this activity with the meeting room lights either off or very dim. You can also ask participants to turn their chairs and face away from you during the introduction. If you use this option, debrief the introduction by saying, "Clearly, you heard what I was saying to introduce this activity. However, you couldn't see me." Then ask the following questions:

- Did it matter that you couldn't see me?
- Was all the information conveyed regardless of your ability to see me?
- What made it less comfortable not seeing me?
- Why would we prefer to see each other?
- How can we become more comfortable conveying information in spite of not seeing each other?

Debra A. Dinnocenzo, M.A., is a published author with a unique approach to the effective marketing of her books. When Debra published her first book, *101 Tips for Telecommuters* (Berrett-Koehler, 1999), she met the marketing and promotion challenge head-on by establishing a highly successful virtual model for book publicity. The virtual PR model was employed again to support the publication of a second book coauthored by Debra, *Dot Calm: The Search for Sanity in a Wired World* (Berrett-Koehler, 2001). Debra brings to book marketing success the book marketing expertise she utilizes herself, along with a wealth of experience in marketing, sales strategy, and collateral product development and sales.

Debra Dinnocenzo, M.A.
Book Marketing Success
10592 Peny Hwy., Suite 310
Wexford, PA 15090
Phone: 724.940.1051
Fax: 724.940.1052
Email: info@bookmarketingsuccess.com
Website: www.bookmarketingsuccess.com

Picture That

Submitted by Deborah Dumaine

Objectives

- To practice improving visual design to clarify written communication.
- To see logical organization expressed visually in more than one way.
- To understand that text is often not the best way to explain concepts.

Audience

Best with 3 groups of 4–5 learners (12–15 total).

Time Required

10 minutes.

Materials and Equipment

- Three pieces of flip-chart paper, or the equivalent amount of space on a whiteboard.
- Two to three different colored markers for each group.
- An untitled, unformatted paragraph (roughly twenty lines long) written by you. The paragraph should be one block of text, in narrative form, and should include some geographical content specific to your business. Use such details as streets, cities, states, names of buildings, names of companies, and specific addresses. For example, you could write a paragraph that:
  - Describes sales opportunities in different parts of a large city.
  - Compares activities at distribution centers throughout the city.
  - Evaluates potential new office locations in your city.

Area Setup

If you are using flip-chart paper, learners will need enough table or wall space to work.

Process

1. Deliver the following lecturette:

   Today's readers are drowning in a sea of information. Most managers read or write a million words a week. What is the role of graphic depiction in writing?

   - *To summarize information in a visual*
   - *To clarify ideas for the reader*
   - *To make complex concepts more accessible*

   Many writers don't think about document design—they simply write paragraphs. Incorporating visual elements, such as charts, pictures, and color, more effectively engages the reader and simplifies concepts. For example, think of a time when you had to assemble something. If the directions didn't include pictures, they were probably difficult to follow.

2. Divide learners into teams of four or five individuals and give each team flip-chart paper (or space on a whiteboard), markers, and a copy of the draft paragraph.

3. Tell teams that they are to turn the prose into a visual representation. Tell them to discuss how to reorganize the paragraph visually so that it makes more sense.

4. Have each team appoint one member to sketch out its new design on flip-chart paper or whiteboard, clearly indicating which kind of information goes where.

5. Facilitate discussion as teams present their solutions to the whole group. Ask the groups to vote on the best solution and discuss why it works.

6. Debrief with these questions:
   - What did you learn from this exercise?
   - How can you transfer what you learned back to the workplace?
   - What might you do differently in the future?

 nsider's Tips

- Learners do not need to rewrite the paragraph—just sketch out their reorganization with an example or two. You will find that learners get really engaged by this exercise. The activity generates an amazing number of possible solutions and is a great way to stimulate creative thinking.
- Learners might rewrite the paragraph as
  - A map
  - A graph, chart, or table
  - An outline
  - A bulleted or numbered list

Deborah Dumaine and Better Communications® (BC) have improved the corporate writing of ninety thousand people since 1978. Deborah is the author of *Write to the Top: Writing for Corporate Success* (Random House, 2004) and the *Instant-Answer Guide to Business Writing* (iUniverse, 2003), and wrote *Harvard ManageMentor*'s business writing section. Deborah pioneered her firm's proven writing process, which helps clients write 30–50 percent faster and improve the quality of their documents.

Deborah Dumaine, President
Better Communications
1666 Massachusetts Avenue
Lexington, MA 02420
Phone: 781.862.3800
Email: ddumaine@bettercom.com
Website: www.writetothetop.com

Mute Instructions

Submitted by Jaime Galvez

Objective

- To use an energizing and creative process to introduce the components of communication.

Audience

Up to 12 participants.

Time Required

10–20 minutes.

Materials and Equipment

- Communication slides or content posted on a flip chart.
- Flip chart.
- Markers.
- Paper and pencils.

Area Setup

Chairs should be pushed aside so that center is clear.

Process

1. Introduce the elements of communication. (Refer to the figure for examples of slides.)
2. Ask for a volunteer to help demonstrate nonverbal communication. Have the participant direct his or her team to form a machine. However, the volunteer must do this without speaking. He or she may use the flip chart, markers, and other resources to convey the message.
3. Once the machine is formed, tell the team members they all are to "move," making the noise of that machine. Each participant must act out his or her part or section of the machine. They each will also make the sound of that corresponding part. Have the machine start to operate (and to move if applicable, as in the case of a vehicle).

4. Debrief the exercise with the following questions:
    - What happened? What did you observe?
    - Why do you think that occurred?
    - How does this relate to communication?
    - What happens if one of the parts of the machine is not working with the other parts? How is this similar to communication?
    - How will you communicate differently as a result of this activity?

Insider's Tip

- This is particularly useful when you are discussing the components of communication and need to energize the group at the same time.

Jaime Galvez was born in Cajamarca, Peru, where he lived until the end of high school. After one year of studies in psychology at Lima University, he departed to the United States to pursue his studies. He attended Pasadena City College, where he graduated with an A.A. degree in business management. Jamie also acquired a certificate in advanced bookkeeping at a business school in Los Angeles. Jaime currently works for Yanacocha/Newmont as a senior trainer delivering bilingual courses on interaction skills development.

Jaime Galvez
Minera Yanacocha
AV. Camino Real 348
Torre El Pilar Piso 10
Lima 27
Peru
Phone: 51.7.6884000
Email: Jaime.galvez@newmont.com

Sample Slides

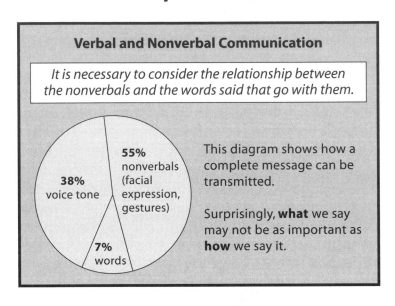

Verbal and Nonverbal Communication

It is necessary to consider the relationship between the nonverbals and the words said that go with them.

55% nonverbals (facial expression, gestures)

38% voice tone

7% words

This diagram shows how a complete message can be transmitted.

Surprisingly, **what** we say may not be as important as **how** we say it.

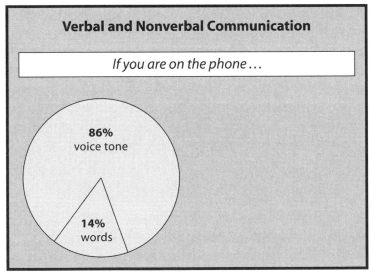

Verbal and Nonverbal Communication

If you are on the phone …

86% voice tone

14% words

Domination Identification

Submitted by Kristina Gow

Objectives
- To be conscious about the methods of domination.
- To identify specific instances and examples of domination techniques.
- To discuss ways to deal with domination.

Audience
For the best results, the size of the group should be 15–20 participants.

Time Required
2–4 hours.

Materials and Equipment
- Flip chart.
- Markers in a variety of colours.

Area Setup
The room should be arranged with four or five tables for group work.

Process
1. Deliver the following mini-lecture:

   Berit Ås, a professor from Norway, has identified and defined the five most common "techniques of domination." She focused the perspective on the techniques being used by men against women. They can, however, also be used with a focus on how people, both men and women, treat each other. Sometimes, we even use these techniques ourselves without thinking they will hurt anyone.

   The five techniques of domination are
   - *Invisibility. You are forgotten, run over, or not treated with any real interest.*
   - *Ridiculing/belittling. You are made fun of.*
   - *Withholding information. You don't get the information you need.*
   - *Dual punishment. It doesn't matter what you do; whatever it is, it's wrong.*
   - *Creating shame and guilt. This is both ridiculing and dual punishment.*

   Write the five methods on the flip chart as you describe each.

2. Ask participants if they have ever experienced any of the five techniques and if they have any questions.
3. Divide the participants into work groups of four or five participants each.
4. Have them discuss each technique and provide an illustrative example of each type of domination. Tell them they will have about half an hour.
5. Ask each group to create a role play about one of the techniques. Identify a given technique for each group to work with. Ensure that as many techniques will be modelled as possible. Use these instructions to clarify:
   - Ask them to develop a role play that illustrates something that can happen in reality.
   - Someone should be treated badly and will not be able to stand up for herself or himself.
   - State that after the role plays, the group will discuss what someone could do in that type of difficult situation.
   - During the role play, participants should consider both verbal and nonverbal communication.
   - Players should choose names other than their own.
   - The role play should be only 3–6 minutes long.
6. Ask if there are any questions. Then tell the group that they will have 30–40 minutes to plan their role play before presenting to the larger group.
7. When the groups are ready, present the people in the role plays by asking their new names and inviting them to start. When the role play is finished, lead an applause.
8. After each role play, facilitate a dialogue about what happened by asking questions such as these:
   - Can this happen in reality?
   - How do you think this person feels?
   - What can she or he do in this situation?
   - Could anybody else in the situation have reacted differently?
   - Do we use this technique ourselves without knowing it?
   This could be discussed in the large group or first in pairs. The time spent on each role play should be about 20 minutes.

9. Continue through the rest of the role plays in the same way. After each is completed, finish the exercise by summarising what participants have discussed and what they have learned from this exercise. Ask how they anticipate using what they have learned.

10. Afterwards, it is nice to have a positive short poem or story to read for the participants.

 nsider's Tips

- This exercise is best used by a group whose members know each other—for example, people who work together.
- It is good to start with a positive exercise, perhaps a warm-up—for example, about friendship.
- If you have not worked with role plays before, I recommend that you read a book with more instructions than are included here.
- If you are familiar with the forum play method (which comes from Augusto Boal, Brazil) you can use that method instead of role plays.

Source

The methods of domination have been published in books, magazines, and brochures. The exercise itself, however, was created by me and has not been previously published.

Kristina Gow works with pedagogic leadership, diversity, gender, and ethics and has written a book for teachers about how to talk to teenagers regarding identity, relationships, and HIV/AIDS. All Kristina's courses use a variety of dialogue methods—for example, values clarifications, creative exercises, role plays, and forum play.

Kristina Gow
Wisdom Education
Trollyckan 4, S-471 60 MYGGENÄS
Sweden
Phone: 0046.70.5627855
Email: kristina.gow@visdom.se

Metaphorically Speaking

Submitted by Ann Herrmann-Nehdi

Objectives

- To provide a unique and powerful way to allow participants to go beyond a superficial introduction in a training setting.
- To learn to use metaphor in a practical application to share and communicate more effectively.
- To introduce the differences that make each of us unique.

Audience

Any size. If the group is large, have the participants share in small groups. If there are fewer than 10–15 participants, they may share with the total group.

Time Required

10–40 minutes, depending on the number of participants and the process—small group process (shorter) versus individual sharing with total group (longer); allow 2–3 minutes per person.

Materials and Equipment

- Toys or playful objects.
- Any object the participants have with them (keys, calendar, phone, pen, wallet, or others).
- Work-related objects easily available (pens, paper clips, CD, mouse pad).
- Paper and pens or pencils for participants.

Area Setup

Display the objects around the room.

Process

1. Ask everyone to select an object that interests them or intrigues them. Do not explain why at this point.
2. Ask participants to play with or explore the object and write down its attributes (at least three: colorful, shiny, hard, soft, moving parts, worn, new, and so on).

3. Next ask participants to "connect" the three attributes to *who they are* as a person.

    "I am like [the object] in that/because _____.

    Example: "I am like this Slinky in that I am flexible, yet I have a core structure that keeps me in line."

4. Have participants "introduce" themselves to others and explain the connections.

Insider's Tips

*   This is a surefire way to get people opening up very early in a program and sharing traits and aspects of their personalities. I have used it for twenty years and never had it backfire. It works well with people who do not know each other at all or with intact groups where people already know each other.
*   The use of metaphor allows participants to easily convey or depict aspects of themselves that they may not normally verbalize in an introduction.

Ann Herrmann-Nehdi is CEO of Herrmann International, publisher of the Herrmann Brain Dominance Instrument (HBDI), which is based on extensive research on thinking and the brain. Multiple applications of whole-brain technology include creativity, strategic thinking, problem solving, management and leadership, teaching and learning, self-understanding, communication, and team and staff development. Ann seeks to apply the principles of whole-brain technology to her varied responsibilities: from day-to-day operations to sales to workshop design and presentations. Having resided in Europe for thirteen years, Ann brings a global perspective to the company. Since joining Herrmann International USA nineteen years ago, Ann has expanded the network of international offices to sixteen, spanning Europe, the Pacific Rim, and Latin America. Her personal goal is to promote better understanding of how individuals and organizations think and become more effective, as well as to enhance learning and communication technologies worldwide through the application and development of the whole-brain concept.

Ann Herrmann-Nehdi
Herrmann International
794 Buffalo Creek Road
Lake Lure, NC 28746
Phone: 828.625.9153
Email: ann@hbdi.com
Website: www.hbdi.com

Open Their Fists

Submitted by Elliott Masie

Objectives
- To demonstrate how language can lead a group down a path.
- To loosen up a group and create some safe physical contact and laughter.

Audience
I have used this in a group as small as 9 and as large as 10,000.

Time Required
3 minutes.

Materials and Equipment
- Just your voice and your hands.

Area Setup
Any.

Process.
1. Ask participants to pair up. They may turn to their neighbors, or you can use any other creative way you choose.
2. Ask them to pick one person to be A and one person to be B.
3. Ask the person who is A to make a fist and to place it in front of the other person.
4. Tell B that they have 16 seconds, without drawing blood (due to insurance regulations), to open the fist of A.
5. Say, "Ready, set, go," and call time at 16 seconds.
6. Ask the following questions:
   - How many used force or violence?
   - How many used tickling?
   - How many bribed with money?
   - How many just requested that the person open his or her fist?

> **Editor's Note**
> Most people will answer with the first three, and only a few with the last.

7. Point out that this group of professionals all (or mostly, depending on people's approaches) took the *more complicated* and *conflict-based* approach.
8. Then take responsibility for the fact that *your language* led them there ("Make a fist," "without drawing blood").
9. Explain how language can lead us down a path. For example, if someone says, "I need to have a course on this," we start talking about a course. In contrast, if someone says, "How do we help them learn this?" we begin thinking of many other options.

 nsider's Tip

- Keep it fast and keep it light.

Source

I learned this activity from the master of creative and humorous activities, Dr. Joel Goodman, head of the Humor Project in Saratoga Springs, New York.

Elliott Masie is an internationally recognized futurist, analyst, researcher, and humorist on the critical topics of technology, business, learning, and workplace productivity. He is the editor of *Learning TRENDS by Elliott Masie,* an Internet newsletter read by over forty-six thousand business executives worldwide, and a regular columnist in professional publications. He is the author of a dozen books, including the recently authored free digital book *701 E-Learning Tips* (Webcite, 2004). He is the host of Learning 2006, a new global conference. Elliott heads the MASIE Center, a think tank in Saratoga Springs, New York, focused on how organizations can support learning and knowledge within the workforce. He leads the Learning CONSORTIUM, a coalition of 191 Fortune 500 companies (including JPMorganChase, Target, UPS, National Security Agency, McDonald's, Sears, Bank of America, and the U.S. Departments of Defense and Labor) cooperating on the evolution of learning strategies.

Elliott Masie
The MASIE Center
P.O. Box 397
Saratoga Springs, NY 12866
Phone: 518.587.3522
Email: emasie@masie.com
Website: www.masie.com

Line Up!

Submitted by Agnieszka Niziol-Kaplucha

Objectives
- To introduce a communication module or activity while at the same time providing an energizer for the learners.
- To improve communication or to build teamwork.

Audience
Very effective for a group of 8 to 15. If the group is larger, divide into smaller subgroups.

Time Required
Average time is 15 minutes for the activity and 30 minutes for observing the film and processing the event.

Materials and Equipment
- Blindfolds (bandanas) for every participant.
- Cards with numbers on them.
- Video camera (optional but highly recommended).

Area Setup
A large, safe open space: if outdoors, a large lawn; if indoors, a large area without furniture or a hallway.

Process
1. Before your session, create a set of numbered cards starting with 0, then 1, 2, and so forth so that you have enough for every participant.
2. Invite participants to select a card and to memorize it. Tell them to remember their number, but not to tell anyone else.
3. Invite participants to gather in the designated place. Ask them to spread around the designated area so that they are not all in one space and there is no one who is far away from the group.

4. Tell participants that from this moment until the completion of the task they are not allowed to produce any vocal sound. Coughing, hemming, murmuring, and other such sounds are forbidden as well.

5. Distribute the blindfolds and ask everyone to put them on. Tell them that their assignment is to line up in order according to the numbers each selected from the card deck. You will most likely hear some moaning, so remind them that the speech restriction is still valid.

6. Videotape the activity. Pay attention to the body language used by the participants despite their being blindfolded, observe with your camera what causes the communication chaos, what means of communication the participants develop, and other pertinent discussion points. Pay special attention to the person with number 0.

7. When the task is completed, let the participants remove the blindfolds and say their numbers aloud in order starting with 0.

8. Return to the training room to debrief the exercise. Show the video made during the exercise. Allow for laughter. Then discuss how they managed to accomplish the task. Ask questions such as these:
   - What *effective* communication techniques were used?
   - What communication techniques were ineffective in this situation?
   - What was difficult? What was easy?
   - How did you feel when I told you that you would be blindfolded?
   - What did you learn from this activity?
   - What can you take back to the workplace to implement?
   Add any other question based on the learning module that follows this activity.

Insider's Tips

- Before you introduce the exercise to the participants, ask if anybody suffers from claustrophobia. If there is such a person, ask the individual to be the observer.
- You may need to remind the participants to remain quiet and not produce vocal sounds.
- During the activity, observe and film the participants who have difficulties getting together with the group. Pay attention to the natural leaders of the group and their behavior.
- Be prepared with a box of Kleenex for tears of laughter!

Source

I have no idea of the origin of this activity. I got it ages ago from somebody during a conversation about training in general.

Agnieszka Niziol-Kaplucha is an independent HR development consultant helping organizations in Central Europe, Russia, and the Middle East improve the quality of people management. She has been in the business of adult education for the past fifteen years. She is the coauthor of a vocational high school curriculum on how to enter a job market, developed to help young adults adjust to the political and economic changes in Poland.

Agnieszka Niziol-Kaplucha
ANK Konsulting
Kadlubka 33a
Poland
Phone: 0048.22.6624920
Email: aniziol50@hotmail.com

Four Facts

Submitted by Bob Pike, CSP, CPAE

Objectives
- To encourage participants to learn something about each other.
- To introduce a variety of communication topics.

Audience
Any number, divided into groups of 6.

Time Required
20 minutes.

Materials and Equipment
- One copy of the Four Facts worksheet for each participant.
- Pencils.

Area Setup
Space for each group of six to communicate.

Process
1. Ask each participant to complete the top of the page, listing four facts. Three of the facts should be true about the person and the fourth false. Ask them not to share the facts.
2. Have participants list on their worksheets the names of the other participants in their small group.
3. Ask each group to complete the following steps, in order, one at a time. Have each person read the four statements in order aloud. As each person reads the four statements, the other participants should list next to his or her name the number of the statement they think is false about the person and why.
4. Once each person has completed sharing the statements, have the other five participants tell which statement is false and why. Then the person who shared the four statements reveals which one is actually false.
5. Do this for each of the participants in the group.

90 World-Class Activities by 90 World-Class Trainers

6. Conclude the discussion by asking the following questions:
   - Were you surprised at some of the "facts" that people shared? Which? Why?
   - How good were you as a group and individually at picking the false statement? What does this tell you about making assumptions and judgments about people?
   - Were some of the statements made by different people similar? What reasons can you give for this?
   - Were some of the facts quite different? What reasons can you give for this?

 ## Insider's Tip

- This activity can be used as an icebreaker, an energizer, or a team builder, or to introduce any number of different topics, such as communication, influencing others, communication style, judging, diversity, and others.

Bob Pike, CSP, CPAE, has well earned his reputation as "the trainer's trainer." He's been a trainer since 1969 and is most well known as the editor of the *Creative Training Techniques Newsletter.* He personally delivers consulting value and training keynote addresses more than 150 days each year. Bob has earned the rare Certified Speaking Professional (CSP) honor from the National Speakers Association and has shared his message with more than one hundred thousand people around the world. Bob received his CPAE (Council of Peers Award of Excellence) and was inducted into the Speakers Hall of Fame. Bob has served on ASTD's national board of directors. The new edition of Bob's *Creative Training Techniques Handbook* (HRD Press, 2005) is a best-seller with over one hundred thousand combined copies of all editions in print. He has written or edited over twenty books, including *50 Creative Closers* (Pfeiffer, 1998) and *One-on-One Training* (Pfeiffer, 1999), seminars, and training videos. His video by the BBC, *Creative Training and Presentation Techniques,* won the Best Business Video award from the Special Interest Video Association.

Bob Pike, CSP, CPAE
The Bob Pike Group
7620 West 78th Street
Edina, MN 55439
Phone: 952.829.1954
Toll-free: 800.383.9210
Fax: 952.829.0260
Email: bpike@bobpikegroup.com
Website: www.bobpikegroup.com

Four Facts

List four facts. Three should be true about you. One should be false.

1.

2.

3.

4.

List the names of your small group here. As each person reads his or her four statements, record the one you believe is false and why.

1. Name _____ Statement number _____ is false because

_____.

2. Name _____ Statement number _____ is false because

_____.

3. Name _____ Statement number _____ is false because

_____.

4. Name _____ Statement number _____ is false because

_____.

5. Name _____ Statement number _____ is false because

_____.

90 World-Class Activities by 90 World-Class Trainers. Copyright © 2007 by John Wiley & Sons, Inc.
Published by Pfeiffer, an Imprint of Wiley. www.pfeiffer.com

The Shape of Things to Come

Submitted by Suzanne Adele Schmidt, Ph.D.

Objectives

- To break the ice and warm up the group.
- To introduce the concept of typology when used in conjunction with MBTI, DISC, or another social or communication style instrument.

Audience

25 is an ideal size for this exercise.

Time Required

If 25 people, 20 minutes (5 minutes for setup, 5 minutes for discussion, 5 minutes for debrief, and 5 minutes to get people to and from their seats).

Materials and Equipment

- Signs (with the actual shape) for each shape to be posted around the room:
  - Box.
  - Triangle.
  - Rectangle.
  - Circle.
  - Squiggle.
- Ten copies of each of the five different shape description handouts (available at www.it-serve.co.uk/shapes), in envelopes.
- Prepared flip-chart pages with the shapes on one page and the discussion questions on another page.

Area Setup

Open space in the back of the training room with five shapes posted around the room. Place envelopes with copies next to the respective signs.

Process

1. Introduce this activity by giving some background as follows:

   "Dr. Susan Dellinger is the author and creator of the Psycho-Geometrics™ System, a unique method of analyzing human personality based on preferences for shapes. She developed this system in 1978 when she was human resource development manager

for General Telephone and Electronics Data Services. Her system has been presented to over a million people in twenty-two countries. We are going to draw on her shape typology today."

2. Say, "Here are the five shapes (refer to the prepared flip chart with shapes). Choose a shape that represents you at work. In just a moment, you will find your shape on the wall in the back of the room and group around the shape with others who have chosen the same shape."

3. Have participants form groups based on the shape they chose. Once they are in their groups, ask them to spend 5 minutes discussing the following questions you have posted on a flip chart:
   - Why did you choose the shape you did?
   - How does the shape represent you at work?
   - What is your best guess about the attributes of the shape that you have chosen?

4. Allow people a few minutes for gathering around the shapes and then give a signal to begin discussion. After the discussion, ask each group to report out. After each report-out, read a few lines of the description for each type, as follows:
   - Box—hard worker; dependable; detail oriented; loves to collect data; likes to work alone.
   - Triangle—interested in upward mobility; leadership type; energetic; task oriented.
   - Rectangle—a shape in transition; can't decide what shape it wants to be; exploring; takes risks.
   - Circle—interested in harmony; mission at work is to get people to feel good about themselves; pleasers and nurturers.
   - Squiggle—innovative and unique; tends to be disorganized; likes to have many things going at once.

5. Encourage participants to take a copy of the description of their type in the envelopes and to go online to take the inventory and learn more about Dr. Susan Dellinger and her work. Her URL, www.it-serve.co.uk/shapes, appears at the bottom of the handout.

6. You may wish to take a break after this activity. Although it is based on research, you will most likely have a number of disbelievers. Therefore, I recommend that you keep the activity less serious so that you do not take time and energy away from the rest of the session.

 **I**nsider's Tips

- I use this activity most often when introducing groups to the Myers-Briggs Type Indicator. If using it with the MBTI, introduce the concept of typology before doing this exercise. Otherwise introduce it as an icebreaker.
- As the author of this activity, I always choose a circle and this is confirmed when I complete the inventory as a circle. I recommend that you as the trainer complete the inventory before the training event so that you can speak about your experience with this.

Source

This activity is based on shape typology concepts developed by Susan Dellinger, Ph.D., though I do not believe it has ever been published.

Suzanne Adele Schmidt, Ph.D., is the cofounder of Renewal Resources, a consulting firm dedicated to the renewal and revitalization of individuals and organizations. She has spent the last decade of her work focused on helping others lead more balanced and productive lives at work. She is the coauthor of *Running on Plenty at Work: Renewal Strategies for Individuals* (Renewal Resources Press, 2003).

Suzanne Adele Schmidt, Ph.D.
Renewal Resources
18920 Falling Star Road
Germantown, MD 20874
Phone: 301.601.1990
Fax: 301.540.1990
Email: suzanne@renewalatwork.com
Websites: www.renewalatwork.com
         www.runningonplentyatwork.com

## Chapter 4

Conflict and Collaboration

What comes to mind when I say the word *conflict*? Arguments? Clashes? Discord? Anger? Disagreement? Hostility? Opposition? Contention? Distrust?

All of these are indeed aspects of conflict. But we shouldn't forget that conflict can also lead to clear understanding, healthy relationships, satisfying resolution, win-win solutions, and creative processes.

Conflict is natural in any situation. It is neither good nor bad. It just is. There isn't a question of whether conflict will exist in your organization, your work, or your personal life. You know the answer is that conflict will be there. It's how you respond to conflict that will make a difference. As a trainer, you help others understand how to manage conflict appropriately, presenting your participants with another way to view the world.

Although I could easily have titled this chapter "Conflict Management" or simply "Conflict," I consciously chose "Conflict and Collaboration." I included the second half because collaboration is the real message coming from our contributors.

We are so lucky to have Tom Crum, author, international trainer, and conflict resolution expert, as a contributor to this collection. His activity will create a meaningful experience for your participants. Herb Kindler and Joe Willmore add their expertise with two more short activities that prove that collaboration will win out over conflict. Darryl Sink has contributed a set of practice scenarios that you may build into a workshop. Even better, he has shared a job aid to assist participants in determining strategies for resolving conflict. Richard Whelan shares a magic trick that you can use to explain that things may not always be as they first appear—much like conflict. You might be able to use this attention grabber to introduce a module on conflict management.

Each of the five activities gives you another tool to help participants appreciate the wisdom of embracing win-win principles in their lives.

Force Follows Force Blindly

Submitted by Thomas Crum

Objectives

- To demonstrate the knee-jerk response of resisting or fighting when pressured in a conflict situation.
- To illustrate that it takes only one person to initiate de-escalation in a conflict situation and to shift an adversarial relationship into a partnering one.

Audience

Any size.

Time Required

5 minutes.

Materials and Equipment

- None.

Area Setup

Any setting. Works best when presenter walks up to a participant seated in the audience or asks for a volunteer.

Process

1. Ask a volunteer to stand facing you, holding out his or her arm toward you, and to make a fist.
2. Casually place your fist against the volunteer's fist and increase pressure. In almost all cases, the volunteer will push back.
3. Ask why the volunteer is pushing. The usual response is, "because you are." Gradually decrease your pressure while you are talking with the volunteer.
4. Ask why the volunteer stopped pushing (he or she usually will). The person's response is typically, "because you did."

5. Talk about the idea that *force follows force blindly,* and how it creates a problem in conflict when you want to be persuasive. For every unit of time or energy you spend on being "right," the other side will tend to use an equal and opposite amount of time and energy "defending" their position. The result is that both sides get entrenched in the belief that "I won't do anything to reconcile this conflict until 'they' back off." The last part of this exercise reveals that, in reality, it takes only one side to begin the resolution process, not both sides.

 nsider's Tips

- This exercise works best when you subtly increase or decrease your pressure. Volunteers will correspondingly alter their pressure without realizing that they are doing so.
- If you have been working with a group on win-win principles, team building, or any theme on working together, this exercise shows how easy it is to fall back on old behaviors under pressure.

Source

I discuss this activity in *The New Conflict Cookbook* (Aiki Works, 2000), written by my colleagues Judith Warner and Christine Steerman and me.

Thomas Crum is the author of *Journey to Center* (1997) and *The Magic of Conflict* (1998) (both published by Simon & Schuster). His newest book, *Three Deep Breaths* (Berrett-Koehler), was published in 2006. Tom has developed an in-depth technology to turn conflict into powerful relationships, stress into vitality, and pressure into peak performance. He conducts trainings throughout the world and includes principles and movements of aikido and other mind-body arts in his presentation.

Thomas Crum
Aiki Works Inc.
P.O. Box 7845
Aspen, CO 81612
Phone: 970.925.7099
Email: Judy@aikiworks.com
Website: www.aikiworks.com

The Cost of Conflict

Submitted by Herb Kindler, Ph.D.

Objective

- To present a fun activity that teaches strategies for handling conflict and disagreement constructively.

Audience

Any size.

Time Required

About 15 minutes.

Materials and Equipment

- Play money (three $1,000 bills) or three real $1 bills.

Area Setup

Any setting as long as participants can see and hear the three volunteers.

Process

1. Ask for three volunteers. You may want to reassure these participants that they will not be embarrassed participating in this activity.
2. Announce that the activity will last no longer than *7 minutes.* At this point ask for a volunteer to be the timekeeper. Instruct the timekeeper to call out when 5 minutes have elapsed, 6 minutes, and, if necessary, 7 minutes.
3. Inform everyone about the rules of the game as follows:
   - "I am giving each player $1,000." (You may use either play money or single dollar bills. Use real money only if you feel generous, because you won't get your money back. You may use higher-denomination bills to make the game even more realistic.)
   - The objective of the game is to redistribute the money so that *at least one player gets no money.* It is also okay for two players to get no money. If the objective is not reached before 7 minutes have elapsed, the timekeeper gets all the money.

90 World-Class Activities by 90 World-Class Trainers

- No deals can be made by which money is returned after the conclusion of the game. For example, one player can't say to the others, "Give me your money to invest, and I'll pay you back (perhaps with dividends) at some future time" or "Give me your money, and I'll buy lunch today."
- Also, as the pressure builds and the game objective has not been reached, a player may be tempted to say, "Here, take my money." Therefore, you (the trainer) should say, "Releasing your money would ease tension, but would limit the potential learning from this game. Therefore, don't just give your money away."

4. Before starting the game, if you use play money, say, "Because we are not using real $1,000 bills, to make the game more realistic, I would like each of the three players to say what they really would do with $3,000 if he or she were to receive all the cash." After each person suggests how he or she would spend $3,000, you start the game-clock ticking.

5. What you may observe:
- Typically, much of the allotted time is spent by the players trying to convince one another that their use of the money is most worthy (or that their circumstances are most desperate). This *smoothing-persuading* strategy almost never works.
- Sometimes a *collaborative* strategy works in which all funds are given to one person who promises to donate it to an agreed-on charity.
- As the clock ticks down, a *decision rule* is sometimes used, such as "paper-rock-scissors" or flipping coins for quick resolution.
- Rarely, except for college students, is *force* used. A student, after waiting 6 minutes, may grab the money and try to hold it for another minute.

6. Debrief the activity using these questions:
- What did you observe?
- What conflict management strategies did you observe?
- What worked? What didn't work?
- What did you learn from this activity?

Insider's Tips

- This exercise is a good introduction to reviewing a variety of conflict management strategies while also energizing your training program.
- For a detailed examination of nine strategies for conflict resolution, you may want to provide trainees with my book *Managing Conflict* (3rd ed., Crisp Learning, 2005). Another book of mine, with several related exercises, is *Leadership Mastery for Turbulent Times* (Course Technology PTR, 2005).

Herb Kindler, Ph.D., has conducted hundreds of leadership and conflict management training programs in the United States and abroad. An MIT graduate with his Ph.D. from UCLA, Herb was a CEO in industry before becoming a professor of management. His clients include Boeing, Symantec, the U.S. Navy, Thai Airways, IBM, Mattel Toys, General Motors, Lawrence Livermore National Laboratory, BBDO, Starbucks, UCLA, and UC Berkeley. He is the author of seven books.

Herb Kindler, Ph.D.
Herb Kindler & Associates
427 Beirut Avenue
Pacific Palisades, CA 90272
Phone: 310.459.0585
Email: HerbKindler@aol.com

Resolving Conflict: Easy as ABCD

Submitted by Darryl L. Sink, Ed.D.

Objective
- To provide a job aid that helps participants select the most appropriate conflict resolution strategy.

Audience
Conflict management class, divided into 4 teams. Maximum of 24 participants in class.

Time Required
45–75 minutes.

Materials and Equipment
- One copy of the Conflict Resolution Strategies Job Aid for each participant.
- One set of the twelve conflict scenarios for each team.

Area Setup
Any classroom setup that allows room for small teams to work. If used for a distance learning session, have participants work in teams allowing a day to complete the assignment.

Process
1. Open with the following: "Conflict in teams is natural and plays off the different goals of the various team members. This activity will provide you with conflict resolution strategies and will give you the opportunity to practice applying the strategies. The four conflict resolution strategies are *Agree, Bargain, Control,* and *Delay.*"
2. Provide a copy of the Conflict Resolution Strategies Job Aid for each participant. Tell the participants that they are going to overview the job aid using a "teach-back" process. Divide the group into four teams and assign each team A, B, C, or D. Each team will read its section of the job aid and teach it back to the rest of the larger group. For example, the A team will teach the rest of the group about the Agree strategy. Tell each team that you would like members to come up with an example of the strategy they will teach back to the group. Allow the teams about 5–10 minutes to prepare for their teach-backs.

Conflict and Collaboration

3. Starting with the A team, have the team explain the strategy it was assigned (Agree) and when to use the strategy, and provide an example. Continue with the B team (Bargain), the C team (Control), and the D team (Delay). Ask if there are any questions.
4. Hand out one set of the twelve conflict scenarios for each team. Assign the scenarios you would like each team to complete. Explain that they are to read the scenario and make a team decision about which strategy to use.
5. Once teams have completed their assigned scenarios, review a selected few with the larger group. Some participants may want you to provide correct answers. (1 = B; 2 = A; 3 = C; 4 = D; 5 = D; 6 = A; 7 = A; 8 = C; 9 = B; 10 = A; 11 = D; 12 = C)

Insider's Tips

- To shorten the amount of time, you can assign fewer scenarios to each team.
- You may have participants first complete the activity alone and then share their ideas with the rest of their team.
- If you use this in a distance learning activity, assign pairs to complete the activity and then share and "discuss" their ideas in the chat room prior to submitting the work to you.

Source
This is one of my original published activities.

Darryl L. Sink, Ed.D., is president of Darryl L. Sink & Associates, Inc. With twenty-five years of experience designing and developing great learning experiences, Darryl specializes in learning and performance consulting and custom training design and development. Darryl is the author of six comprehensive guides to instructional design and development and has designed and developed over a thousand custom-designed training programs. He is a contributing author to ISPI's *Handbook of Human Performance Technology* (Pfeiffer, 1999) and is the recipient of ISPI's Professional Service Award. He was twice awarded ISPI's Outstanding Instructional Product of the Year Award.

Darryl L. Sink, Ed.D.
Darryl L. Sink & Associates, Inc.
60 Garden Court, Suite 101
Monterey, CA 93940
Phone: 831.649.8384
Email: Darryl@dsink.com
Website: www.dsink.com

Conflict Resolution Strategies Job Aid

Directions: Use this job aid to select the appropriate strategy for resolving conflict.	
Strategy	**When to Use This Strategy**
Agree Ignore your own needs while satisfying the needs of another.	1. The issue is not important. 2. You realize you are wrong. 3. The issue is within the other person's technical domain. 4. The other person lacks a strong self-image. 5. You want the other person to learn from making a mistake. 6. You want the other person to agree with you on some other important issue later. 7. The team is not very cohesive.
Bargain Negotiate for a win-win resolution of the conflict.	1. The issue is important. 2. Different members have the technical skills required for solving the problem. 3. Collaborative problem solving is likely to increase members' commitment. 4. You want members of the team to learn from each other. 5. The team is cohesive and can focus on the problem without personality conflicts.
Control Insist that the other person do what you want.	1. The issue is important. 2. You are sure you are right. 3. You have greater technical competence in the area than the other person. 4. You are dealing with a manipulative person. 5. You have the support of the rest of the team.
Delay Ignore the issue temporarily.	1. The issue is not critical. 2. You don't have all the necessary information to make a definite decision. 3. The team does not have the technical competence. 4. You don't have a tight deadline. 5. You cannot get what you want. 6. You need time for the team members to calm down.

90 World-Class Activities by 90 World-Class Trainers. Copyright © 2007 by John Wiley & Sons, Inc.
Published by Pfeiffer, an Imprint of Wiley. www.pfeiffer.com

Conflict Scenarios: A, B, C, or D?

Directions: Read the following scenarios and decide what conflict resolution strategy would be most appropriate for each. Circle the conflict strategy that is most appropriate for each situation.

Scenario 1

You are the project coordinator, and you are meeting with several other members of your instructional development team to make some important decisions about the media for the course. Your preference is that the course should be delivered as a workshop with a subject matter expert (SME) as the instructor. Your CBT specialist feels that everything should be packaged as a self-instructional tutorial. The SME wants a set of training manuals and reference documentation. Nobody appears to be entrenched in his or her position.

Your Response

Which conflict resolution strategy is most appropriate for this situation?

Agree   Bargain   Control   Delay

Scenario 2

You are discussing revisions to a course. Cathy, your graphic designer, recommends that the margins be wider. You are happy with the current margin width. Cathy's changes are no big deal. They will not require major time or budget commitments because they just involve a one-shot change in the style sheet. Cathy is somewhat emotionally attached to her preference and is resentful of the other members of the team for frequently shooting down her ideas.

Your Response

Which conflict resolution strategy is most appropriate for this situation?

Agree   Bargain   Control   Delay

Scenario 3

You are the project coordinator, and today you are acting as a referee in a dispute between Linda, your instructional designer, and Jim, your evaluator. They are discussing changes to the course based on evaluation data. Jim has done an excellent job of presenting the data, but his suggested revisions indicate a lack of understanding of instructional design principles. Linda's prescriptions are much more effective, but Jim does not want to do the additional analyses to provide in-depth information for the revisions. Jim is manipulating you to take his side by appealing to your instincts as a technical specialist.

Your Response

Which conflict resolution strategy is most appropriate for this situation?

Agree   Bargain   Control   Delay

Scenario 4

You are a project coordinator, and you are involved in a dispute between your instructional designer and the media designer. They are shouting at each other about the choice of the appropriate media. Personally, you feel that you don't have enough information from the field to make a logical choice. For example, you are not sure how many of the training centers have access to interactive video equipment.

Your Response

Which conflict resolution strategy is most appropriate for this situation?

Agree   Bargain   Control   Delay

Scenario 5

You are the project coordinator, and your team is being split into two hostile camps over a very trivial conflict about the color of the dividers that separate one module from the next in the binder. The two groups are at each other's throat, trying to win final approval for their color choices.

Your Response

Which conflict resolution strategy is most appropriate for this situation?

Agree   Bargain   Control   Delay

Scenario 6

You are in charge of a new course development team. Members of the team do not know each other. Some of them are located far away from your office. John is the program evaluator in your team. He is a fresh graduate from a big midwestern university and is full of academic ideas related to research design. You want a simple needs analysis, but John wants an elaborate study using a stratified random sample and collecting a wide variety of qualitative and quantitative data using several different strategies. You feel that John's plans are impractical and unnecessary. However, you do have plenty of time, and you feel that if you give John enough rope, he will learn the realities of real-world projects soon.

Your Response

Which conflict resolution strategy is most appropriate for this situation?

Agree   Bargain   Control   Delay

Scenario 7

You are the instructional designer, and you are having some problems with Harold, your subject matter expert. Harold has a unique way of defining technical terms. You are not a technical expert, but you know enough about the content to feel that these definitions are unnecessarily complex. The definitions are to be included only in the glossary at the back of the book. You will need Harold's support later to make a case for leaving out the module on skills, which is likely to become obsolete in the very near future.

Your Response

Which conflict resolution strategy is most appropriate for this situation?

Agree   Bargain   Control   Delay

Scenario 8

You are the project coordinator, and you have a problem with Larry, your instructional designer. You are working under tight deadlines, and you feel that Larry should complete his task analysis quickly and get started on the design of the materials. If necessary, he can conduct additional analyses later. The rest of the team agrees with you. Larry is worried about not having enough time later.

Your Response

Which conflict resolution strategy is most appropriate for this situation?

Agree   Bargain   Control   Delay

Scenario 9

You are a writer working with a specialist to design an interactive video course. Although you are a competent scriptwriter, you are new to this interactive video business. The video specialist knows a lot about the technical capabilities and limitations of the medium, but she does not know much about good scripts and visual impact. In working with her, you have several differences of opinion on how exactly something should be done. However, both of you have mutual respect and trust in each other's judgment in your areas of expertise.

Your Response

Which conflict resolution strategy is most appropriate for this situation?

Agree   Bargain   Control   Delay

Scenario 10

You are the project coordinator, and you are having some problems with your media designer, Mark. Mark is a very competent person, but he is not committed to the project. He offers his ideas, but if anybody comes up with even a minor objection, Mark withdraws and lets the other person have his or her way. You are discussing with Mark how to lay out the CBT screen, and it is clear that Mark is competent but indifferent. You wish he'd show more interest in the task. You know that Mark's behavior is affecting the quality of the team's work.

Your Response

Which conflict resolution strategy is most appropriate for this situation?

Agree   Bargain   Control   Delay

Scenario 11

You are the project coordinator, and you don't feel that David, the subject matter expert, knows his technical area. You are talking with him about the issue of whether the course should include a final module on optional peripherals. David does not think so, partly because he has not studied the topic. You feel that these peripherals may become a critical component in future sales. However, you do not have enough information or technical expertise to make a final decision. There is enough work currently to keep the other team members occupied.

Your Response

Which conflict resolution strategy is most appropriate for this situation?

Agree   Bargain   Control   Delay

Scenario 12

You are a subject matter expert, and you have considerable clout over the way the project is being implemented. You are having some difficulties with Sheila, your writer. You agree with Sheila that all content should be communicated in plain English, but you disagree with some of her explanations, which are factually inaccurate. Although she is an extremely competent writer, you have grave doubts about her understanding of the technical topic.

Your Response

Which conflict resolution strategy is most appropriate for this situation?

Agree   Bargain   Control   Delay

Magic Matters

Submitted by Richard T. Whelan, M.A.

Objectives

- To provide a brief experience that sets the stage for recognizing that things aren't the way they first appear.
- To lighten up the workshop environment by letting participants laugh and relax from the start.

Audience

Any size.

Time Required

Approximately 10–15 minutes.

Materials and Equipment

- A large coin, such as a quarter.
- An empty 1-pound coffee can (metal), which has the label painted or covered.

Area Setup

The area should be set up on a level floor, like a classroom setting—not a stage or lecture hall. You should be able to walk among the seated participants easily so that they can see what you are doing, and you are in control of what is happening with this trick.

Place the empty coffee can in a location that can be seen by everyone, but it should not be the center of attention.

Process

1. Allow the participants in your class or workshop to seat themselves where they like, so that they are comfortable and ready to begin.
2. Introduce yourself and tell the participants what they need to know about the purpose of the class or workshop, but do not start your presentation.
3. While speaking, slowly walk toward the coffee can. Prior to arriving at the can's location, reach into your pocket and carefully remove the quarter—so no one can see you do this—with your left hand. (I am assuming you are right-handed. If you are not, simply reverse the hand directions.) Pick up the can by

placing your left thumb on the outside of the can and your remaining four fingers on the inside of the can. The quarter you have in your left hand will be held against the inside of the can between your fingers and the can so that no one can see it.

4. Tell the participants that in their workplaces, things are not always what they seem to be. At times, problems may appear in places that are least expected, and you are going to show them a simple example of this.

5. While walking among the participants, quickly show them the inside of the can and then turn it upside down and shake it, so they see that nothing is inside it. Then stop near one of the participants and tell them you are going to catch a falling coin in the can.

6. With your right hand, reach into your pocket and then remove it as if you were removing a handful of coins. Your hand is empty, but you are pretending it is full of coins. Place your right hand in front of one of the participants and ask her to remove a quarter. If she looks at you in a strange manner or states there are no coins, say, "Of course there are," and place your hand in front of another person, telling him to remove a quarter. As he "picks up" the coin, you may say, "Not a dime, a quarter—thank you." Then ask him to flip the quarter into the air, saying that you are going to catch it in the can.

7. Hold the can above your eye level and move it around as if you were actually following the flight and descent of the coin. You may comment on the height the coin has reached or its "hang time." Then stop moving the can and move your fingers that are holding the coin, allowing the coin to be heard dropping to the bottom of the metal can. Take the can with your right hand and turn it over so that the participants can see the real quarter dropping into your left hand; hold it up so everyone can see it.

> ## Editor's Note
>
> The participants may ask you how the trick was done. Just look at them in a quizzical manner, shrug your shoulders, and say, "Simple. I showed you an empty can, you took one of my quarters (which I made sure to get back from you) and flipped it in the air, and I caught it in the can." Then put the can down and continue with the next portion of your class or workshop presentation. It is important not to tell anyone how magic tricks are performed. (Magicians who learn tricks are often required to sign a legal contract never to reveal a trick's secret.)

8. Now ask the participants, "Tell me what you just saw happening." Don't let them tell how they think it happened, but what they *saw* happening. You may have to direct the comments so that the response includes their seeing an empty can, taking an invisible coin and flipping it into the air, seeing you "watch" it, hearing it drop into the can, and then actually seeing a quarter.

9. Ask them how this relates to problems or conflicts that may arise in their workplaces. Allow several participants to offer ideas until you get comments relating to looking for something in a location, not seeing anything, and then later discovering it was actually there.

10. Finish the trick by stating, "Remember: always look carefully, as things may not be what they appear to be."

 **Insider's Tip**

- Practice this trick alone several times so that you become completely comfortable with it and can practice the "banter" (talking) you do during its performance. Then try it among family, friends, or coworkers until it feels almost like second nature to you. You'll find it a lot of fun and something you can do on occasions other than workshops, such as at parties or family gatherings.

Richard T. Whelan, M.A., is a comprehensive HR coordinator, certified mental health counselor, and a published freelance writer. He designs, develops, and delivers HR and technical workshops for businesses, organizations, and agencies in the public and private sectors, both nationally and internationally.

Richard T. Whelan, M.A.
Chesney Row Consortium for Learning & Development
520 Collings Avenue, Suite B823
Collingswood, NJ 08107
Phone: 856.858.9496
Email: MrPerker@aol.com

Cross the Line

Submitted by Joe Willmore

Objectives

- To create a forum for participants that allows new insights into collaboration and conflict.
- To quickly energize a class of participants with a short, physical, interactive experience that has versatile application.

Audience

Requires at least 2 people but can be done with much larger groups. The activity will be completed in pairs, so if there is an odd number of participants, the extra person can serve as an observer who walks around and looks for insights from other pairs.

Time Required

1 minute to explain and set up, 1 minute to conduct, and whatever time to debrief that you choose to use.

Materials and Equipment

- None.

> **Editor's Note**
>
> This activity requires participants to stand up, so anyone using a wheelchair or walker will have difficulty participating.

Area Setup

Participants need to be able to stand up in pairs facing each other approximately 3 feet apart, with no tables, chairs, or obstacles between them. Some room to spread out is desirable.

Process

1. Tell all participants to stand and to pair up with someone.
2. Once participants have had approximately 20 seconds to stand and pair up, tell them, "We're going to play a game. Stand about 3 feet away from your partner so you face each other. Imagine an invisible boundary or border or demilitarized zone that runs from your left to your right halfway between you and the person you're facing. The way you win this game is to get your

partner to cross over to your side of the line. You can't use physical force or threat. Otherwise, any other inducement or incentive is fair game. You've got 45 seconds—GO!"

3. Keep track of the time. Do not give participants more than 60 seconds to play the game. As they play, observe pairs to see what strategies people are trying.
4. Make a loud signal when time is up to get participants to stop playing.
5. Debrief the activity with these questions:
   - What happened in your pair?
   - How many of you got your partner to cross the line?
   - What worked?
   - What didn't work?
6. Usually at least one pair figures out that they can *both* win by each crossing over to the other's side of the line (win-win). Point this out as an example of collaboration or out-of-the-box thinking.

 **Insider's Tips**

- Typically, many others will treat this as a "win-lose" activity. You'll see guilt, bribes, persuasion, and manipulation all attempted by other pairs. You can ask *why* they chose those strategies as well as what worked or didn't work. This can set up a discussion on sales, competition, cooperation, manipulation, supervision, and influence.
- Even some pairs who agreed to cross the line had trust issues. You might hear, "I won't cross the line until you do it first!" "No, you do it first!" "No, it was my idea." Use this to talk about trust and reciprocity.
- It's important to introduce the activity as a game or contest. That's because most of us hold the mind-set that a game or contest is something in which you keep score, something that someone wins and another has to lose and that is competitive. You can examine assumptions people make about games, contests, and competition (and how this applies to teams or work settings). Point out that even though it was never clear what people "won" by "winning this game," for many of them winning the game became very important. You will find that some people offer money or food or promises to do projects at work in order to "win." This is also a good activity to talk about cross-cultural behavior, nonverbal behavior, and negotiation.

- Whatever you do, keep it quick. The activity doesn't benefit from lots of explanation and setup. It's much more revealing if people just react to the rules (rather than get a chance to strategize).
- This is a great energizer in a long class or meeting—it gets everyone up and moving, involves some competition and cooperation, and usually gets a couple of laughs from people. You can use it as a change of pace and then go back to the original work with a reenergized group of participants.
- A variation of this activity (and I don't know to whom to attribute it) is to arm wrestle. The winner is the person who can press the other person's arm to the table the most.

Joe Willmore is president of the Willmore Consulting Group, a performance improvement firm located in northern Virginia. He is a former member of the ASTD board of directors, a facilitator for ASTD's HPI program, and the author of *Performance Basics and Managing Virtual Teams* (ASTD Press, 2004).

Joe Willmore
Willmore Consulting Group
5007 Mignonette Court
Annandale, VA 22003
Phone: 703.855.4634
Email: Willmore@juno.com

Chapter 5

Creativity

If your organization is like most, it is going through change—lots of it! Competition is intensifying, the war for talent is escalating, technology is accelerating, and challenges of every kind are multiplying. Along with these changes come problems—new problems that need new solutions and new ways of thinking. Organizations need knowledgeable people to clearly assess what the changes mean; they require creative people to spawn new ideas.

Einstein, one of the smartest people who ever lived, stated that "imagination is more important than knowledge." Therefore, it would stand to reason that we ought to spend some time determining how to be more creative.

Ever needed to get your employees' or participants' creative juices flowing? Wonder how to engage their right brains? The activities in this section are fun, fast moving, and, well, creative!

I had fun just reading the activities in this section. M. K. Key provides a great way for participants to practice with two well-known creativity tools. Lenn Millbower's energizing activity is a great way to warm participants up to the idea of creativity and gives "out of the box" a whole new meaning! Mimi Banta shares a solid (or scrambled, depending on the results) hands-on activity that challenges our creative problem solving. And leave it to Steve Sugar to look at things from a different vantage point. I hope you all see the richness in his adaptation of the old standby, Bingo. And I must admit to laughing out loud when reading Andy VanGundy's activity—what a playful way to practice thinking on your feet. This is so much fun you could use it as a game at your next party!

Each of the five provides an opportunity to practice creativity-generating techniques. They all get those creative juices flowing!

Creativity and Collaboration Eggsperiment

Submitted by Mimi Banta

Objectives
- To illustrate the value of having many different viewpoints and ideas from which to build the best solutions.
- To encourage teamwork.
- To have lots of fun!

Audience
Divide a large group into smaller teams of 5–7.

Time Required
45 minutes include setup, construction, and debrief.

Materials and Equipment
For each team:

- One egg.
- Four balloons.
- Ruler.
- Fifteen index cards.
- Eight straws.
- Ten paper clips.
- Two Styrofoam cups.
- Roll of Scotch tape.
- Six sheets of newspaper.
- 1 meter of string.

Area Setup

Each team needs space to complete construction away from the others. The group needs access to an outdoor or indoor hallway a minimum of 5 meters long for the test.

Process

1. Divide the group into teams of 5–7. Tell the teams that their challenge is to use materials to construct a casing that will protect the shell of an egg from breaking. Inform them that they will have 30 minutes for construction and that after they have constructed the protective casing they will test it out. State that their goal is to be able to toss a raw egg in its protective casing a distance of at least 4 meters. The egg must land on the floor or the ground without breaking.
2. Distribute the materials to each team and tell the teams to begin.
3. Allow 30 minutes for construction.
4. Allow the teams to test their casings.
5. Debrief the exercise using the following questions:
   - Did your group engage in any planning?
   - Could you improve your process?
   - What variations occurred in the ways different groups approached the challenge?
   - What role did creativity play in your solution?
   - Did everyone contribute ideas to the final product?
   - How did you tap into each group member's ideas?
   - What is the result of having different viewpoints?
   - How does this apply to the workplace?

 nsider's Tip

- If you have multiple groups, after they have built their separate casings, you may wish to tell them that the company cannot support the testing of more than one prototype. Tell them they must combine their ideas and come up with a single casing.

Mimi Banta is a facilitator and organization development consultant with over twenty years of experience. Her consulting practice offers a full-service approach that assists organizations in defining vision and purpose, implementing strategic initiatives, coaching executives, and determining training plans that achieve new levels of employee performance. Mimi's educational background is in psychology and adult education. She has published research in the *Personality and Social Psychology* bulletin and has national speaking experience on the importance of line management's involvement in human resource development. In addition to Netspeed Leadership, she uses a variety of organizational consulting tools to help her clients reach their objectives.

Mimi Banta
Netspeed Leadership Consultant Partner
Banta Training Services
905 Dalebrook Drive
Alexandria, VA 22308
Phone: 703.780.3542
Email: Mbanta@cox.net
Website: www.netspeed.com

Doubling Up on Creativity

Submitted by M. K. Key, Ph.D.

Objectives
- To learn how to conduct a simple scientific experiment.
- To examine team productivity using two idea-generating creativity tools.
- To practice using brainstorming and nominal group technique.

Audience
Any size.

Time Required
40–50 minutes.

Materials and Equipment
- An overhead transparency (see the sample experiment overhead) with an overhead marker and projector.
- A stopwatch.
- Four objects selected from this list: paper clip, ballpoint pen, empty water bottle, rubber band, ruler, or any other commonplace object in a classroom or office.
- One copy of the Nominal Group Technique and Brainstorming handout for each participant.
- Flip charts and markers for each table.
- Blank sheets of paper and pencils at each table.

Area Setup
Even numbers of tables, as long as the number of participants in each table subgroup is equal and no group is larger than eight people

Process
1. Explain that the group is about to conduct a "simple experiment."
2. Provide a brief tutorial on brainstorming and nominal group technique. Use the handout as a basis for your discussion.

3. Divide the room in half (equal number of tables in Group 1 and Group 2) and explain that one half will be using brainstorming, and the other half, the nominal group technique. There must be an equal number of people at each table (rearrange them if not).

4. Provide these instructions: "Here is a chance to practice what we have just learned, brainstorming and nominal group technique. I want you to generate as many ideas as possible with your tablemates; the only thing that counts is quantity. There is an easel at each table. Select a recorder now." (Pause until a person is selected and poised by the flip chart.)

5. Continue by saying, "This is a timed exercise. Half the tables [designate which ones] will use nominal group technique. The other half will use brainstorming. You will have 5 minutes to list your ideas. For the nominal group, you will have 1 minute to write down your ideas and then move to Step 3."

6. Now give the objective, which is to generate all possible uses for Object 1 (for example, a paper clip) for one half of the room and for Object 2 (for example, a water bottle) for the other half.

7. Call out "Go." For the nominal group technique tables, let them know when they are 1 minute into the exercise, so that they might start calling out their ideas and move to Step 3.

8. After 5 minutes, ask all to stop and total their ideas. Sum these numbers of ideas across Group 1, then across Group 2. Record the totals on the overhead under Round 1.

9. Now ask them to try the other tool in the second round, with two new objects.

10. Repeat Steps 7 and 8, recording the total ideas under Round 2.

11. Subtract the difference between Round 2 and Round 1 and write that total in the third column.

12. Debrief the exercise by asking for observations about what made a difference in the quantity (their productivity): Was it the tool, the object, the people, the conditions, or the order?

13. Then ask for their theories about why this occurred: a warm-up effect, hearing and bouncing off of other people's ideas, getting feedback by seeing their recorded scores on the overhead, the effect of quiet time before group time, and so on.

14. Liken this experience to their work experience outside the classroom. What are the conditions for creativity? Some common suggestions are (a) use a warm-up when productivity is called for; (b) provide a degree of tension, such as timing and feedback; (c) allow teams interaction time as well as quiet time;

(d) don't write and edit at the same time; and (e) use dual recorders to keep up with the creative output.

 ## nsider's Tips

- Use this exercise early in the day. It works well as an opener for team-building, creativity, and statistics courses, or simply to teach the tools to a group.
- Try variations on the experiment: vary the feedback component (don't record the number of ideas until all have finished); standardize the object, so that all have the same one.
- Keep the tension and the humor up, pointing out some of the more unusual uses for objects.

M. K. Key, Ph.D., a licensed clinical-community psychologist, has over thirty years of experience in organizational quality. She teaches, consults, and speaks on such topics as leadership, customer value management, tools for change, corporate culture, team development, mediation of conflict, and creativity. She received her doctoral, master's, and bachelor's degrees (Phi Beta Kappa, *cum laude* and honors in psychology) from Vanderbilt University. She has served for years as adjunct associate professor of human and organization development at George Peabody College of Vanderbilt. In addition to numerous professional articles, she has authored the book *Managing Change in Healthcare: Innovative Solutions for People-Based Organizations* (McGraw-Hill, 1999), coauthored with Terry Deal *Corporate Celebration: Play, Purpose and Profit at Work* (Berrett-Koehler, 1998), and authored *Thought Packages That Produce Results: Just-in-Time Modules for Continuous Improvement* (Quorum Health Resources, 1997).

M. K. Key, Ph.D.
Key Associates
1857 Laurel Ridge Drive
Nashville, TN 37215
Phone: 615.665.1622
Email: keyassocs@mindspring.com
Website: www.mkkey.com

EXPERIMENT OVERHEAD

	Round 1	Round 2	Difference
Nominal Group and Brainstorming	(Object 1)	(Object 3)	
Brainstorming Only	(Object 2)	(Object 4)	

Nominal Group Technique
and Brainstorming

Nominal Group Technique

A group decision-making technique designed to generate a large number of ideas through contributions of members working individually.

How to Conduct a Session Using Nominal Group Technique:

1. Clarify the nominal group objective.
2. Individually list as many ideas as possible.
3. Call out ideas from the lists in turn around the group.
4. Record each idea on a flip chart.
5. Pass when all ideas on a list have been presented.
6. After all ideas are listed, clarify each idea and eliminate exact duplicates.

Brainstorming

A group decision-making technique designed to generate a large number of ideas through interaction among team members.

How to Conduct a Brainstorming Session:

1. Clarify the brainstorming objective.
2. Call out ideas in turn around the group.
3. Record each idea on a flip chart.
4. Build on and expand the ideas of others.
5. Pass when an idea does not come quickly to mind.
6. To generate as long a list as possible, resist stopping when ideas slow down.
7. After all ideas are listed, clarify each idea and eliminate exact duplicates.

What's in the Box?

Submitted by Lenn Millbower, B.M., M.A.

Objectives
- To help participants begin thinking beyond their normal limitations and to demonstrate adaptive thinking skills.
- To create a metaphor for thinking out of the box.
- To warm up to brainstorm an organizational issue.

Audience
Up to 24 participants; any team or work group tasked with thinking creatively or beginning a brainstorming session.

Time Required
30–45 minutes.

Materials and Equipment
- A sealed cardboard box (large enough to be held with two hands, but not so large as to be unmanageable).
- A sign inside the box that states "Your Imagination!"
- Masking tape (20–40 feet).

Area Setup
Place tape on the floor in two parallel lines 3 feet apart and long enough to accommodate half of the participants standing on each line.

Process
1. Open the activity by stating, "Organizations are often unable to create new ideas because of the confines they place on themselves. Thinking 'out of the box' is required for reinvention. This activity helps you envision solutions beyond those you would normally consider."
2. Divide the participants into two groups. Direct each group to stand on one of the lines, with both groups facing the same direction in a single-file line.

3. Give the box to the participant at the front of one of the lines (line one) and explain that the two groups will play "What's in the Box?"
4. Explain the procedures. The participant at the front of line two (without the box) will ask the participant holding the box (line one), "What's in the box?"
5. The participant holding the box (line one) will respond with a made-up answer as he or she hands the box to the participant asking the question in line two.
6. The participant now holding the box (line two) must react to whatever is "in the box." For example, an elephant in the box would mean that the box is extremely heavy.
7. The participant who surrendered the box (line one) moves to the back of his or her group's line.
8. The participant at the front of line one repeats the question, "What's in the box?"
9. The participant holding the box (line two) must respond with a different answer that relates to the first item reputed to be in the box. For example, if an elephant was the first item, peanuts could be the next item because elephants eat peanuts. That participant hands the box to the participant in line one.
10. The participant who surrendered the box (line two) moves to the back of his/her group's line.
11. The participant now holding the box (line one) must react to the new item in the box.
12. Repeat this procedure until each participant has taken two turns, ensuring that no participant repeats an answer already given. Invite everyone to sit down.
13. Debrief the experience, focusing first on the participants' emotional reaction to the experience and then on the wide variety of items that were "in the box."
14. Ask the participants if they would like to know what is really in the box. Open the box, displaying the sign that says "Your Imagination!"
15. Conclude by saying, "When you started this activity, your imagination was in the box. But as you've seen, your imagination cannot be held by any box. You have been thinking outside the box, so your imagination is 'box-free'! Let's keep the momentum going and turn our thinking toward the reason we are here today."
16. Begin a creative brainstorming session on the organizational need that is the focus of the session.

Insider's Tips

- Use the following questions to encourage a rich follow-on discussion:
  - Did you enjoy the activity? What was fun about it?
  - Were you able to imagine what was in the box?
  - Was it hard to come up with new items for the box?
  - Did you notice that the items in the box became more improbable over time?
  - Did the improbability of those items really being in the box stop you from imagining them being there?
  - What conclusions can you draw from this information?
  - What are you going to do differently as a result of those conclusions?
- The activity may also be run with the participants formed in a circle and passing the box first left, then right, and then at random.

Lenn Millbower, B.M., M.A., the Learnertainment® Trainer, is an expert in the application of entertainment techniques to learning events. He is the author of several works, including *Show Biz Training* (American Management Association, 2003) and *Training with a Beat* (Stylus Publishing, 2000). Through Offbeat Training®, Lenn helps organizations reinvent events with show-biz techniques that increase results.

Lenn Millbower, B.M., M.A.
Offbeat Training
329 Oakpoint Circle
Davenport, FL 33837
Phone: 407.256.0501
Email: lennmillbower@OffbeatTraining.com
Website: www.offbeattraining.com

Scavenger Bingo

Submitted by Steve Sugar, M.B.A.

Objectives
- To introduce new team members while kicking off group work.
- To spur creative thinking and problem-solving talents within the team.

Audience
6 or more.

Time Required
25–60 minutes.

Materials and Equipment
- One Bingo sheet for each team.
- Pens or pencils for each team.
- Timer (optional).

Area Setup
Any.

Process
1. Introduce this activity by saying,

   Bingo is one of the most user-friendly and popular classroom games. We know it in many forms—from the visual game board of the TV game show Jeopardy *to the countless fill-in-the-frame templates created for icebreakers and topic-related scavenger hunts. Scavenger Bingo is an easy-to-use icebreaker or creative activity.*

   Movie buffs may recall the famous scavenger hunt opening to the 1936 movie My Man Godfrey, *with William Powell and Carole Lombard. Of special note was the excitement created by sending players scurrying all over New York City in search of obscure and hard-to-get items. Although obviously staged, the energy created by this activity was infectious.*

2. Say, "So now let's experience our own Scavenger Bingo." Divide the class into teams of three or more players each and distribute a Bingo sheet to each team.

3. Instruct the teams to identify or locate an item suggested by each clue on the Bingo sheet.
4. For each item located, the team marks an X through the appropriate space on the Bingo sheet.
5. Teams continue to identify, locate, and mark as many items as they can until time is called.
6. The team with the most spaces marked when time is called wins.

# Insider's Tips

- This activity serves as an excellent creativity exercise as well as icebreaker.
- You can use this game to debrief team activities.
- You can use the activity to promote a dialogue about interpretations, perceptions, and thinking out of the box. The following are some examples of creative responses to the clues:
  - "Notched" as a dime or quarter.
  - "Etching" as a dollar bill.
  - "Clubby" as a Costco or AAA card.
  - "Pie" as a dessert item or graphic (pie chart).
- To create Bingo game cards with different clue patterns, consider using "Zingo," easy-to-use software that randomly sorts and prints your game sheets (www.thiagi.com).
- The activity is easily "filled" with topic-related items or clues. Simply select the size of the matrix (from 3 × 3 to 6 × 6) and then create enough clues to fill each square. My version of this standard opening activity is a combination of Autographs (the "find someone who" activity) combined with Thiagi's famous Beyond Bingo.

Source

I originally developed this for my fortieth Bucknell reunion dinner (June 2002). I was tired of Autographs and noted that many colleges, including my own University of Maryland, use Autographs in their orientation sessions. Carol Willett and I rewrote Scavenger Bingo for *Games That Boost Performance* (Pfeiffer, 2004). I currently use this exercise as the "get-acquainted dyad" as I have my Maryland students get acquainted with their textbook. It is very powerful.

Steve Sugar, M.B.A., is a teacher and the author or coauthor of five Jossey-Bass/Pfeiffer books on games, including *Games That Teach* (1998), *Games That Teach Teams* (2000), *Primary Games* (2002), *Retreats That Work* (2002), and *Games That Boost Performance* (2004). Steve is currently a faculty member of the University of Maryland, Baltimore County, and has taught on the faculties of Johns Hopkins University and the New York Institute of Technology. He is a frequent speaker at international teaching conferences. He holds a B.A. in economics from Bucknell University and an M.B.A. in economics and statistics from George Washington University.

Steve Sugar, M.B.A.
10320 Kettledrum Court
Ellicott City, MD 21042
Phone: 410.418.4930
Email: ssugar@starpower.net

Scavenger Bingo

etching	facial metal	wild thing	sandy	sticky
flowery	silvery	notched	musical	colorful
silky	heirloom	tattoo	woodsy	star quality
toothy	noisemaker	plastic	pie	half-something
poetic	government form	fruity	clubby	scratchy

Scavenger Bingo

scratchy	etching	wild thing	sandy	notched
facial metal	woodsy	clubby	musical	silky
silvery	poetic	colorful	star quality	toothy
fruity	flowery	plastic	tattoo	pie
half-something	heirloom	government form	sticky	noisemaker

Scavenger Bingo

tattoo	scratchy	fruity	toothy	colorful
silvery	facial metal	sandy	sticky	musical
government form	half-something	heirloom	wild thing	notched
star quality	clubby	plastic	poetic	woodsy
etching	flowery	pie	noisemaker	silky

Scavenger Bingo

flowery	fruity	sandy	toothy	etching
clubby	facial metal	noisemaker	half-something	wild thing
tattoo	silvery	star quality	pie	heirloom
government form	notched	plastic	colorful	poetic
silky	woodsy	musical	sticky	scratchy

Tell Me Why

Submitted by Arthur B. VanGundy, Ph.D.

Objectives
- To practice creative thinking during performance evaluations.
- To evaluate the ability of employees to think on their feet.
- To create a playful atmosphere conducive to creative thinking.

Audience
Small groups of 4–6 people each.

Time Required
30–40 minutes.

Materials and Equipment
- One pad of paper and a pen or pencil for each interviewer.
- One copy of the Tell Me Why handout for each interviewer.
- One copy of the Tell Me Why Interview Rating Form for each interviewer.
- One flip chart and markers.
- Novelty prizes for first-, second-, and third-place winners (plus extras in case of ties).

Area Setup
A room large enough to accommodate small groups seated around tables.

Process
1. Briefly review the objectives with all participants.
2. Divide the participants into groups of four to six people.
3. Assign a number to each group and tell the groups to select one member to be interviewed.
4. Distribute one copy of the Tell Me Why handout and the Tell Me Why Interview Rating Form to each of the remaining group members (the interview team).

> **Editor's Note**
> The interviewee should not see the interview questions.

5. Instruct each person on the interviewing teams to take turns asking the interviewee each of the ten questions—in the order listed on the handout—until all questions have been asked.

6. Before telling them to start asking the interview questions, note that the team members doing the interviewing should evaluate the interviewee's responses to each question using the Tell Me Why Interview Rating Form.

7. Instruct the interview teams to start asking questions.

8. When all groups have finished, have them tally the results so that there is an overall average rating for each interviewee across all ten questions.

9. On the flip chart, list the numbers assigned to each group.

10. Ask each group to report the score they gave the interviewee, and record it beside the group number.

11. Review the results and announce the first-, second-, and third-place winners.

12. Facilitate a brief discussion of the exercise and the results. Use the following questions:
    • How did you feel about this activity?
    • What did you learn?
    • How does this relate to other times when you have had to think on your feet answering questions out of left field?
    • What can you transfer back to the workplace?

 nsider's Tip

• Be sure to emphasize that this is designed to be a fun exercise to practice quick, improvised thinking. Not everyone will do equally well, but there are no "correct" (or incorrect) answers.

Source

This exercise was inspired by an exercise created by my friend Jacquie Lowell (www.jacquielowell.com), and has not been published elsewhere.

Arthur B. VanGundy, Ph.D., is considered a pioneer in idea-generation techniques and has written thirteen books, including *101 MORE Great Games & Activities* (Pfeiffer, 2004), *101 Creativity and Problem Solving Activities* (Pfeiffer, 2005), and *Framing Strategic Innovation* (in progress). Clients include Hershey Foods, MBNA, and the Singapore government. He has received leadership service awards from the Creative Education Foundation and the Singapore government.

Arthur B. VanGundy, Ph.D.
VanGundy & Associates
428 Laws Drive
Norman, OK 73072
Phone: 405.447.1946
Email: avangundy@cox.net

Tell Me Why

1. In our last staff meeting, you seemed to spend most of the time just staring out the window. Why?

2. We understand that you sent a secret memo to your boss saying that you were looking for another job. Why?

3. We saw you having dinner and dancing with your married boss last night. Why?

4. Your projected expenses for your last business trip were $1,250, but you submitted an invoice without receipts for $2,500. Why?

5. We noticed that you've installed a very large safe in your office. Why?

6. Your administrative assistant says that you make him remove and save all postage stamps from incoming mail. Why?

7. Donald Trump just called and said you sent a letter to him addressed to "Donald Tramp." Why?

8. For the last week, you have come into work at 10:00 A.M. and left at 2:00 P.M. Why?

9. All of our petty cash is missing, and our records indicate you were the last one to withdraw any. Why?

10. Security tapes in your office show that a chimpanzee sits in your office chair every night. Why?

Tell Me Why Interview Rating Form

Please rate this person's responses to the questions according to how well you thought he or she answered each one. (For example, were the responses convincing and creative?)

Question 1
    Not very well   1   2   3   4   5   Very well

Question 2
    Not very well   1   2   3   4   5   Very well

Question 3
    Not very well   1   2   3   4   5   Very well

Question 4
    Not very well   1   2   3   4   5   Very well

Question 5
    Not very well   1   2   3   4   5   Very well

Question 6
    Not very well   1   2   3   4   5   Very well

Question 7
    Not very well   1   2   3   4   5   Very well

Question 8
    Not very well   1   2   3   4   5   Very well

Question 9
    Not very well   1   2   3   4   5   Very well

Question 10
    Not very well   1   2   3   4   5   Very well

Chapter 6

Customer Service

By now most of you have heard the quote from the Nordstrom employee handbook that states, "Use your good judgment in all situations. There will be no additional rules." This elegantly simple rule has led the retailer to be one of the most successful in the business. How can you help the organizations you work with achieve this same kind of success?

Customer service pays; it does not cost. Good—nay, *excellent*—customer service is something we have all come to expect as basic to any exchange. Organizations often have a handle on how much it costs to acquire a customer, but they do not appreciate the cost of losing a customer. My experience indicates that it costs five to six times more to acquire a new customer than it does to maintain a current customer. Poor customer service is expensive; excellent customer service is invaluable.

Excellent customer service is provided by competent, well-trained employees. Hire good people, give them the tools to do their job, treat them as the professionals they are, and provide them with the authority to make decisions in the best interest of your customers.

Our two contributors are "best in class" when it comes to customer service. Chip Bell, author of the best-seller *Managing Knock Your Socks Off Service,* shares a creative approach to gaining a new perspective on delivering service. Bill Rothwell, with student Dennis Gilbert, has developed a process to discover and use what is important to an organization's customers to improve service.

Use one of these two activities and your organization will be well on its way to delivering knock your socks off service. Hey—isn't there a book by that name?

Special Delivery

Submitted by Chip R. Bell, Ph.D.

Objectives

- To have an opportunity to see the service delivery processes through a new, fresh perspective.
- To have an opportunity to go outside the industry one works in to invent service delivery processes that are more comfortable for customers.
- To gain ideas for improving a troublesome service delivery process.

Audience

Anybody wishing to improve service quality. No limit on size of audience. I have done this activity with an audience of 10 and one of 1,000.

Time Required

20 minutes to do the task plus added time to report out after each of the 4 steps; could take 30–45 minutes overall (depending on how much discussion you want in the total group).

Materials and Equipment

- None. A set of slides with prompts helps guide the activity, but is optional.

Area Setup

Any.

Process

1. Have participants form small groups (five or six people) and select a service delivery process they know needs improvement to be more comfortable for customers. You might suggest one that could be improved and that perhaps has been the target of customer complaints. (Give them 5 minutes simply to agree on one.)

2. Ask the groups to pick a positive ending emotion or feeling. Use a slide with a seed list of emotions the groups might consider. Bottom line, you are asking them, "If your goal is world-class service, what feeling or emotion would you like customers to have after going through this targeted service delivery process?" Examples of ending emotions you might have on a slide: Confident, Proud, Cared For, Unique, Frugal, Smart, Elite/Rich, Efficient, Special, Happy, Like a Kid, Secure, Pampered, Responsible, Patriotic, Neighborly, Like Family, Healthy, Like a Partner, Wise, Clever, Strong. Give them 2 minutes to select an emotion appropriate to the customer and the process.

3. Ask the group, "What service provider does a 'world-class' job of making their customers feel that same way?" For example, FedEx works to make customers feel confident, Disney World makes guests feel "like a kid," Wal-Mart makes customers feel frugal, Pinkerton makes clients feel secure, Mary Kay Cosmetics makes customers feel pampered, and Nordstrom makes customers feel cared for. Select a dozen or so examples to put on a slide. Give participants 5 minutes to think of several examples from their experience.

4. Now ask, "How would you guess one of the selected service providers would reinvent the chosen process to make your customers feel the way you've described?" You may wish to provide an example: if the service delivery process selected were "our billing process," the desired ending emotion or feeling was "confident," and the selected exemplar was FedEx, then the question for this step would be, "How would FedEx reinvent our billing process to make our customers feel confident?" Give them 8 minutes to complete this task.

5. Ask each group to report out its ideas. Ask what participants might do differently as a result of this activity.

 nsider's Tip

- With more time you get more report-out discussion of what each group selected after each of the five steps in the exercise.

Source

A version of this activity is on my website.

Chip R. Bell, Ph.D., is founder of the Chip Bell Group and manages the Dallas, Texas, office. Chip is the author of several best-selling books, including *Customers as Partners* (Berrett-Koehler, 1994), *Managing Knock Your Socks Off Service* (AMA, 2000), *Service Magic* (Kaplan Business, 2003), *Managers as Mentors* (Berrett-Koehler, 2002), and his latest book, *Magnetic Service: Creating Passionately Devoted Customers* (Berrett-Koehler, 2003).

Chip R. Bell, Ph.D.
The Chip Bell Group
1307 West Main Street, Suite B-110
Gun Barrel, TX 75156
Phone: 214.522.5777
Email: chip@chipbell.com
Website: www.chipbell.com

A Customer Service Dream

Submitted by William J. Rothwell, Ph.D., SPHR, FLMT, CTDP, with Dennis E. Gilbert

Objectives

- To connect participants with customer service as viewed by the organization and as viewed by the customer.
- To use what is important to customers to formulate strategies for improving customer service and retention.

Audience

Ideal for groups of 20–30, and most effective for client training where all participants are from the same organization. Variations of the intervention can accommodate participants from different organizations. Minimum audience should be 8–10 participants.

Time Required

Approximately 2½ hours.

Materials and Equipment

- One envelope containing Question One for each participant.
- One envelope containing Question Two for each participant.
- One copy of the Discover and Dream Data Sheet for each participant.
- One copy of the Discover and Dream Chart for each facilitator.
- A pen or pencil for recording thoughts for each participant.
- A clipboard or writing surface for each participant.
- A flip chart.
- Masking tape for posting flip-chart pages.

Area Setup

The room should support small breakout groups and the ability to reconvene as part of a single, larger group.

Process

1. Provide a 5- to 10-minute introduction to the activity. The emphasis behind the introduction is to discover positive customer service themes or processes. The end result of the entire activity should leave participants with a renewed and invigorated appreciation for customer service. This can subsequently lead to strategies for developing improved customer service or identifying additional training activities.

2. Hand out sealed envelopes containing Question One. Each envelope should have an identifier for establishing small groups of three or four participants. For example, envelopes could be distributed for group A, B, C, and so on. For variation you can use colors, clip art, or stickers on the envelopes. Shuffle the envelopes so that participants move around to find other members of their group.

3. Tell participants to wait to open the envelopes until their entire group is assembled. Participants then follow directions as described for Question One. Allow 10 minutes.

4. Have the group reconvene as one large group and gather the predominant ideas from all groups. Record the ideas on a flip chart under the label "Lens [or View] of the Organization." The idea is that these data represent customer service through the eyes of the organization.

5. Hand out sealed envelopes containing Question Two. Each envelope should have a new identifier for establishing small groups of three or four participants. Again, the envelopes could be distributed for group A, B, C, and so on; groups could also be distinguished using colored markers, clip art, or other identifiers. Shuffle the envelopes so that participants form new groups.

6. Tell participants to wait to open the envelopes until their entire group is assembled. Participants then follow directions as described for Question Two. Allow 10 minutes for this step.

7. Reconvene the large group and gather the predominant ideas from all groups. Record the ideas on a flip chart under the label "Lens [or View] of the Customer." The idea is that these data represent customer service through the eyes of the customer.

8. Take this opportunity to compare and contrast the data collected through the two-question process. Point out differences and similarities in the collected data and, if applicable, remind participants of internal and external customers and the importance of seeking excellence in customer service.

9. Take several minutes to provide an overview of the activity's next step. Give each participant a Discovery and Dream Data Sheet. Ask participants to spend several minutes reading the Discover and Dream Data Sheet and to begin to formulate and record their thoughts.

10. Have the group form subgroups of five to seven participants. Tell the subgroups that once they have gathered in a work space, they should begin to share their thoughts.

11. Participants should record highlights of each story that is told. What is the main theme of the story? What are some of the feelings that each participant has individually described? After all group members have briefly told their stories, one member of the group serves as the facilitator for the group. This person collects common themes from the group and records them on the Discover and Dream Chart. This will take about 45 minutes.

12. Bring all participants back together to debrief the activity. Post the flip-chart sheets showing the lens of the organization and the lens of the customer. Using a clean flip-chart sheet, collect the common themes and feelings from each group facilitator.

13. After this collection process, engage the entire group in discussing the procedures, processes, or cultural themes that they would create in their organization if they had no obstacles. Use this time to discuss future training or learning opportunities and focuses for improved customer service programs. Further encourage discussion by comparing and contrasting themes from the various groups. Focus on common findings and ask participants how they may be able to encourage improved customer service in their organization after considering all data collected from this activity. Anticipate that this discussion will take 45 minutes.

Insider's Tips

- Encourage as much participation and discussion as possible.
- Consider anecdotal stories to stimulate activity when you are confident in the delivery of such stories.
- As the trainer, observe all activities as much as possible. Do not allow participants to stray into negative stories or bad experiences. The intent is to discover the positive energy and themes that would improve existing conditions within the organization.

William J. Rothwell, Ph.D., SPHR, FLMT, CTDP, is Professor in Charge of Workforce Education and Development on the University Park campus of Pennsylvania State University, where he heads up a graduate emphasis in workplace learning and performance. Author, coauthor, editor, or coeditor of more than fifty books on human resources, workplace learning, and related fields, Bill was a training director in government and in business for many years before assuming his current role at Penn State. He runs his own consulting company, Rothwell and Associates.

Dennis Gilbert is the managing director of workforce development and continuing education (WDCE) at Pennsylvania College of Technology in Williamsport, Pennsylvania. He is an accomplished trainer, facilitator, and speaker.

William J. Rothwell, Ph.D., SPHR, FLMT, CTDP
Pennsylvania State University
Human Resource Development
605 C Keller Building
State College, PA 16802
Phone: 814.863.2581
Email: wjr9@psu.edu
Website: www.rothwell-associates.com

Discover Customer Service— Question One

What does customer service mean to *you*?
Think about your entire organization. If you were asked to define the important parts of customer service, what would they be? What does good customer service mean to you?

  Spend about 5 minutes to record three to five of your own thoughts, then discuss them with your group for another 5 minutes. Total time: 10 minutes.

1.

2.

3.

4.

5.

Discover Customer Service—
Question Two

What does customer service mean to *our customers*?
Think about what it is like being the customer. Think about what you would want or expect from your experience with using a product or service that your organization produces or supplies. Consider all interactions between your organization and the customer. What would you expect when you telephone, email, walk in, Webshop, or engage with your organization in any manner?

   You are now a customer; you are asked to define the important parts of customer service. What is important to you—the customer? Spend about 5 minutes to record three to five of your own thoughts, then discuss them with your group for another 5 minutes. Total time: 10 minutes.

   1.

   2.

   3.

   4.

   5.

Discover and Dream Data Sheet

The purpose of this activity is to share stories about an exceptional customer service experience in your past.

Think about a time when you experienced exceptional customer service. Formulate the experience in your mind, and recall the details as vividly as possible. Tell the story about that experience. What happened? What are some of the feelings that you were experiencing? What were the contributing factors to the experience? Who was involved? What did you do that may have contributed to this experience?

Describe three procedures, processes, or cultural themes that you would create in your organization to support the kind of experience you described above, assuming you were to have no obstacles.

1.

2.

3.

Discover and Dream Chart

Group facilitator: What are the common themes captured from the storytelling? Review themes and encourage continued discussion as you capture the feelings expressed on the chart below.

Feelings or Recurring Themes and Highlights		
Theme	**Feelings**	
Theme	**Feelings**	
Theme	**Feelings**	
Theme	**Feelings**	

Chapter 7

Diversity and Differences

Whether one is working in the international arena where one needs to understand hidden cultural assumptions that interfere with effective intercultural interaction or working domestically in an environment that is becoming ever more culturally diverse, it is certain that interacting and communicating effectively across cultures is emerging as a critical skill of the twenty-first century.

As a trainer, consultant, executive coach, performance consultant, or course designer, and whether you work internally or are an external provider, you have already bumped into this growing need. You will be asked to enhance the effectiveness of many people whose work brings them in contact with people from other countries and other cultures.

Further, the very role you hold requires you to model the skills of one who understands, respects, and appreciates diversity. You interact with a culturally diverse workforce, and even if you haven't yet begun traveling internationally, there's a very good chance that you will.

The contributors for this chapter have produced a creative array of activities for a variety of situations. Read Carol Friday's (Saudi Arabia) short bio, and you will understand why this might be her favorite activity. Her activity will lead to interesting dialogue. Phil Green's (United Kingdom) Animal Magnetism is an activity that should loosen up even the most reserved person in your group, not to mention that it is a great way to introduce diversity. Julie O'Mara, one of the world's leading authorities on diversity, has updated her Diversity Crossword Puzzle, an activity for which she is recognized. Thanks for the update, Julie. Edwina Pio (New Zealand) has created an activity using parables that gets to the heart of diversity in the workplace in a safe and secure manner.

As organizations develop their workplace strategies, they are looking for ways to maximize and capitalize on workplace diversity and to help their employees understand how cultural factors affect outcomes. These activities will give you a start.

Building Cross-Cultural Awareness

Submitted by Carol J. Friday, M.A.

Objectives

- To demonstrate or explain two "surface" behaviors from a culture different from your own.
- To explain two "hidden" beliefs or concepts from a culture different from your own.

Audience

Intended for groups of individuals from at least two different cultures. Group size should be 15–20, although the activity easily can be adapted for more or fewer. The activity works best if there are several nationalities or subcultures in the session. (It also can work with cross-generational groups.)

Time Required

30–45 minutes, depending on the number of participants.

Materials and Equipment

- Instructions written on a flip chart or handout.
- Two sets of cards. One set has printed "surface" or obvious cultural behaviors and cultural elements (for example, gestures of greeting; holiday customs; common business attire). Another set of cards has printed "hidden" cultural beliefs or concepts (for example, importance of time; meeting style; nature of friendship; concept of personal space in the workplace; concept of leadership).

Area Setup

Room can be set up with tables for small group work. However, this activity can also work with other configurations. Participants can move their chairs to work together before the group call-out work.

Process

1. Explain briefly that cultural differences exist on two levels: one is on the surface, where they are obvious; the other is hidden below the surface, where they are not as obvious to see and understand.

2. Place participants into groups of two or three, with at least two different cultures represented in each group.

3. Have each person take four cards, two from the "surface" cultural behavior pile and two from the "hidden" cultural belief pile.

Editor's Note

If you have a large group, you may want each person to take only one card from each pile.

4. Explain that working in the groups, each person will ask another person from a different culture to explain two surface behaviors and two hidden beliefs from his or her cultural point of view. Allow about 10 minutes for this step.

5. Reconvene the larger group and have participants demonstrate or explain two surface behaviors and explain two hidden beliefs or concepts *from a culture different from their own* to the greater group. Anticipate that this step will take 30–45 minutes depending on the size of the group and the amount of discussion.

6. Allow questions and discussion and expect a lot of laughter!

Insider's Tips

- Make as many different cards as you can. It makes the session more interesting if no similar situations are repeated.
- It helps if you are generally familiar with the customs and beliefs of the participants' cultures.
- A demonstration is helpful. You as facilitator can choose a volunteer. Each of you chooses one card from either pile. Then you ask questions of the volunteer to understand his or her viewpoint about the cultural points. For example, you might ask, "Kim, how do you celebrate the New Year in Korea?" Then Kim asks you a question based on the card he chose. For example, "Please demonstrate how businessmen shake hands in New York." Explain that during the activity to follow, participants will explain to the complete group what they have learned.

Source

This exercise may have been done by someone somewhere, but I do not know of any source offhand.

Carol J. Friday, M.A., is a leadership and learning consultant. She recently coordinated and facilitated a major leadership development program at a large oil company in the Middle East. Previously she helped design, develop, and implement the company's global e-learning initiative. She has worked in Korea, Iran, and the United States as a corporate trainer, business consultant and coach, HRD program developer, and learning consultant. She particularly enjoys addressing multicultural workforce challenges. She holds a master's degree and several professional certificates.

Carol Friday, M.A.
Saudi Aramco Leadership Forum
P.O. Box 5781
Dhahran 31311
Saudi Arabia
Phone: 966.3.876.1551
Email: carol.friday@aramco.com

Animal Magnetism

Submitted by Phil Green, B.Ed., Adv. Dipl. in Primary Ed., Cert. Ed.

Objectives

- To introduce group members to one another, stimulate communication, and set a tone of warmth, collaboration, and good humour.
- To put participants at ease and prepare them for an action-filled session.
- To introduce such topics as diversity, difference, trust, or empathy.

Audience

This activity works for an audience of up to 20 organised into groups of 3, 4, or 5.

Time Required

20 minutes for a group of 20.

Materials and Equipment

- Sheets of newspaper.
- Litter bins or plastic refuse sacks (one per table).
- Pen and paper for each participant.
- Prizes (optional).

Area Setup

Any.

Process

1. Deliver the following instructions:

   To get us all in the right mood for this session, we're about to create some animals from newspaper. I stole this idea from our family party games, so be prepared for some fun. Think about an animal that you can relate to at this time, and plan to create that animal. To make this game a little more challenging, there are three important rules:
   - *You may not use scissors nor cut or shape the newspaper with any other device or implement.*
   - *You may not draw guidelines or features, nor may you colour your product.*
   - *Absolutely no talking as you work.*

2. Tell them that they are probably wondering how they can create an animal. Tell them that they will tear the newspaper as skillfully as they can and that they will have just 1 minute in which to create their animals.

3. Say, "Tear out from your newspaper the shape of the animal that best represents you, or how you are feeling right now. At the end of one minute I'll ask you to hold up your animal so the rest of the group can identify it or at least have a good guess."

4. Tell them that points will be awarded. Say, "Here's how you can win valuable points. Each time your animal is correctly guessed, you gain one point. If you make a correct guess of someone else's animal, you win one point. But if you cheat in any way—by speaking or miming or animating your animal to give out obvious clues—then you lose five points." Continue with "Now, be warned—some people set out feeling comfortable like cats or dangerous like tigers or timid like mice, but their tearing skills may make them finish up as snakes or wiggly worms!"

5. Ask if there are any questions. Then state again that they have 1 minute to create their animals.

6. Once all have completed the task, ask each participant to number notepaper from 1 to 20 (for a group of twenty). Assign a "person number" to each participant. Have each in turn hold up his or her animal for scrutiny for a few seconds.

7. Remind all the others in the group to write their guess, or leave a blank, by the person's number.

8. When all have presented their newspaper animals, ask all participants to name their animals in order. Let group members mark their immediate neighbour's guesses.

9. The winner is the one with the most points. (Of course, you may want to have some kind of prize.)

10. Ask each person why he or she identifies with the animal he or she has created. Continue the discussion depending on what content you are introducing.

Insider's Tips

- Make sure all can see each effort from where they are seated—very tiny animals may need to be paraded around.
- Be prepared to manage lots of riotous laughter.
- Do not tolerate put-downs.

- Be aware that this trivial-seeming exercise provides safe engagement for a very wide range of learner styles, cognitive skills, and perceptual modality—requiring, as it does, skills in listening, presenting, motor co-ordination, observation, metaphor, and empathy. It can serve very well in the context of training managers and trainers where you may wish to reinforce the message of diversity or "different strokes for different folks."

Phil Green, B.Ed., Adv. Dipl. in Primary Ed., Cert. Ed., coaches new and experienced entrants to the field of training design. Widely published in the United Kingdom and overseas, he runs regular workshops and seminars on themes connected with improving performance for individuals, groups, and organisations. A regular commentator for learning forums in the United Kingdom, Phil serves on the committee of the E-Learning Network.

Phil Green, B.Ed., Adv. Dipl. in Primary Ed., Cert. Ed.
Optimum Learning Ltd
Tapton Park Innovation Centre
Brimington Road, Chesterfield
Derbyshire S41 0TZ
United Kingdom
Phone: 44.01246.541904
Email: philgreen@mail.com

Diversity Crossword Puzzle

Submitted by Julie O'Mara

Objectives
- To create knowledge of terminology and concepts of diversity.
- To increase awareness of diversity issues.

Audience
8–36 participants.

Time Required
45 minutes.

Materials and Equipment
- One copy of the Diversity Crossword Puzzle for each team.
- One copy of the Diversity Crossword Puzzle clues for each participant.
- One copy of the Diversity Crossword Puzzle key for each participant.

Area Setup
Best if participants are at table groupings of three or four.

Process
1. Announce the purpose and give a brief overview of the activity.
2. Instruct the participants to form teams of three or four people.
3. Distribute a copy of the crossword puzzle clues to every participant. Give each team a copy of the crossword puzzle and instruct the members to work as a team to complete it. Tell the participants that if the answer is more than one word, they should not leave a blank space between the words. Allow 20 minutes for this step.
4. When all teams seem to have solved as much of the puzzle as possible, reconvene the group and distribute a copy of the crossword puzzle key to each participant. Ask them to check their answers.
5. Debrief this activity by leading a discussion on the participants' reactions to some of the words and concepts. Ask questions such as the following to start the discussion:

- Which terms or meanings were unfamiliar to you? What insight did you gain from learning about them?
- Which terms are controversial? Why? What do they signify to you?
- Which concepts usually cause resentment? Why?
- Which concepts are most misunderstood? What can be done to help people understand them?
- What items surprised you? Why?
- Name one term or definition you want to study about and reflect on following this session.

Mention that there is controversy today over terminology and that many people see "politically correct" as absolutely the right thing to be, whereas others see it as avoidance of the true issues or as "going overboard" on diversity issues.

6. Close the activity by asking participants the following questions:
   - How does the learning from this activity apply to your organization?
   - What will be different if you apply your learning?

 nsider's Tips

- Do some additional study so you are prepared to answer questions and provide additional commentary on the words and clues.
- Use this activity early in a session before you've given participants much information, or use late in a session as a review and "quiz." It can also work as pre-work done individually.
- You can make this into a competition among table groups and offer a prize for the first team that completes the puzzle.
- You can also create your own crossword puzzle customized to a specific topic or dimension of diversity. There are several crossword puzzle makers on the Internet that will create the puzzle grid in just a few minutes after you key in your words and clues.

Source

I developed this activity to increase awareness of diversity issues. A similar activity was published in my book *Diversity Activities and Training Designs* (Pfeiffer, 1994). This is a new puzzle reflecting today's diversity issues.

Julie O'Mara specializes in leadership, facilitation, and diversity. She is coauthor of *Managing Workforce 2000: Gaining the Diversity Advantage* (Jossey-Bass, 1991) and author of *Diversity Activities and Training Designs* (Pfeiffer, 1994). Known for strategic thinking, she is writing a book on diversity best practices around the world. She is a former national ASTD president.

Julie O'Mara
O'Mara and Associates
5979 Greenridge Road
Castro Valley, CA 94552
Phone: 510.582.7744
Email: Julie@omaraassoc.com
Website: www.omaraassoc.com

Diversity Crossword Puzzle

Diversity Crossword Puzzle Clues

Across

1. Being placed in a position of little importance. Often used in reference to any-one not in a dominant group, especially if they are considered unimportant or "lesser than."

6. An umbrella term coined by this community to include all persons with diverse gender behaviors and identifications, including cross-dressing, transsexual, transgenderist, androgyne, and intersex persons.

7. An unreasonable fear or hatred of foreigners or strangers.

8. A science that helps shed some light on how men and women communicate.

9. If current trends continue, this religion will become the world's most popular religion sometime in the mid-21st century.

10. A person of Latin American or Spanish-speaking descent; in some geographi-cal regions, this term is preferred over the term *Hispanic.*

11. U.S. legislation passed in 1972 that has made a significant difference in the participation of girls and women in athletics.

13. A dimension of diversity that includes size, dress, body ornamentation, and attractiveness. Many assumptions about people are made based on factors of this dimension.

14. A dimension of diversity that addresses various age groups and how they interact in the workplace.

15. One thing in return for another. Often used when discussing sexual harass-ment. It is the ultimate in sexual harassment when someone asks for sex in return for something of value, such as a promotion.

17. A clearly agreed-on set of these helps managers and employees know what to do on a daily basis to help achieve an organization's diversity goals.

20. Name of a character from a song written and sung by Daddy Dan Rice in his 1832 minstrel act. The term eventually came to mean *Negro* and was used to describe laws that were passed by legislatures of the U.S. southern states that created a racial caste system.

21. Many _____ _____ were blocked from access to health care until Title VI of the U.S. Civil Rights Act of 1964, which said they could not be legally barred from health services delivery.
22. Extreme anger. Often used to describe the feelings of people who have been oppressed for a long time.
23. A term used in diversity work to describe an unearned advantage of members of a dominant culture. Those who benefit from these advantages are often not aware of them because they are taken for granted. However, people who don't have these benefits are very conscious of them. Two types of this term are *white* and *heterosexual*.
24. A subtle feeling or conflict as a result of diversity.
25. A member of the generational group born in the 1960s or 1970s. There is much controversy about the beliefs, behaviors, and age demographics of this group, of which about 35 percent in the United States are nonwhite or Hispanic.

Down
2. To incorporate the negative cultural values, mores, motives, beliefs, etc., that another identity group believes about your group. You come to believe that those negative messages are true about your group.
3. What one must have to be an effective manager of diversity.
4. A root cause of conflict and discrimination against homosexuals in the workplace.
5. The world's largest religion followed by about a third of those with a formal religion.
12. A person's self-identification with maleness or femaleness.
14. A mind-set that helps expand one's thinking to address diversity issues from a worldwide perspective rather than from the perspective of any one country or region.
16. According to Dr. Roosevelt Thomas, what is really needed to describe jobs, rather than conveniences, preferences, and traditions.
18. Hatred, dislike, or mistrust of women.
19. Term used to describe disabilities that are not obvious and are frequently misunderstood.

Diversity Crossword Puzzle Key

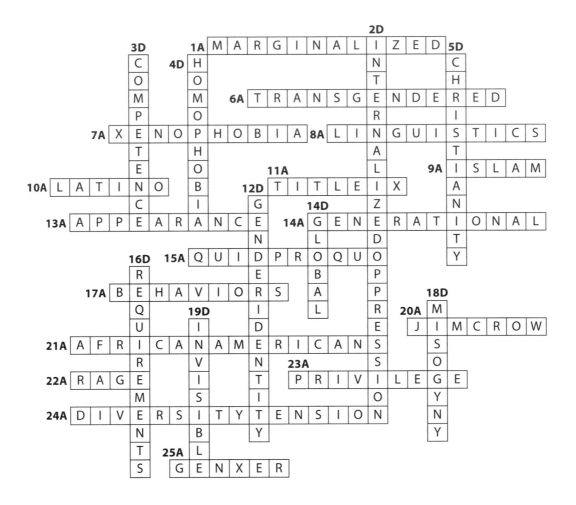

Inspirational Parables in the Multiethnic Swirl

Submitted by Edwina Pio, Ph.D.

Objectives

- To identify and analyse diversity management practices in the workplace through the construction of parables.
- To promote listening skills and instill respect for dialogue and diversity through the creative presentation of parables.

Audience

9–50 participants.

Time Required

Approximately 90 minutes, depending on the size of the audience.

Materials and Equipment

- One copy of the Inspirational Parables in the Multiethnic Swirl Lecturette for the facilitator.
- One copy of Constructing Inspirational Parables for each participant.
- One copy of the Inspirational Parables in the Multiethnic Swirl Suggested Readings for each participant.
- Paper and pens or pencils for each participant.
- If the audience is technologically savvy, laptops can be used along with projection facilities for the presentation.

Area Setup

A room large enough for concentrated group work, with groups varying in size from three to five people per group.

Process

1. Deliver a brief lecturette using the notes provided.

2. Form groups of three to five participants. Try to ensure diversity in each group with reference to ethnicity, gender, and age. Have the participants in each group introduce themselves.

3. Announce that each group is to construct one inspirational parable based on "difference" in terms of ethnicity. The parable must be related to workplace experiences or perceptions—for example, entering the workforce, conducting job interviews, staying in the workforce, managing a multiethnic team, or working overseas. The parable must be inspirational.

4. Hand each participant the Constructing Inspirational Parables sheet and announce that each group will work independently for 25–30 minutes to construct their parables and plan their presentations. Emphasize that all members of the group should participate in the presentation and that each group will have 4 minutes for presentation.

5. Respond to any questions from the participants and be available should any group seek clarification while the participants construct their parables. After 25 minutes, give the participants a 5-minute "get set" reminder before calling time.

6. Have each group present its parable. When all the groups have finished presenting their parables, ask for 2 minutes of silence so that participants can jot down their impressions and learnings in the construction and presentation of their parable, as well as in listening to the parables presented by others.

7. Lead a discussion on the need for dynamic diversity management and the significance of sharing inspirational parables. Ask these questions:
   - How did you feel about this activity?
   - What did you learn about yourself?
   - How did this activity help you understand diversity concerns?
   - How can you transfer this learning to the workplace?

8. Conclude by giving participants the Inspirational Parables Suggested Readings. Thank the participants for weaving their personal experiences of the multiethnic swirl and sharing their thoughts in the session.

 nsider's Tips

- Keep the structure in terms of instructions and clarifications on the word *inspirational* and the concept of parables fairly loose and unstructured to give space for the participants' perceptions and experiences to emerge.
- Encourage creative presentations, including song, dance, theatre.
- Focus on the word *inspirational* and the layers of meaning that are possible when constructing and interpreting parables.
- If the group size is small, ask each group to construct two parables.

Edwina Pio, Ph.D., is Senior Business Faculty, Auckland University of Technology, New Zealand, and visiting professor at Boston College, MA. She is widely traveled, and her work takes her to Asia, America, Europe, and Oceania. She specializes in diversity management research and implementation and is a regular contributor to the *Pfeiffer Annuals* and other international journals.

Edwina Pio, Ph.D.
Faculty of Business (Management)
Auckland University of Technology
Private Bag 92006
Auckland 1020
New Zealand
Phone: 64.9.921.9999, ext. 5130
Email: Edwina.pio@aut.ac.nz

Inspirational Parables in the Multiethnic Swirl Lecturette

Parables have been used since time immemorial to transmit knowledge and information about the world, and they have been used by all cultures. The etymology of the word *parable* is from the Greek *parabola* and *paraballein,* which mean "to compare or place beside."

A parable is a short story about the behaviour of human beings with an ethical slant in the story. Parables have many layers of meaning and allow space for the listener to make his or her own conclusions and applications in life by conveying a sense of paradox and stretching the logical, rational mind.

Parables can be varied in subject matter—for example, entering the workforce, conducting job interviews, staying in the workforce, managing a multiethnic team, working overseas, mentoring, and working on multiethnic project groups or multi-ethnic interview panels and boards. Inspirational parables are meant to exert an enlivening, animating, hopeful, and/or optimistic mood in the listener, often leading to thoughtful action and/or mindful behaviour change.

Parables can help to deconstruct discourse and incorporate a variety of perspectives, for they acknowledge multiple voices and can set the scene for multi-faceted communication.

In an organizational context, they can be the source for norm and value sharing and can have the potential to evoke reflection and dialogue by adding value to exploring difference.

Parables can serve as an invitation to understand and appreciate the dynamic nature of diversity in the workplace, particularly in the context of international population mobility and significant demographic changes in countries as well as in the nature of doing business and the diversity of workforce projections.

Effective diversity programs involve being in synch with the business plans of the organization, deciding what the program will achieve, and assessing the resources required within the context of the particular country's legislative and business framework as well as the organization's human resources policies.

Inspirational Parables in the Multiethnic Swirl Lecturette (continued)

Diversity management needs to be clearly articulated and measurable if a continuously supportive work environment for employees is to be achieved. Ernst & Young, Hewlett Packard, IBM, Lucent Technologies, McDonald's, Pepsi, and PriceWaterhouseCoopers are companies with interesting and successful diversity programs. For those individuals who feel marginalized or are perceived as different, corporations that elucidate diversity policies are generally easier places to work in, for they believe that diversity makes good business sense and implement such beliefs in practice. Hence people feel valued for their contribution irrespective of their ethnicity or other differences, and this helps craft the culture of the organization.

Organizations across the globe are becoming more keenly aware that dynamic diversity management implies changes in many aspects of the company's culture and that such dynamism is more than cultural celebrations and must be tied to the strategic goals of the company. Diversity management is about creating an environment where there is dignity and respect for all so that every individual can be encouraged to learn and contribute to the competitive advantage of their organizations.

Constructing Inspirational Parables

The Concept

A parable is a short story about the behaviour of human beings with an ethical slant in the story. Parables have many layers of meaning and allow space for the listener to make his or her own conclusions and applications in life while conveying a sense of paradox and often stretching the logical, rational mind. Parables can be varied in subject matter—for example, entering the workforce, conducting job interviews, staying in the workforce, managing a multiethnic team, working overseas, mentoring, or working in a multiethnic project group.

Inspirational parables are meant to exert an enlivening, animating, hopeful, and/or optimistic mood in the listener, often leading to thoughtful action and/or mindful behaviour change.

Steps in Construction

1. Each participant in the group can share his or her own story and perceptions of an incident with reference to ethnicity in the workplace.
2. The group members can decide which elements of the shared stories they would like to use in the construction of their parable.
3. A title for the parable is often a helpful focusing point.
4. Identify what you want the audience to know.
5. Identify what you want the audience to remember.
6. Use word pictures and descriptive phrases to illustrate your parable.
7. Target approximately 400–500 words.
8. Plan your presentation to make it memorable for yourself and the audience.

Inspirational Parables in the Multiethnic Swirl: Suggested Readings

Publications

Bell, E. L., & Nkomo, S. M. (2001). *Our separate ways: Black and white women and the struggle for professional identity.* Boston: Harvard Business School Press.

Cox, K. (2001). Stories as case knowledge: Case knowledge as stories. *Medical Education, 35,* 862–866.

Denning, S. (2004). Telling tales. *Harvard Business Review, 82*(5), 122–129.

Orbe, M., & Harris, T. (2001). *Interracial communication: Theory into practice.* (Belmont, CA: Wadsworth).

Pio, E. (2005). Rich traditions: Managing diversity. In E. Biech (Ed.), *The 2005 Pfeiffer annual: Training* (pp. 19–30). San Francisco: Pfeiffer.

Sole, D., & Wilson, D. (2002). Storytelling in organizations: The power and traps of using stories to share knowledge in organizations. *Training and Development, 53*(3), 44–52.

Stockdale, M. S., & Crosby, F. J. (Eds.). (2003). *The psychology and management of workplace diversity.* Malden, MA: Blackwell.

Websites

http://oeo.od.nih.gov/diversitymgmt

www.apsc.gov.au/publications01/diversityguidelines.htm

www.ethnicmajority.com/workplace.htm

www.ilr.cornell.edu/library/subjectGuides/workplaceDiversity.html

www.inform.umd.edu/EdRes/Topic/Diversity/Response/Workplace/

www.shrm.org/diversity/

www.workplacediversity.info/

Chapter 8

Leadership

Probably no topic has more books and articles published about it than leadership. Leadership is studied from a business, military, and personal perspective. Books examine leadership in terms of trust, credibility, the heart, intelligence, vision, change, commitment, honesty, stewardship, and performance. And authors still debate whether leadership is a science, an art, or a bit of both.

Who are the leaders of today and the recent past? Mohandas Gandhi, Winston Churchill, Abraham Lincoln, Franklin Roosevelt, Martin Luther King Jr., Margaret Thatcher, Nelson Mandela, Bill Gates, Rudy Giuliani? And who will be the leaders of the future? Trainers, consultants, and coaches have a huge job to prepare the world's future leaders. Are you prepared to do that?

The first three contributors focus on activities that provide clarity about what a leader represents. Marjorie Blanchard offers an activity in which leaders define their points of view. Marlene Caroselli uses quotations from various leaders to stimulate discussion about the topic of leadership. Jim Kouzes, whose leadership resources have been used by over one million professionals, contributes an activity to help participants see the connection between clarity of personal values and commitment.

Jean Lamkin tells us how leaders can use a "board of encouragement" to develop a leadership development action plan. Bob Preziosi teaches us how to play Leadership Bean Bag Volleyball to raise awareness of leadership characteristics. Lorraine Ukens uses a twenty-first-century activity, Laser Beam Bounce, to observe the leader's role in a team.

Which of our future leaders are you currently working with?

Developing Your Leadership Point of View

Submitted by Marjorie Blanchard, Ph.D.

Objectives
- To help leaders both define and share their leadership point of view.
- To help the people on whom the leader has an impact know what the leader expects and what can be expected from the leader.

Audience
About 20 people per facilitator, in groups of 5.

Time Required
3–4 hours.

Materials and Equipment
- One copy of the Your Leadership Point of View Group Directions for each participant.
- Paper and pen for each participant.

Area Setup
Round tables with five chairs for each group.

Process
1. Provide each participant with a copy of the directions and tell them that they will think and write notes about who and what has influenced them regarding their beliefs about their leadership role and their values related to that role. Ideally this includes their models for leadership and what they learned from both negative and positive experiences. Encourage them to accompany major points with a story or example versus just proselytizing. They should also think and write about what others can expect from them and what they expect, again with examples if possible. The goal for each participant is to share and get feedback from fellow team members and distill their leadership point of view down to something they could communicate in 8–10 minutes.

2. Tell them they have 20 minutes to begin their descriptions. Tell them it is important that each of them prepare as though he or she were actually addressing a group back home.
3. After the 20 minutes have ended, have each group begin the feedback step. One by one, participants share their leadership point of view with tablemates and get feedback. Ideally, each person has at least three opportunities to share and get feedback. After two rounds you may wish to reshuffle the groups so participants have a new audience.
4. This exercise can be expanded by having each participant share his or her leadership point of view with the entire group. This takes about 20 minutes per person, but it is a great bonding experience for a team of leaders. Each leader is then expected to deliver his or her leadership point of view to the appropriate team back on the job.

nsider's Tips

- It is helpful for the facilitator to read three or four leadership points of view from prior classes or groups. Also, it is helpful for the facilitator to sit in with each group for enough time to be sure they are on track.
- The biggest problem is that participants try to say too much and do not use examples. It is best to say much less and have a story or example for each major point.

Source
This activity has been included in several of the Ken Blanchard Company workbooks.

Marjorie Blanchard, Ph.D., cofounded the Ken Blanchard Companies in 1979 with her husband, Ken Blanchard. From 1987 to 1997, she served as president of the firm, spearheading its growth to $30M and over 200 employees. Today, Margie leads Blanchard's innovative Office of the Future. She writes and speaks on life balance, retention, and leadership.

Marjorie Blanchard, Ph.D.
Ken Blanchard Companies
125 State Place
Escondido, CA 92029
Phone: 769.489.5005
Email: margie.blanchard@kenblanchard.com
Website: www.kenblanchard.com

Your Leadership Point of View
Group Directions

This exercise will help you define your personal leadership point of view. As you work through this exercise, imagine that you are addressing a group at your company or department. Use the time guidelines to stay within the schedule.

Round 1

20 minutes: Write several paragraphs that describe who or what has influenced you regarding your beliefs and values about your leadership role. Include thoughts about your leadership model; what you've learned from positive and negative experience; what others can expect from you and what you expect from others. Add examples and stories to clarify your points.

75 minutes: Each team member reads what he or she wrote to his or her team. Team members provide feedback to the individual. As feedback is provided, listen carefully, take copious notes, and accept the feedback graciously. Each person is allowed a maximum of 15 minutes.

Round 2

15 minutes: Use the feedback and rewrite your leadership statement.

50 minutes: Again read what you wrote and obtain feedback from your team. Each person is allowed 10 minutes.

Round 3

10 minutes: Use the feedback and rewrite your leadership statement one last time.

50 minutes: Read your leadership statement and listen for comments that will help you polish your final leadership point of view.

Quotable Leaders

Submitted by Marlene Caroselli, Ed.D.

Objectives

- To familiarize participants with great thoughts from great leaders.
- To stimulate discussion via sharing of participants' insights.

Audience

This activity works best if the group is divided into teams of 4–6 participants.

Time Estimated

20 minutes.

Materials and Equipment

- One copy of the Do You Think Like the Great Thinkers? worksheet for each participant.
- One copy of the Answer Sheet for Do You Think Like the Great Thinkers? for the facilitator.
- Token prizes. (I like to distribute "knowledge-prizes": used books or copies of magazine articles relevant to the subject matter.)

Area Setup

Table groups are ideal for this exercise.

Process

1. Distribute the worksheet and allow about 10 minutes for teams to discuss and vote (collectively) "Agree" or "Disagree" for each statement.
2. Process the activity by asking the following:
   - What did you learn from the activity?
   - What did you learn about yourself?
   - How does this activity relate to what you want to know?
   - How can you apply this information?
3. Go over the answers.
4. Award prizes to the team(s) that had a perfect score—in other words, their thoughts paralleled exactly the thoughts of great leaders.

Insider's Tips

- Sometimes, if a team that came close to winning wishes to argue a point, I encourage the participants to do so. If their presentation is indeed persuasive—in other words, their thinking is the opposite of the great leader's thinking but is convincing nonetheless—I grant them the point. The test, after all, is designed to see if they think the way great leaders think. But that's not to say that the great leaders are always right or that their viewpoint is the only one that makes sense. (For example, with regard to the quotation from Mother Teresa, business leader Jim Collins would take exception: he encourages us to have BHAGs—Big, Hairy, Audacious Goals.) So if a team thinks differently but thinks well, it deserves the credit.
- Ask participants to identify bold statements that influence their leadership.
- Although the topic focuses on quotations from leaders, the activity will work in courses dealing with supervision, management, ethics, communication, interpersonal skills, administrative support, team building, and many other topics.

Marlene Caroselli, Ed.D., author of fifty-five business books, is an international keynote speaker and corporate trainer for Fortune 100 companies, government agencies, educational institutions, and professional organizations. In 1984, she founded the Center for Professional Development, an organization dedicated to helping working adults enhance their professional skills. Among her clients are Lockheed-Martin, Mobil Chemical, Magnavox, Allied Signal, the New York State Education Department, UCLA, and the United States Office of Personnel Management.

Marlene Caroselli, Ed.D.
Center for Professional Development
Fetzner Square
80 Greenwood Park
Pittsford, NY 14534
Phone: 585.249.0084
Email: mccpd@frontiernet.net
Website: www.caroselli.biz

Do You Think Like the Great Thinkers?

Bold statements typically have great impact on an audience. And if the statements resonate, they can be quite influential. You'll have 10 minutes to discuss the following bold statements with your team. As a group, you'll make a collective "Agree" or "Disagree" choice as to whether each of these statements is what the speaker said.

1. "Wealth is the control of knowledge."

2. "Knowledge is more important than imagination."

3. "If you have gone a whole week without being disobedient, you are doing yourself and your firm a disservice."

4. "It's better to give directions than direction."

5. "Money is the most powerful motivator of outstanding performance."

6. "Organizations should engage in tribal storytelling."

7. "Psychology accounts for 95 percent of workplace success."

8. "Creative minds cannot survive bad training."

9. "A great leader need only depend on himself or herself."

10. "It's impossible to do great things, so we should stick with small goals."

90 World-Class Activities by 90 World-Class Trainers. Copyright © 2007 by John Wiley & Sons, Inc.
Published by Pfeiffer, an Imprint of Wiley. www.pfeiffer.com

Answer Sheet for Do You Think Like the Great Thinkers?

1. Agree. These are the words of economist Lester Thurow.

2. Disagree. Einstein actually said, "Imagination is more important than knowledge."

3. Agree. Management guru and avowed rebel Tom Peters encourages the asking of questions when things don't seem quite right.

4. Disagree. General George Patton advised would-be leaders to "give direction, not directions."

5. Disagree. The research of Frederick Herzberg (and numerous others) shows that people perform best when tasked with challenging work and when their work is appreciated.

6. Agree. Author and former CEO of Herman Miller Furniture, Max DePree, says (in *Leadership Is an Art*) that we need to keep alive the best of our organizational stories.

7. Agree. Hatim Tyabji, CEO of Verifone, asserts that the key to individual and organization success is an understanding of human behavior.

8. Disagree. Austrian psychoanalyst Anna Freud maintained that "creative minds have always been known to survive any kind of bad training."

9. Disagree. Teton Sioux chief Lone Man asserted, "I have seen that in any great undertaking, it is not enough for a man to depend simply upon himself."

10. Agree. It was Mother Teresa who said, "We can do no great things, only small things with great love."

Credo Memo

Submitted by Jim Kouzes

Objectives
- To help participants see the connection between clarity of personal values and commitment to an organization.
- To help participants express their personal values to their constituents in their work setting.

Audience
Participants interested in improving their leadership skills.

Time Required
60 minutes.

Materials and Equipment
- Prepared flip chart to match Impact of Values Clarity on Commitment.
- Paper and pens.
- One copy of the Impact of Values Clarity on Commitment handout for each participant.
- One copy of the Your Credo Memo handout for each participant.
- One copy of the Clarifying Your Values handout for each participant.

Area Setup
Workspace with tables and room for small group work.

Process
1. Begin by saying,

    Let's talk about the say part of "Do What You Say You Will Do." Leaders can't do what they say if they have nothing to say. They can't walk the talk if they have no talk. They can't practice what they preach if they have no sermon. The place leaders must start earning and sustaining their credibility and becoming role models is with finding their voice. They have to clarify their values and beliefs. They have to be clear about the core principles that guide them in their work and personal life. Only then can they choose the actions that are consistent with those principles. We also know that a person's clarity around his or her personal values directly affects the level of commitment that person has toward his or her organization.

2. Show the prepared flip-chart page with the blank Impact of Values Clarity on Commitment matrix. Hand participants a copy of Impact of Values Clarity on Commitment.

3. Ask participants what they think the relationship is between a leader's clarity about personal values and his or her clarity about the organization's values. "Which combination of the two factors—clarity about personal values and clarity about organizational values—contributes most to a person's level of commitment to an organization?" Elicit several responses. Then write "6.26" in the top right-hand corner of the matrix.

4. Explain that using a scale of 1 to 7, with 1 equaling low commitment and 7 equaling high commitment, Jim Kouzes and Barry Posner found that the score here was 6.26, indicating that the highest level of commitment comes when an individual has clarity about both the organization's values and his and her own personal values. Ask, "Does that surprise you?"

5. Ask, "Which combination do you believe contributes the next highest level of commitment?" Elicit a few responses. Then write "6.12" into the bottom right-hand corner of the matrix. Explain that "being clear only on your personal values, even when you are not so clear about the organization's, is crucial to organizational commitment. Notice that there is only a small difference between clarity on both sets of values and clarity on only personal values."

6. Ask, "Which combination of clarity on personal and organizational values contributes the least to organizational commitment?" Elicit a few responses. Then enter the final two figures into the matrix: 4.87 in the upper left and 4.90 in the lower left. Say, "Although many people believe that the combination of low clarity on organizational values and low clarity on personal values would contribute least to organizational commitment, it's actually the combination at the upper left of the matrix—high clarity on organizational values and low clarity on personal values."

7. Ask participants what message they take from these findings. Elicit several responses. Make this point if participants do not mention it: "Commitment to the organization comes more from clarity of personal values than clarity of organizational values." Ask *why* clarity about values leads to greater commitment. Elicit a few responses. Make this point if participants don't mention it: "People with clear values are quicker to realize that their values are (or are not) consistent with those of their organization. Without clarity, we might be unhappy without an understanding of or conviction about the source of our discomfort."

8. Add this point: "Before you take a group off on a retreat to develop organizational values, first make sure that people are clear about their personal values. You can see from this matrix that clarity around organizational values by itself does not produce high levels of commitment. In order to have commitment, people must know what they personally value."

9. Make a transition to the next step by saying, "Because clarity of personal values is so important to organizational commitment, everyone in the organization should have the opportunity to clarify his or her personal values and examine the fit between personal and organizational values. That includes, you, the leader. You need to do this first for yourself. Your ability to DWYSYWD (do what you say you will do) is going to depend on how clear you are about your values and how well they fit with the organization's values. The next step in this activity will take us in this direction."

10. Explain that participants will now have the opportunity to express their values in a way that will help guide the actions of their associates: they will complete a credo memo. Ask, "What is a credo?" Expect responses to include the following:
    - A statement of your values and beliefs
    - From the Leadership Practices Inventory (LPI) question 26, your philosophy of leadership
    - A creed, a set of fundamental beliefs

11. Explain that *credo* comes from the Latin for "I believe." It is also the word root of "credit" and "credibility." When you are given "credit," the lender is saying, "I believe you can repay this debt." In a similar way, when constituents grant us credit or credibility, they are saying, "I believe in you. I believe you will keep your promises to us to do what you say."

12. Hand each participant a copy of Your Credo Memo. Explain that this activity will give them an opportunity to clarify their values and express them to their constituents.

13. Say, "Imagine that you are about to take a six-month sabbatical. Your team will be managing without you. Before you leave, you have just enough time to write a memo explaining the key values and guiding principles you would like people to use when making decisions and taking actions during your absence. Think about what you would like to say and then use this page to write your memo."

14. Urge participants to imagine that the scenario is real and to respond as if it were actually going to happen. Remind them to avoid simple, catchy slogans like "Just Do It" and to be as clear as they can in communicating their values. Give participants 5–8 minutes to write their memos.

15. When they are finished, hand them a copy of Clarifying Your Values and ask them to share what they wrote, either with a small group or with a partner if time is tight: "Read your credo memo aloud to your colleagues (or partner). Ask them to tell you what values they heard. Did they match what you intended?"

16. Debrief the activity by asking these kinds of questions:
    - What did people in your group (or your partner) say in their credo memos? Responses might be similar to these:
        - I trust you to do what is right.
        - Work together as teams.
        - When in doubt, think about the customers' needs.
    - Who heard a memo that they think the entire group would benefit from? Ask whether the writer would be willing to share his or her memo with the group.
    - How many of you have ever published your values, beliefs, and leadership philosophy for your people? What happened?
    - How closely do your behaviors actually model what you wrote in your credo memo? For example, if your group found your memo, but it did not have your name on it, would they know you had written it, because your behaviors so closely model what you wrote? Why or why not? (You might add, "If your group found your memo and it did have your name on it, would they scratch their heads in amazement, wondering how you could say something so different from the way you act?")

> **Editor's Note**
>
> These two questions may be for reflection only; participants do not have to answer them publicly.

Source

This activity was published in *The Leadership Challenge Workshop Facilitator's Guide* (Jossey-Bass, 2005).

Jim Kouzes is the coauthor with Barry Posner of the award-winning and best-selling book, *The Leadership Challenge* (Jossey-Bass, 2003), with over one million copies sold. He's also an executive fellow at the Center for Innovation and Entrepreneurship, Leavey School of Business, Santa Clara University. The third edition of *The Leadership Challenge,* released in fall 2002, debuted as number four on the *BusinessWeek* best-seller list, the only third edition of any book ever to make that list. *The Leadership Challenge,* available in eleven languages, has been a selection of the

Macmillan Executive Book Club and the Fortune Book Club. It's the winner of the 1989 James A. Hamilton Hospital Administrators' Book and the 1995–96 Critics' Choice Award, and was a *BusinessWeek* best-seller in 2001 and 2002. Jim and Barry have also coauthored *Credibility: How Leaders Gain and Lose It, Why People Demand It* (Jossey-Bass, 1993), *The Leadership Challenge Workbook* (Pfeiffer, 2003), and *The Leadership Challenge Journal* (Pfeiffer, 2003). The *Leadership Practices Inventory* (LPI) (Jossey-Bass, 2003), a 360-degree questionnaire assessing leadership behavior, has been the basis of more than 250 doctoral dissertations and academic research projects. *The Wall Street Journal* has cited Jim as one of the twelve best executive educators in the United States. Jim served as president and then as CEO and chairman of the Tom Peters Company from 1988 to 2000.

Jim Kouzes
The Leadership Challenge
117 Casa Vieja Place
Orinda, CA 94563
Phone: 925.254.8699
Fax: 925.254.6606
Email: jim@kouzesposner.com
Website: www.leadershipchallenge.com

Impact of Values Clarity on Commitment

What happens when individuals are clear about their own and their organization's values?

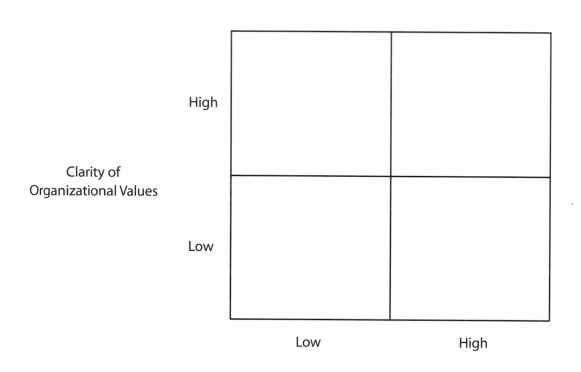

Clarity of Organizational Values — High / Low

Clarity of Personal Values — Low / High

Your Credo Memo

Clarity of values enables us to feel more confident in our voice. It makes us feel strong and assured. Because clarity of values is so important to the credibility of leaders, we're going to ask you to write your own credo memo.

Imagine that your organization has afforded you the chance to take a six-month sabbatical, all expenses paid.

You will be going to a beautiful island where the average temperature is about 80 degrees Fahrenheit during the day. The sun shines in a brilliant sky, with a few wisps of clouds. A gentle breeze cools the island down in the evening, and a light rain clears the air. You wake up in the morning to the scent of tropical flowers.

You may not take any work along on this sabbatical. And you will not be permitted to communicate with anyone at your office or plant—not by letter, phone, fax, e-mail, or other means. It's just you, a few good books, some music, and your family or a friend.

But before you depart, those with whom you work need to know something. They need to know the principles that you believe should guide their actions in your absence. They need to know the values and beliefs that you think should steer their decision making and action taking.

You are permitted no long reports, however. Just a one-page memorandum. If given this opportunity, what would you write on your one-page credo memo?

Take out one piece of paper and write that memo.

Clarifying Your Values

Dialogue assists clarification. The purpose of this step is to help you in gaining greater clarity about your guiding beliefs.

1. Select a partner. The person whose birthday is closer to today's date will start the conversation.

2. Each of you will have the chance to tell your partner about your values and beliefs. For the next few minutes, simply have a conversation about what you really care about.

3. While your partner is talking, your task is to listen and to pay attention to what your partner is saying. Listen for understanding. If you are not clear, ask questions for clarification. Again, the purpose of this activity is to gain clarity about each other's guiding beliefs.

4. After each of you shares your values, express appreciation for what the other expressed and how she or he expressed it. The task is really simple: just thank the other person for what he or she said and how he or she said it.

90 World-Class Activities by 90 World-Class Trainers. Copyright © 2007 by John Wiley & Sons, Inc.
Published by Pfeiffer, an Imprint of Wiley. www.pfeiffer.com

Board of Encouragement

Submitted by Jean G. Lamkin, Ph.D.

Objectives

- To create a personal action plan for leadership development.
- To strengthen the plan through feedback from "board" members.

Audience

Each "board" is composed of four people. If possible, each person on the board has been identified as having a different profile—for example, a harmonizer, a driver, an analyzer, and an adapter. (This exercise may be used for any communication or social assessment instrument that results in multiple designations, such as the MBTI or DISC.) The variety of styles on the board ensures that the feedback will be generated from a broad set of perspectives.

Time Required

35 minutes per person, with 5-minute breaks between people; about 2½ hours total.

Materials and Equipment

- One copy of the Individualized Board Meeting Format for each participant.
- Four copies of Board Member's Feedback for each participant.
- One copy of Catch the Moment for each participant.
- One copy of the Leadership Development Action Plan for each participant.

Area Setup

Small tables that seat four. An informal outdoor patio area works well.

Process

1. Form boards of four and assign a location for each board. Give each person a copy of the Individualized Board Meeting Format and overview the process with them. State that they will proceed in order of their birth date starting with January 1. Once they are settled in their assigned locations, tell them that they can follow your instructions (steps) on the format handout.
2. The focus person overviews his or her situation by reflecting on strengths and areas for development.
3. The three board members ask questions. Note that the more questions the better and that follow-up questions are okay. The focus person can pass if he

Leadership

159

or she doesn't want to answer the question, but should note what it was. Allow about 10 minutes for this step.

4. Distribute the handouts to participants. Assign 5 minutes of silence during which:
   - The board members summarize their thoughts and recommendations using the Board Member's Feedback form.
   - The focus person uses the Catch the Moment form to list two thoughts and ideas.
5. The next 15 minutes are spent in dialogue as each board member communicates his or her ideas, leading to an open group dialogue. The board focuses on coming together in a solidified oneness in an attitude of support, affirmation, and trust.
6. Take a 5-minute break (mandatory).
7. Repeat this process with the remaining three board members.

 ## Insider's Tips

- Use an assessment that will give participants good feedback on their styles and strengths.
- The participants should be a cohort group in a long-term development program that will bring them together several times. This activity creates a strong bond between the board members, and they should be encouraged to communicate after leaving the session. At a subsequent session, they review their plans and progress using the same process. They develop new plans to go forward.

Source
This activity was developed by Gary J. O'Malley and Lee Ellis of RightPath Resources. You may contact the company at www.rightpath.com.

Jean G. Lamkin, Ph.D., is the director of career development for the Landmark Publishing Group of Landmark Communications, Inc. Her customers include newspapers, cable television stations, and new ventures operations. This activity is part of the curriculum created for the Weather Channel's Emerging Sales Leaders Program in 2005.

Jean G. Lamkin, Ph.D.
Landmark Communications
150 W. Brambleton Avenue
Norfolk, VA 23510
Phone: 757.446.2913
Email: jlamkin@lcimedia.com

Individualized Board Meeting Format

Each board member will be the "focus" for 30 minutes. Order yourselves according to birth dates beginning with January 1. Follow the five steps.

1. 5 minutes—Action Plan Overview
   - The first focus person overviews his or her situation by reflecting on strengths and areas for development. This may be based on a previous assessment.

2. 7 minutes—Questions Only
   - Board members ask the focus person questions, and the focus person provides brief responses.
   - Remember:
     - The more questions the better.
     - Follow-up questions are okay.
     - The focus person can pass if he or she doesn't want to answer.

3. 5 minutes—Silence
   - Board members summarize thoughts and recommendations using Board Member's Feedback form.
   - Focus person uses Catch the Moment form to note thoughts, ideas, and key questions.

4. 15 minutes—Dialogue
   - Each board member communicates his or her ideas.
   - Begin an open group dialogue.
   - Allow the focus person the last 3 minutes to capture actions on the Leadership Development Action Plan form.

5. 5 minutes—Mandatory Break

Board Member's Feedback

Individual's Name _____

Board Member's Name _____

1. Here's what I am hearing:

2. Here's what I am thinking:

3. Here's what I am suggesting:

Catch the Moment

Remember, effective board members:

     Care

     Dare to ask

     Tear down walls

     Wear well

Key Questions:

1.

2.

3.

4.

5.

Essential Principles/Ideas/Reminders:

Leadership Development Action Plan

Struggles I face:

       Why this occurs:

       What I can do about it:

Strengths I will use:

As a leader, I must remember:

As a result of my board's feedback, I plan to take the following actions:

1.

2.

3.

4.

5.

I will continue to involve the following people in my growth and development:

Signed _____ Date _____

Leadership Beanbag Volleyball

Submitted by Robert C. Preziosi, D.P.A.

Objectives
- To raise awareness of leadership qualities and characteristics during the launch of a leadership training program.
- To provide an energizer to introduce the topic of leadership.

Audience
This activity is designed for a group of 12–16 participants in a leadership development program.

Time Required
About 20–25 minutes.

Materials and Equipment
- Two easels with flip-chart pads.
- Flip-chart markers.
- Roll of 1-inch masking tape.
- One beanbag approximately 3 by 3 inches.
- Bags of wrapped candy for prizes.

Area Setup
An empty area approximately 30 by 30 feet. Position easels in corners along a common wall.

Process
1. Divide the room space in half to form a volleyball court. Use masking tape on the floor to identify two different playing areas.
2. Divide the participants into two equal teams. Have each team line up on opposite sides of the court and arrange themselves into volleyball team positions.
3. Explain to all participants that they are going to play a game of Beanbag Volleyball.

4. Toss the beanbag to one of the teams as preparation to start the game and explain the rules of the game.
   - The game begins when one team member makes a "soft" underhand toss to the directly opposite player on the other team.
   - If the player on the other team catches the beanbag, she or he has a right to name one characteristic of a successful leader.
   - The facilitator writes the characteristic on that team's flip chart and makes a reinforcing comment.
   - The teams alternate throwing and catching with a catch required to name different characteristics. If the beanbag isn't caught or is dropped, the right to name a characteristic is lost. Characteristics may not be repeated during the game.
   - A characteristic on one team's flip chart may not be on the other team's flip chart.
   - Throwing and catching the beanbag is rotated among all players on both teams.
   - One round is completed when everyone has had an opportunity to throw and catch the beanbag.
   - Play two complete rounds.
   - The team with more characteristics after two rounds is pronounced the winner. If the two teams are tied, both are declared the winner. Provide candy to the winners.
5. Conclude the activity by calling everyone's attention to the lists and make "bridging" comments to translate to the next activity in the session.

 **nsider's Tips**

- Make sure that all the beanbag tosses are thrown softly and underhand.
- Relate the flip-chart lists to the actual content of the training program.
- Be certain to allow flexibility for anyone with a disability.
- Encourage teams to clap each time a team member catches the beanbag.

Robert C. Preziosi, D.P.A., is a professor of management in the Huizenga School of Business at Nova Southeastern University. He is a former HR director and a VP of management development, currently teaching nontraditional graduate students in HR, HRD, and leadership. Bob has been training trainers for over twenty years and is the editor of the *Pfeiffer Annuals* on HRM and management development. He is a frequent presenter at professional and academic conferences.

Robert C. Preziosi, D.P.A.
Huizenga School of Business
3301 College Avenue
Ft. Lauderdale, FL 33314
Phone: 954.262.5111
Email: preziosi@huizenga.nova.edu

Laser Beam Bounce

Submitted by Lorraine L. Ukens, M.S.

Objectives
- To examine the role of the leader in the group process.
- To observe how the collaboration of individual efforts contribute to the team effort.

Audience
Several groups of 6–10 persons each.

Time Required
20–30 minutes.

Materials and Equipment
- A laser pointer for each group.
- A small pocket mirror for each participant.

Area Setup
A large open space.

Process
1. Direct the participants to form groups of six to ten persons each. Select one person from each group to act as the group leader.
2. Distribute a laser pointer to each group leader and a mirror to all remaining participants. Explain that the goal of the activity is for the group members to use the mirrors to transmit the laser beam from person to person until all the mirrors are reflecting the beam, which will be started by the leader, who shines the laser pointer onto the mirror of the first person. Stress the importance of safety in directing the laser beam so that it does not shine into anyone's eyes. To prevent this from occurring, the mirrors should be held at waist level.

3. Signal for the activity to begin and allow approximately 10 minutes for the groups to work on the task. Make note of which groups are able to accomplish the task and the various methods used.

4. Lead a concluding discussion based on the following questions:
   - What approach did your group take to accomplish the task? Was it successful? Why or why not?
   - What factors influenced a group's ability to succeed? How did the achievement of each individual contribute to the overall success of the group?
   - How important was the role of the leader? Why? What happens when the leader shifts position?
   - How can we relate what occurred in this activity to the overall concept of leadership within the group process? How does it relate to group member collaboration? To teamwork in general?
   - How is a laser beam like a company vision? Is the vision of your organization clear and straightforward, or does it waver, dim, or extinguish? In what ways and why?
   - What is the leader's role in sharing the vision?
   - What concluding remarks can you make regarding leadership?

Insider's Tips

- Be aware of the safety issues of using laser pointers in this activity. There is very little danger as long as the beam is not pointed directly at someone's eyes. The majority of the laser pointers used in the United States use Class 2 or 3a diode lasers in the 630–680 nm wavelength (red), with a maximum power output of between 1 and 5 mW. The length of exposure to visible lasers is usually limited by the *eye's* blink reflex, which normally occurs within a quarter of a second. *Do not* use laser pointers that emit a green beam.
- The most efficient way to accomplish the task is to have group members form two lines facing one another and spaced very close together, and then relay the beam back and forth from one person to the other.
- As a variation, you can direct the members of each group to form a circle and relay the beam from person to person until it makes a complete circuit around the group.

Source

I published this activity in *The New Encyclopedia of Group Activities* (Pfeiffer, 2004).

Lorraine L. Ukens, M.S., is a consultant specializing in team building and experiential learning. She is the author of several training activity books, consensus activities, and games that make learning interactive and fun. Lorraine earned her B.S. in psychology and M.S. in human resource development from Towson University in Maryland.

Lorraine L. Ukens, M.S.
Team-ing with Success
25252 Quail Croft Place
Leesburg, FL 34748
Phone: 352.365.0378
Email: ukens@team-ing.com
Website: www.team-ing.com

Chapter 9

Organizations and Process Improvement

"**O**rganizations are the world's 21st-century dilemma. They are magnificent and mad, wonderful and wretched, crazy and compelling. They make so little, and so much, sense." Thus begins Geoff Bellman's book *The Beauty of the Beast.* Geoff's observations throughout the book about our love-hate relationship with organizations encourage all of us to better understand our huge responsibility to make them better for the future.

How do we do that? Organizations need to change: adapt to new customer and stakeholder demands, transform to meet the challenges of global competition, and shift to address the needs of their workforce. Process improvement is one of the tools that assists organizations in making the required changes. Whether you call the change *process improvement, quality improvement, business reengineering,* or *lean six sigma,* it is the method used to reinvent organizations to keep up with change coming from every direction. We need to help leaders of organizations understand the corporate culture and what they are doing to themselves by not looking far enough into the future.

Very experienced people work in the important world of improving organizations. Our three experts have well over a hundred years of experience among them. Mary Broad shares a process for diagramming complex systems. Richard Chang, viewed by many as a process improvement guru, delivers a powerful activity straight from his successful workshops. The activity makes the point that everyone must work together and that process improvement is a continuous effort that must start and end with customer satisfaction. Jack Zenger, a world-renowned leader in leadership development and organizational change, shares his favorite activity for examining an organization's culture and issues.

171

The three excellent activities take time and require experience and expertise to deliver successfully. They are a true gift from three of the best practitioners in the profession.

Organizational turbulence will never cease. Change is here to stay. Successful organizations will continue to reinvent themselves, continue to improve their processes, continue to examine their culture, and continue to address the issues that prevent them from going from good to great (and that's another book!).

Diagramming a Complex System

Submitted by Mary L. Broad

Objectives

- To clarify relationships among stakeholders in a complex organizational system who support improved performance in a particular group in the system.
- To identify other allies in the system who also support the improved performance, as well as to identify possible "adversaries" who will need either to be persuaded to join or to be neutralized.

Audience

2–10 decision makers who support improved performance in the complex system, and who have contacts and relationships with decision makers in other parts of the system.

Time Required

Initially 2–3 hours, but further refinement and revision of the diagrammed system can go on for months.

Materials and Equipment

- Examples of diagrams of other complex systems.
- Flip charts.
- Masking tape.
- Markers.
- Digital cameras to capture results.

Area Setup

Any conference room with some uninterrupted wall space for hanging flip-chart pages, and room for participants to walk around and add to or revise the system diagram as it evolves.

Preparation

Before the session, identify the complex system to be diagrammed: a multinational organization or a formal or informal group of organizations who share a common goal for improved performance. Examples include the following:

- The National Weather Service (NWS) as a central component with geographically dispersed weather stations within the organization, plus other commercial users of NWS data (TV and radio stations, consulting organizations) and the public at large, whose performance in responding to weather warnings needs improvement.
- Disaster Response systems being established in major cities and other jurisdictions, with components that include local and state government bodies; transportation systems; health and medical facilities; police, fire, safety, and health first responders; neighborhood residents; and many other groups, with the goal of developing collaborative disaster responses.

Process

1. Bring together representatives of major known components of the system for the purpose of identifying stakeholders and defining desired performance of key groups, authority or influence relationships, and levels of support.
2. Gain agreement on purposes and uses for the diagram of the system; clarify that the diagram will evolve as new insights are gained and that perfect accuracy is not necessary at the start.
3. Get agreement on styles of boxes for types of system components (rectangles, circles, ovals, and so on) and connecting lines and arrows (solid lines for authority, dotted lines for influence). (Use an example, such as the one provided at the end of this activity.) Post these on a flip chart.
4. Suggest a modified brainstorming process, with a participant sketching out a rough draft of the system as group members suggest components. At the same time, others will suggest revisions and adaptations.
5. Identify specific stakeholders in each system component by name, if possible, and list them on a separate flip-chart page.
6. Date the diagram and capture the latest version by digital camera so that the image can be sent electronically to all stakeholders as the performance improvement effort evolves for a specific group in the complex system.

 nsider's Tips

- Assure diagramming participants, and other stakeholders to whom the diagram is sent, that the diagram may never be completely accurate, but that it will be a useful tool to conceptualize how the system functions.
- Don't let a graphic artist "prettify" the diagram until it is 98 percent complete; it should look like a rough draft to encourage additions and revisions as the complex system forms and is acknowledged.
- In the early stage, you may wish to use Post-its, which can be moved around more easily until the diagram achieves some sense of stability.

Source

The importance of diagramming complex systems is emphasized in my recent book *Beyond Transfer of Training: Engaging Systems to Improve Performance* (Pfeiffer, 2005), and several examples of complex system diagrams are shown there, but the process of developing the diagram is not spelled out.

Mary L. Broad is an internationally recognized performance consultant. She helps organizations recognize complex systems within which they operate, and identify key stakeholders throughout the system who can help or hinder performance improvement initiatives. Mary is widely published; her most recent book is *Beyond Transfer of Training: Engaging Systems to Improve Performance* (Pfeiffer, 2005). She has served on the ASTD board of directors and is an adjunct faculty member at George Washington University.

Mary L. Broad
Performance Excellence
3709 Williams Lane
Chevy Chase, MD 20815
Phone: 301.657.8638
Email: marybroad@earthlink.net

Example: Simplified Diagram of a Complex System to Deliver Mental Health Services in the State of Georgia, United States

Note: Rectangles and rounded boxes in gray are key components of the complex system, the delivery system for mental health services delivered during 1999–2001 by the Georgia State Mental Health Services system. Other components are identified that influenced that system, either through authority (solid-line arrows) or influence (dotted-line arrows). This diagram is a simplified version of the more precise and comprehensive system as it existed at that time.

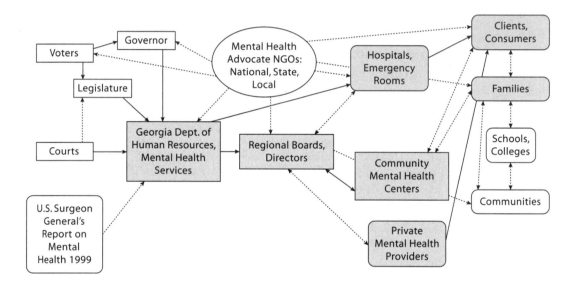

Process Improvement in Action

Submitted by Richard Chang, Ph.D.

Objective
- To demonstrate how important it is for suppliers, producers, and customers in the process chain to understand customer requirements.

Audience
10–12 participants.

Time Required
60–90 minutes.

Materials and Equipment
- One set of Lego® System 4153 (or equivalent).
- To create the "Lego Car," every Lego kit must include the following:
  - Four wheels.
  - Two axles.
  - Steering wheel.
  - Seats.
  - Lots of other pieces.
- Large notepad.
- One copy of the Process Improvement in Action handout per participant.
- One copy of the Exercise Debrief per participant.
- Four flip charts, prepared as described in the Preparation section.

Area Setup
Three separate breakout rooms or areas are required. If necessary, a classroom large enough for the teams to be able to work separately without overhearing each other could be used.

Preparation

Before the activity, prepare the four flip charts as follows:

1. Flip chart one: Divide one sheet with three lines, as follows:

   Line one: Design Team _____

   Line two: Production Team _____

   Line three: Sales Team _____

2. Flip chart two: Round 1 instructions:
   a. Design team has approximately 5 minutes to design a car.
   b. One member of the design team passes drawing to production team.
   c. Production team has approximately 7 minutes to produce car with the Legos and pass it on to sales team.
   d. Sales team has approximately 3 minutes to sell the car to the customer.
3. Flip chart three: Round 2 instructions:
   a. Sales team has approximately 3 minutes to meet with the design team to discuss "problems" with the car.
   b. Design team has approximately 4 minutes to review the car and pass it on to the production team.
   c. Production team has approximately 3 minutes to produce the redesigned car and pass it on to the sales team.
   d. Sales team has approximately 5 minutes to sell the car to the customer.

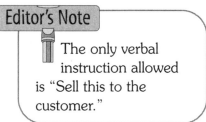

Editor's Note
This can include verbal instructions, such as feature requirements.

4. Flip chart four: Round 3 instructions:
   a. The three teams come together as a group for approximately 3 minutes to discuss ideas and plan for producing the car.
   b. The teams have approximately 7 minutes to produce the car as a group.
   c. The teams sell the car to the customer as a group.

Editor's Note
The only verbal instruction allowed is "Sell this to the customer."

Process

1. Tell participants there will be three rounds in the exercise with separate instructions for each round. The teams will be operating separately for the first two rounds. Poll the group to see which participants are the most

experienced with Legos. (You will need to have at least two of the "Lego pros"—identified during your poll—on the production team.)

2. Divide participants into three different teams: design, production, and sales teams. The breakout for a class of twelve participants should be as follows:

Design team   4
Production team   5
Sales team   3

(The sales team has a smaller team simply because their role does not allow for active participation by more than four participants.)

Provide each participant with a copy of the Process Improvement in Action handout as an overview of the activity.

If you have more or fewer than twelve participants, try to maintain an approximately similar ratio. For example:

20 Participants		**10 Participants**	
Design team	6	Design team	3
Production team	10	Production team	5
Sales team	4	Sales team	2

3. Tell participants that, depending which team they are on, their separate tasks will be to design, produce, and sell a Lego model car to their customer (role-played by you, the facilitator).

4. While the teams are working, keep track of the time to ensure handoff to the next team within the allocated time. Tell the teams that they may want to appoint a timekeeper in their group.

5. Instructions for Round 1:
   - Show flip chart one, and assign the team members to each of the three respective team categories.
   - Show flip chart two to highlight the instructions for Round 1. Read aloud the time constraints for each phase (5 minutes for design, 7 minutes for production, and 3 minutes for sales).
   - Break the teams into their separate groups. Provide the following direction to the teams:
     - While the design team is working, the production team can get organized.
     - While the production team is building, the design team can improve their process.
     - While both the design and production teams are working, the sales team should strategize.
   - Provide the design team with a large notepad to communicate their drawing to the production team.

- Tell the design team that one member will pass their drawing to the production team. It must be a picture only—no written words are allowed—presented with only a single verbal instruction: "Produce this."
- Remind the design team that they have approximately 5 minutes to design their car.
- Quickly give the design team your specifications for the car. It should be
  - Fast
  - Able to carry plenty of luggage
  - Brightly colored
  - Safe
  - "Classic" looking

  Important: The design team may not ask the customer (you) any questions; do not volunteer any other information. The production and sales teams must not hear your instructions.
- As the teams complete their respective handoffs, direct them to use the remaining time in Round 1 to discuss what they would do differently next time.
- Once the design is passed to the production team, remind the production team that they have 7 minutes to build the car.
- After the 7 minutes are up, the production team passes the car to the sales team with the verbal instruction, "Sell this to the customer." Permit no other conversation.
- Tell the sales team that they have 3 minutes to sell the car to you, without the other teams present.
- When playing the role of the customer, show your dissatisfaction by expressing some of the following points:
  - "This is *not* the car I ordered."
  - "This car doesn't look safe to me."
  - "I wouldn't call this 'classic' looking."
  - "That car doesn't look *very* fast to me."
- The sales team can openly discuss the customer's (your) requirements at this point.
- Bring the entire group back together for instructions for Round 2. Let them see the final product and express your dissatisfaction with it. Permit no other conversation.

6. Instructions for Round 2:
   - Show flip chart three to highlight the instructions for Round 2.
   - The sales team has 3 minutes to meet directly with the design team to discuss "problems" with the car. Have the sales team return to its room or area after that meeting.
   - As the teams complete their respective handoffs, direct them to use the remaining time in Round 2 to discuss what they would do differently next time.
   - The design team has 4 minutes to redraw the car and hand off the new drawing, which can now include verbal instructions, such as feature requirements, to the production team. The handoff can include only one-way communication; no questions can be asked or answered.
   - The production team has 5 minutes to build the redesigned car and hand it off to the sales team, again with the instruction, "Sell this to the customer."
   - The design team can watch the production team, but they cannot say anything.
   - The sales team has 5 minutes to sell the car to the customer (you).
   - Your response is, "This is not exactly the car I want." Provide feedback to the sales team on why it does "not exactly" fit your needs.
   - Bring the entire group back together for instructions for Round 3. Let them see the final product and express your concern that it is "not quite" what you wanted. Permit no other conversation.
7. Instructions for Round 3:
   - Show flip chart four to highlight the instructions for Round 3.
   - All three teams can meet and work together as a group to discuss their ideas and their plans for building the car. Allow 3 minutes.
   - The teams will build the car as a group.
   - The teams will sell the car as a group.
   - Allow 7 minutes for the group to build the car together. Leave the room as they do so, having them bring you in when they are finished.
   - You accept the car as being exactly what you were looking for.
8. Allow 10 minutes for participants to respond to the questions in the Exercise Debrief. An answer sheet has been included with possible answers and some follow-up questions for you.
9. Review the responses.

 nsider's Tips

- You will find this activity both fun and challenging. The best part, however, is the participant learning that results.
- You may need to take 2 minutes to work with the group to make any minor changes that may be necessary after the final round.
- This is an excellent exercise to introduce a process improvement workshop.

Source

This activity is a part of our Continuous Process Improvement training.

Richard Chang, Ph.D., chief executive officer of Richard Chang Associates, is internationally known and highly respected for his expertise in quality improvement, organization development, customer value, strategic planning, measurement systems, team development, performance improvement, product realization, and HR development. In addition, he served as a judge for the prestigious Malcolm Baldrige National Quality Award from 1996 to 1999 and currently serves as the chief judge for the California Awards for Performance Excellence.

Richard Chang, Ph.D.
Richard Chang Associates, Inc.
21072 Bake Parkway, #102
Lake Forest, CA 92630
Phone: 800.756.8096 or 949.727.7477
Fax: 949.727.7007
Email: info@rca4results.com
Website: www.richardchangassociates.com

Process Improvement in Action

Each participant will be a member of a design team, a production team, or a sales team. Your goal is to satisfy the requirements of your external customer.

1. The design team will design a car with pictures only. No written words are allowed.

2. One member of the design team passes the drawing to the production team with the single verbal instruction "Produce this."

3. The production team will produce the car and pass it on to the sales team. The only verbal instruction that's allowed is "Sell this to the customer."

4. The sales team then sells the car to the customer.

Exercise Debrief

On the basis of the group exercise just completed, please respond to the following questions. Be specific in your ideas and responses.

1. Why did your product not satisfy the customer in the first round?

2. What was done differently in the second round? What difference did it make in producing the product the second time?

3. What was done differently in the third round? What difference did it make in producing the product the third time?

4. Of these two elements: (1) using the most efficient process for producing the product or (2) determining customer requirements, which is the more critical for satisfying customers, as demonstrated in this exercise? Why?

5. How was the experience during this exercise similar to (or different from) your own on-the-job experiences?

6. What key lessons have you learned that you want to remember when improving processes in your organization?

Facilitator's Process Debrief: Discuss with Participants

Questions from Exercise Debrief and Possible Answers

1. **Why did your product not satisfy the customer in the first round?**
   Answer: Very little communication between the various teams; unclear requirements; unclear roles; unclear production process.

2. **What was done differently in the second round? What difference did it make in producing the product the second time?**
   Answer: Sales had the opportunity to get a better understanding of the customer requirements. Feedback from sales to design was allowed. Production was able to make a product closer to the customer's requirements, but not good enough to sell.

3. **What was done differently in the third round? What difference did it make in producing the product the third time?**
   Answer: Teams built and sold the car as a collaborative effort. Feedback was offered and questions were clarified and answered. As a result, the teams were able to meet customer requirements.

4. **Of these two elements: (1) using the most efficient process for producing the product or (2) determining customer requirements, which is the more critical for satisfying customers, as demonstrated in this exercise? Why?**
   Answer: Determining customer requirements. You could have the most efficient process imaginable, but if the final product doesn't satisfy customer needs, all your time and energy will be wasted.

5. **How was the experience during this exercise similar to (or different from) your own on-the-job experiences?**
   Answer: Answers will vary. However, participants frequently respond that many times they act without a complete understanding of the expected outcome.

6. **What key lessons have you learned that you want to remember when improving processes in your organization?**
   Answer: Answers will vary, but may include the importance of feedback, two-way communication, and defining specific customer requirements.

Additional Follow-Up Questions

Q: On what could the sales team have spent more time?
A: Rather than defining "areas," like speed and safety, more time could have been spent on specific requirements (for example, "0 to 60 in 8 seconds").

Q: What do you have to do to get specific requirements from the customer?
A: You may have to ask clarifying questions, because the customer doesn't always know what he wants. You may have to restate the question in a different format. For example, if you are trying to clarify the safety requirement and you ask, "Is safety important?" the answer will inevitably be yes. So you may ask instead, "Are you confident that a midsize auto is as safe as a full-size auto?" or "Will a minivan design satisfy your safety requirement?"

Q: What was the production team doing during Round 2 when they were being visited by the design team?
A: Possibly "doing" rather than "listening." Up-front planning is key to making improvements. Don't assume you know what's expected.

Q: What was helpful to you as a production team member during Round 3?
A: Getting up-front requirements.

Q: What was the production team doing or not doing differently when meeting with the sales and design teams?
A: Listening and asking clarifying questions.

Key Points
- Take the time to talk to customers to find out their requirements.
- Internal teams of suppliers, producers, and customers need to work together. Simply handing things off will not satisfy the customer.
- Process improvement is a continuous effort that must begin and end with customer satisfaction.

90 World-Class Activities by 90 World-Class Trainers. Copyright © 2007 by John Wiley & Sons, Inc.
Published by Pfeiffer, an Imprint of Wiley. www.pfeiffer.com

# Training Vehicles

Submitted by Jack Zenger, D.B.A.

Objectives
- To capture the essence of an organization's current culture in an engaging way.
- To get issues out on the table in a visceral way, all the while having fun.

Audience
Any size, divided into small groups of 4–8 at a table.

Time Required
1½–2 hours.

Materials and Equipment
For each table:

- Flip chart pads.
- Easel.
- Felt-tip pens.

Area Setup
Round tables, scattered throughout a large room.

Process
1. Assign each table to create a drawing of a vehicle that best represents how this organization currently functions. A vehicle is anything that moves on land, sea, or air. The vehicle can be a combination of many vehicles.
2. Tell participants that they should first list adjectives and phrases that best capture the essence of how the organization currently functions—what is the current culture of the organization? Then, with those phrases and adjectives in mind, ask them to think of two or three vehicles that best encompass these ideas.
3. Ask the teams to choose one vehicle and have someone draw it with as much detail as possible. The emphasis is not on artwork, but on insight. Tell the group they have 40 minutes to complete this step.

90 World-Class Activities by 90 World-Class Trainers

4. Have each group select a spokesperson to review their objectives and describe their vehicle to the large group. The spokesperson also answers questions from others in the large group.
5. Post the pictures on the walls.
6. At the conclusion, ask the large group to identify what the drawings had in common. What are the common themes underlying how the organization operates?

Variation

Ask each group to make a second drawing of how they would like the organization to be and to make specific recommendations about what is required to make that transition.

 nsider's Tips

- This is a surefire way to get people sharing the "unshareable." It is particularly good for environments where the culture makes it difficult to tell it like it is. The use of metaphor gives "permission" to convey or depict ideas that may be difficult or uncomfortable to verbalize. The same process can be used to explore thoughts about a product, a market, leadership, and so on.
- You could have participants draw several vehicles from different perspectives: that of the employees, leadership, and customer.
- Encourage participants to have fun, be creative, and use a combination of vehicles.
- Suggest that the teams pay attention to the parts of the vehicle. For example, the vehicle may have tires that are flat, it might have a loud horn, or it might be streamlined and sleek.

Source

Source? Who knows! I've long forgotten, though it is not original with me. I have seen it done with animals, but thought that vehicles were more varied and richer. I may have been one of the early users of this exercise with vehicles, but others use it also.

Jack Zenger, D.B.A., CEO of Zenger/Folkman, is one of the leading practitioners in leadership development and organizational change. For fifty years he has been engaged in developing better ways to help people be more effective in organizations and helping organizations become better places for their people. His career includes entrepreneurial activities (as cofounder of Zenger-Miller, Provant, and the Extraordinary Performance Group), academic roles (teaching at USC and the Stanford Graduate School of Business), and corporate executive roles (vice president of HR for Syntex and group vice president of Times Mirror). In 1994 he was inducted into the HRD Hall of Fame. He is the author or coauthor of fifty articles and seven books, including the best-selling *Self-Directed Work Teams: The New American Challenge* (McGraw-Hill, 1990), *Results-Based Leadership* (Harvard Business School Press, 1999) (voted the SHRM 200 Best Business Book), and *The Extraordinary Leader: Turning Good Managers into Great Leaders* (McGraw-Hill, 2002).

Jack Zenger, D.B.A.
Zenger/Folkman
610 Technology Avenue, Bldg. B
Orem, UT 84097
Phone: 435.654.6604
Fax: 435.654.6602
Email: jzenger@zfo.com

Chapter **10**

Self-Management

Time, Meetings, and Values

Are you working more, enjoying it less? Are you working long hours that don't seem to result in getting the job done any better? Are you facing nonstop change and back-to-back meetings at work? Are you looking for balance in your life?

As practitioners, we are often asked to conduct "management" sessions: time management, stress management, meeting management, conflict management. You may wish to step back and examine all of them as one category: self-management. This perspective allows for a systemic view to consider everything that goes into helping employees identify and implement strategies for working in more balanced and productive ways.

Four authors share self-management concepts in this chapter.

Time is one of the few areas in which every one of us is treated in exactly the same way. We each have twenty-four hours every day, seven days in every week, and fifty-two weeks in every year. We cannot save it; we cannot turn it on or off; we cannot replace it. How we choose to spend or invest our hours, days, and weeks is a self-management issue. Jean Barbazette and the team of Benoit Savard and Daniel Genest (both from Canada) have contributed ideas to explore the use of time. We live in a meeting society, and John Purnell draws on his vast experience to share a simple tool to manage meetings more effectively. Understanding the values that you espouse gives you a way to prioritize your time, and Bob Younglove shares an activity to help you identify your values and your priorities.

Each of these authors based these activities on how they effectively manage themselves. Use their activities in your sessions. Better yet, use their concepts for personal self-management.

What's Your Priority?

Submitted by Jean Barbazette

Objectives
- To learn the usefulness of time efficiency (use of correct techniques) as opposed to time effectiveness (selection of correct priorities).
- To identify elements of teamwork that help or hinder task accomplishment.
- To identify how to respond appropriately to incomplete instructions or directions.

Audience
10, or groups of 10.

Time Required
45–60 minutes.

Materials and Equipment
- Thirty poker chips for each group of 10 people (ten each of blue, red, and white).
- Glass, cup, or container for each set of chips.
- Stopwatch.
- Flip chart and marker.
- One copy of the Discussion Questions handout for each person.

Area Setup
Most classroom settings with tables and chairs can be used. Some groups may choose to stand up for the activity. Clearing tables for a free work space is helpful.

Process
1. Divide the class into teams with equal numbers of participants, with no fewer than five per team. Use observers for larger groups.
2. Give each team an equal number of blue, red, and white poker chips in a cup. Ten chips of each color is best. If your purpose for this activity is to work on priorities, provide another ten of the white chips to each group's supply, as this helps emphasize the importance of prioritizing tasks.
3. Explain the rules:
   - The group must pass each chip through all hands and into the cup in 30 seconds.

- The starter must pick up each chip with one hand, move it to his or her other hand, and then pass it to the next person in the group.
- No sliding the chip on the table.
- Only one chip in a hand at a time.
- No more chips may be added to the cup when time is called.

4. Allow groups to practice, strategize, and move chairs, clear tables, and so on. You should be unavailable to participants during their practice time. If there are observers, talk to them in the hallway outside the room and ask them to observe their group's techniques (what helps the process, what hinders the process, examples of teamwork, and so on). Give the observers a copy of the Discussion Questions handout.

5. Conduct the first 30-second drill and have each group count the number of chips that completed the circuit of ten people and ended up in the cup. Also have the groups select names for themselves. Record the scores on a flip chart.

6. Reveal point values: blue = 10, red = 5, white = 1. Many in the group will say, "No fair!" "You didn't tell us that!" That's one of the learning points. If someone asks before this point if the chips have value, say the colors have no importance or avoid answering the question.

7. Record point values on the easel next to the chip count for each group from the first round.

8. At this point most groups want another opportunity to improve their scores. Conduct the drill a second time and tell them that the objective is to improve their point score. Groups may want a few moments to strategize in light of the new information about point values. Ask the group if they have questions. The same point values apply to the second round.

9. Record new scores for points and chip count.

10. Use the Discussion Questions handout for the group members to record their answers as part of this discussion. Participants sometimes need time to gather their thoughts before discussing their reactions with others. Allow individual time to write answers before discussing the questions. In large groups, ask the observers to facilitate a small group discussion of these questions:
   - What do the numbers say about the results of your efforts?
   - What helped or hindered the process (include feedback from observers)? For groups with a teamwork purpose, it may be useful for each team member to rate on a scale of 1–5 the helpfulness of each group member.
   - Discuss priorities, roles different group members played, changing the rules, not knowing all the rules, or other learning points.

11. Process the learning from this activity. Ask small groups to come up with some generalizations about what they learned. What generalizations can be made about group productivity and teamwork from the process? Have groups write, "It is better to _____." (For example, "It is better to slow down and increase productivity by doing 'blue chip' items.)

12. If the concept you want the participants to discover is about teamwork, time management, or listening to directions, ask questions that will help participants discover the concept.

13. Finally, ask participants, "How can you apply this experience to your team, your job?" Write this down and discuss in small groups and then in the large group.

 # nsider's Tips

- You may wish to make the point that supervisors do not always give complete instructions or directions. It is up to the employees to ask questions to get the job done according to the unspoken expectation.

- Consider changing the questions on the Discussion Questions handout, depending on the goal for the group.

Source

This is one of my favorite activities. I published it in *The 2005 Pfeiffer Annual: Training*, under the title "What's Your Priority? Clarifying Instructions."

Jean Barbazette is the president of the Training Clinic, a training and consulting firm she founded in 1977. Her company focuses on training trainers throughout the United States for major profit, nonprofit, and government organizations. The Training Clinic has three international licensees in the Netherlands, Hungary, and Colombia. Jean has authored *Successful New Employee Orientation* (2nd ed.) (Pfeiffer, 2001), *The Trainer's Support Handbook* (McGraw-Hill, 2001), *Instant Case Studies* (Pfeiffer, 2003), *The Trainer's Journey to Competence* (Pfeiffer, 2005), *Training Needs Assessment* (Pfeiffer, 2006), and *The Art of Great Training Delivery* (Pfeiffer, 2006). She is a frequent contributor to *ASTD Training & Development Sourcebooks, McGraw-Hill Training & Performance Sourcebooks,* and the *Pfeiffer Annuals.*

Jean Barbazette, President
The Training Clinic
645 Seabreeze Drive
Seal Beach, CA 90740
Phone: 800.937.4698
Email: jean@thetrainingclinic.com
Website: www.thetrainingclinic.com

Discussion Questions

Directions: Following the poker chip game, use this space to write the answers to these questions:

1. What did you do that helped the process?

2. What did you do that hindered the process?

3. What did other team members do that helped?

4. What did other team members do that hindered?

5. What could have been done differently that would have helped your group get better results?

6. What are some general concepts about teams, time management, or listening to directions that you learned from this activity? Consider phrasing your response using this pattern: "It is better to _____ than to _____."

7. What can you do to be a more effective team member?

8. How can you apply what you learned from this experience to your team? To your job?

Meeting Norms

Submitted by John H. O. Purnell, M.S.

Objectives
- To gain acceptance and accountability for meeting operating norms.
- To demonstrate how operating norms can be introduced to a group.

Audience
A cross-functional group of 12–18 people.

Time Required
Approximately 30 minutes.

Materials and Equipment
- Flip chart and marker.
- One copy of the Operating Norms handout for each participant.

Area Setup
Tables and chairs set up in a U shape.

Process
1. Provide each participant with a copy of the Operating Norms handout. Review the norms with the group. You may also wish to post the norms on a flip chart.
2. During the review of the operating norms, ask for an example of each to gain clarity. Spend 10 minutes clarifying the norms.
3. Ask if anyone has additional norms they would like to add.
4. Ask the group for agreement and approval. Encourage discussion.
5. Debrief (use the debrief if you are teaching others how to use norms) with the following questions:
   - What did you observe as we established the norms?
   - What do you like or not like about the norms we created?
   - What would you do differently?
   - How will you apply what you learned?

Insider's Tips

- The norms can be used in any meeting or training session you may hold.
- The norms can also be used as a discussion topic if you are teaching people to conduct more effective meetings.

John H. O. Purnell, M.S., is a business performance improvement practitioner with over twenty-five years of experience in several diverse domestic and global organizations; his work has resulted in improved productivity, reduced cycle time, cost reduction, speed-enhanced leadership capability, organization alignment, and capacity. Purnell Associates International is a registered minority business enterprise (MBE), and as an acknowledged speaker and leader of diversity events, John has published *Valuing Diversity in the Workplace* (ASTD, 1991). John has received several master certifications: Process Improvement, Quality (ISO9000), Six Sigma Master Black Belt, Lean Manufacturing, Performance Analysis and Design, High Performance Work Systems, and Leadership Development. He has been a speaker at numerous national conferences and received the ASTD Torch Award and Minority Trainer of the Year Award. He also received the Rockford Chamber of Commerce Community Leadership Award. John has served on ASTD's national board of directors. He has B.S. and M.S. degrees from the University of Tennessee, did postgraduate work at the University of Massachusetts, and participated in executive management development at Harvard University and logistics executive development at the University of Tennessee.

John H. O. Purnell, M.S.
Purnell Associates International
4100 Executive Park Drive, Suite 16
Cincinnati, OH 45241
Phone: 513.489.1860
Email: john@purnellassociates.com

Operating Norms

P **Participation:** Expect full participation from all attendees.

R **Responsible:** Each participant shares responsibility for meeting outcomes.

O **Ownership and Accountability:** We all own the results accomplished (positive or negative).

C **Care and Confidentiality:** We must respect each other; do not spread details of the meeting outside without clear agreement from the group on what will be shared. We do not feed the rumor mill.

E **Enthusiasm:** It is important to have fun—but not at the expense of an attendee.

S **Sincerity:** Change often creates uncomfortable feelings among team members. Keep jokes out of the meeting.

S **Success:** Follow these operating norms, and you will have a much greater chance of a successful event or meeting.

Balancing Your Week

Submitted by Benoit Savard, B.Sc., M.B.A., and Daniel Genest, B.Sc.

Objective

- To discover simple and effective ways of balancing weekly personal activities.

Audience

12–20 people.

Time Required

1–1½ hours, depending on the size of the group.

Materials and Equipment

- Thematic cards (see template at the end of the activity) and 24 inches of string per card (you may need two sets, depending on the number of participants).
- One copy of the Analysing Your Week handout for each participant.
- One copy of A Week's Worth of Ideas for each participant.
- One pocket calculator for each participant.

Area Setup

Plan for enough space so that participants can move around and hold discussion amongst themselves.

Process

1. Prior to the session, prepare cards and copy worksheets for the activity. Pierce two holes in the upper portion of the twelve cards and insert a piece of string measuring about 24 inches.
2. At the session, describe the activity and explain the objective.
3. Distribute a copy of the Analysing Your Week handout to each participant and request that they identify the number of hours per week spent on each activity listed (for a total of 168 hours).
4. Explain that they should then identify the number of hours they would ideally like to spend on each activity.
5. Have them calculate the difference (positive or negative) between the actual time spent and the preferred time spent.

6. Request that they select one activity that they could carry out differently (quality) or could carry out using more or less time (quantity). Ask participants to establish an objective regarding this activity and to write it at the top of the worksheet.

7. Hand twelve of the participants a card bearing the name of one of the activities selected and have them put it around their necks.

8. Explain that they have become a resource person on the given theme and that others will consult them on the subject. Make sure that all themes are distributed at least once (twelve themes). If there are more participants than themes, use a second set of cards. Two resource people can cover the same theme.

9. Distribute a copy of A Week's Worth of Ideas to every participant.

10. Invite participants to circulate throughout the room and ask for ideas, tips, or tricks on how they can better accomplish their weekly routine. Ask them to note these ideas on the Ideas worksheet. For example, if one participant is assigned the theme card Sleep, he should identify a way or a trick on how to improve rest periods, which he will share with others who consult him on that theme. The participant will then seek others with a different theme from his to collect practical advice on other themes. Allow about 30 minutes for this step.

11. Reconvene participants and lead a plenary session to share ideas gathered on the week's activities.

 ## nsider's Tips

- Affirm the fact that all the ideas collected will help balance weekly routines no matter which activity participants choose to improve. With just 168 hours in a week, the time adjusted on one activity will invariably affect the time spent on another or several other activities. The tips collected will help ease this transition.

- Encourage participants to be vigilant in estimating the time they spend on activities. The more precise they are, the more efficient they will be in their use of time.

Sources

We used several sources to inspire this activity:

Fletcher, W. (2002). *Beating the 24/7: How business leaders achieve a successful work/life balance.* Chichester, England: Wiley.

Loehr, J., & Schwartz, T. (2003). *The power of full engagement.* New York: Free Press.

Sandholtz, K., Derr, B., Buckner, K., & Carlson, D. (2002). *Beyond juggling: Rebalancing your busy life.* San Francisco: Berrett-Koehler.

Benoit Savard, B.Sc., M.B.A., and **Daniel Genest,** B.Sc., work as a team in developing training seminars for numerous Canadian businesses. Their respective academic backgrounds and professional experience are reflected in the relevance and quality of their accomplishments. Both work for Le Groupe Savard-Martin Inc., a consulting firm specializing in the development of human resources.

Benoit Savard, B.Sc., M.B.A., and Daniel Genest, B.Sc.
Le Groupe Savard-Martin Inc.
65 Belvédère North, Suite 20
Sherbrooke, QC J1H 4A7
Canada
Phone: 819.822.3710
Email: danielg@savardmartin.com

Thematic Cards

Employment

Family

Meals

Thematic Cards

Routine Chores
Leisure/TV/ Music
Sports/ Outdoors

Thematic Cards

Me
Travel Time
Personal Hygiene

Thematic Cards

Sleep
Spouse
Other: _____

Analysing Your Week

Your Name:
Your Objective:

My Weekly Activities	Actual No. of Hours	Actual % of Total	Ideal No. of Hours	Ideal % of Total	Difference (+/-)	Priority (✔)
Employment						
Sleep						
Family						
Spouse						
Leisure/TV/Music						
Sports/Outdoors						
Me						
Travel Time						
Personal Hygiene						
Meals						
Routine Chores						
Other						
Total	168 hours	100%	168 hours	100%		

A Week's Worth of Ideas

My Weekly Activities	Ideas, Tips, and Tricks
Employment	
Sleep	
Family	
Spouse	
Leisure/TV/Music	
Sports/Outdoors	
Me	
Travel Time	
Personal Hygiene	
Meals	
Routine Chores	
Other	

Prioritize Your Values

Submitted by Bob Younglove, M.Ed., M.A.

Objectives

- To determine the priority of individual values and their relationship to job satisfaction.
- To appreciate the diversity of value preferences in others.

Audience

Any size group of participants, especially intact work groups or teams.

Time Required

30–45 minutes.

Materials and Equipment

- One pack of Value Cards for each participant. Each pack of Value Cards includes eighteen cards containing value words and two blank cards for participants to use in listing other values important to them that are not included in the eighteen values.

Area Setup

Table space for each participant to assemble his or her card profile, and enough space for participants to walk around and look at each person's value profile.

Process

1. Give each participant a pack of the Value Cards.
2. Instruct the participants to arrange the cards in a profile from most important value at the top to least important at the bottom.
3. Give them permission to place up to three cards (but no more than three) on the same line, indicating relatively equal value.
4. Tell participants they can use the blank cards to write in values that are important to them but that are not included in the pack.
5. After 10 minutes, or when everyone has completed his or her value profile, ask people to walk around and observe each person's profile to note similarities and differences.

6. Debrief with these questions:
   - What did you observe during the activity?
   - How do different values affect preferences for what you do?
   - How do different values affect how you are treated in the work environment?
   - How do your values compare to how you spend your time?
   - What does this say about your priorities?
   - What will you do differently as a result of this activity?

 nsider's Tips

- Some people find it very difficult to choose among the values and therefore take a long time to arrange the cards in order of importance. It may be helpful to set a time limit and tell people they can always change their ordering later.
- It is often helpful to share your observations and ask how the values relate to job satisfaction. (For example, someone who values recognition may be motivated by praise and incentives; someone who values fairness may be upset about unequal treatment.)
- You might wish to ask people to list the organization's values and discuss how these are consistent with or in conflict with their personal values.
- Suggest that participants could use this activity at home with family members to increase understanding of value preferences.

Bob Younglove, M.Ed., M.A., is a performance coach, keynote speaker, and author of *Sponsor Success: A Workbook for Turning Good Intentions into Positive Results* (American Literary Press, 2002). Bob is vice president of the National Association for Self-Esteem, where he offers workshops for parents, teachers, and coaches on positively influencing kids.

Bob Younglove, M.Ed., M.A.
PATH Associates
19 Coldwater Court
Towson, MD 21204
Phone: 410.821.0538
Email: PATHassoc@aol.com

Value Cards

Value Card **Financial Security Wealth**	Value Card **Peace Freedom from Conflict**	Value Card **Self-Respect Self-Acceptance**
Value Card **Happiness, Joy Pleasure**	Value Card **Good Health Fitness**	Value Card **Knowledge Intelligence**
Value Card **Friendship Acceptance**	Value Card **Love, Affection Intimacy**	Value Card **Freedom Independence**
Value Card **Helping Others Cooperation**	Value Card **Accomplishments Getting It Done**	Value Card **Honesty Truthfulness**
Value Card **Responsibility Taking Care of Self**	Value Card **Excitement, Fun Active Lifestyle**	Value Card **Equality Fairness**
Value Card **Appreciation Recognition**	Value Card **Organization Neatness**	Value Card **Family Relations Home**

## Chapter 11

Solving Problems and Making Decisions

Solving problems and making effective decisions are not always easy for people. In fact, they can be downright scary to some. Faced with a problem, or at least the sense that something is wrong, many people panic. Imparting the skills of recognizing and using a process to move from problem to solution is a talent displayed by many in our profession. Trainers and consultants are always looking for ways to organize a problem-solving event to add energy and to accomplish as much as possible in as little time as possible.

The five contributors to this chapter are true problem solvers and share several of their best activities so that you can benefit.

You can always count on Kristin Arnold for a quick and useful tool. She came through again with her quick test for consensus. Edward de Bono, originator of the Six Thinking Hats and the term *lateral thinking,* delivers an overview of how the Six Thinking Hats process can be used at work. Dave Jamieson takes us through a half-day process that can be used to resolve difficult problems—no lightweight issues allowed! Hank Karp has developed a role play that seems so real you will think it is, which is why it leads to great discussion. Rich Michaels contributes a tool to help participants think metaphorically to gain new insight when problem solving—and have fun to boot!

These activities will be solid additions to any problem-solving event you may conduct in the future.

Test for Consensus: A Straw Poll

Submitted by Kristin J. Arnold, M.B.A., CMC, CPF, CSP

Objective

- To allow a team a preliminary check on a decision without actually agreeing on the final outcome.

Audience

Any size.

Time Required

10 minutes.

Materials and Equipment

- A prepared flip chart with a 5L scale (see figure). Draw the scale near the bottom of the page.

Loathe	Lament	Live	Like	Love

- One removable colored dot for each team member.

Area Setup

A space large enough for team members to see each other and the easel.

Process

1. When aiming for consensus, take a "straw poll" of the team's energy and commitment to a specific outcome using this fun and simple tool.
2. First, ensure a complete understanding of the issue under discussion. Clarify any lingering questions the team may have.
3. Then have each person take one colored dot.

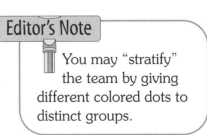

Editor's Note

You may "stratify" the team by giving different colored dots to distinct groups.

4. Refer to the 5L scale on the flip chart. Walk through the definition of each L and ask team members to silently vote on what they think of the solution:
   - You *loathe* it or hate it.
   - You will *lament* it and moan about it in the parking lot.
   - You can *live* with it.
   - You *like* it.
   - You really *love* it.
5. Ask the team members to place their colored dot above the appropriate L so that they build a bar chart. After all have placed their dots on the flip chart, step back and evaluate.
6. Debrief and summarize the activity with these questions:
   - Based on the results of the straw poll, see if the team agrees there is consensus. Consensus is indicated by all votes being at least a Live or better.
   - In the event that there are Loathe, Lament, or just a few Live votes, ask the team as a group why someone voted that way. Be careful not to pick on a specific person, but get the team's feedback on why there isn't consensus.
   - Integrate the new feedback and build a better solution.

 nsider's Tip

- I love using this activity with teams who are starting to finalize a decision, but may not have reached consensus. This is a great way to ferret out information from the group.

Source
I published this activity in *Team Energizers* (QPC Press, 2003).

Kristin J. Arnold, M.B.A., CMC, CPF, CSP, helps corporations, government, and nonprofit organizations achieve extraordinary results. With years of team-building and facilitation experience, Kristin specializes in coaching executives and their leadership, management, and employee teams, particularly in the areas of strategic, business, and project planning; process improvement; decision making; and collaborative problem solving. As a master facilitator, Kristin trains other facilitators. An accomplished author and editor of several professional articles and books, as well as a featured columnist in *The Daily Press,* a Tribune Publishing newspaper, from 1996 to 2004, Kristin is regarded as an expert in team development and process improvement techniques. Her experience and renowned passion for extraordinary teams have enabled her to build a solid clientele that extends throughout North America and Europe.

Kristin J. Arnold, M.B.A., CMC, CPF, CSP
Quality Process Consultants, Inc.
6589 Cypress Point Road
Alexandria, VA 22312
Phone: 800.589.4733 or 703.256.TEAM (8326)
Fax: 703.256.4281
Email: Kristin@extraordinaryteam.com
Website: www.qpcteam.com

Six Thinking Hats® Quick Assessment

Submitted by Edward de Bono, Ph.D.

Objectives
- To provide skills to evaluate an idea, proposal, or solution.
- To experience the Six Thinking Hats® in a practical application.

Audience
The ideal number of people is 6–12.

Time Required
20 minutes.

Materials and Equipment
- Flip chart and marker.
- Prepared flip-chart page. (See Step 2 under Preparation.)
- Timer.
- Notepads and pens for each participant.
- Optional handout providing the White Hat background information on the chosen FOCUS. (See Step 5 under Process for an example.)

> **Editor's Note**
>
> This activity is an application of Edward de Bono's Six Thinking Hats. The facilitator should have formal training in the hats.

Area Setup
Table group or, if more than twelve participants, several tables.

Preparation
1. Prior to the activity, select an idea to be evaluated.
2. Prepare the following flip-chart page prior to starting the activity:
   AGENDA
   - Blue Hat: 2 minutes
   - White Hat: 3 minutes
   - Yellow Hat: 3 minutes
   - Black Hat: 3 minutes
   - Green Hat: 3 minutes
   - Red Hat: 1 minute

Process

1. Post the prepared agenda flip-chart page.
2. Ask someone to be the timer, or use an easy-to-set automatic timer.
3. Write the preselected idea to be evaluated on the flip chart under the heading FOCUS. For example: "Evaluate the idea of asking all employees in a real estate company to dress in uniform." Read the FOCUS idea and post the page on the wall for all to see.
4. Set the timer for 2 minutes and announce "Blue Hat." Say, "The definition of Blue Hat is 'managing the thinking process, thinking about the thinking, facilitating the group.'"

   Explain that the group has been asked to evaluate the FOCUS objectively using Six Hats. As the facilitator, you will wear the Blue Hat, which is managing the thinking and the group process. You will define each hat before the group is asked to use it. You (or your timekeeper) will keep time for the group. You will follow the agenda on the flip chart with a few comments at the end of each hat, so the whole activity will take about 20 minutes.

   Ask if anyone has any questions about how the activity will unfold.
5. Reset the timer for 3 minutes and announce "White Hat." Say, "The definition of White Hat is 'facts, observable information, what is known.' White Hat also includes noting what information is not known but is needed."

   The following kind of information can be provided on a handout or just given verbally:

   - The client is the Country Estates real estate agency.
   - It has five staff members and eight salespeople.
   - It wants to unify its employees and increase the impact of its branding.
   - It is considering mandatory uniforms for all thirteen people.
   - The uniforms are business casual with the company logo and colors.
   - The cost is $98 for each man's uniform and $129 for each woman's set.
   - Employees would be required to buy their own uniforms.

   Ask, "What additional information do you have or would you like to know in order to assess this idea? I will give you 1 minute to jot down your thinking, and then we'll go around for your comments."

   Time 1 minute and then ask someone to offer his or her White Hat. Write each White Hat comment on the flip chart. Many of these may be "White Hat *needed*." When time expires, thank the group for its White Hat thinking. If any of the White Hat questions seem essential, provide answers for the group.

Example: Who thought of this proposal?

Answer: This idea came from a marketing agency that has a great track record in increasing client sales.

6. Reset the timer for 3 minutes and announce "Yellow Hat." Say, "The definition of Yellow Hat is 'benefits, value, why this idea might work, why it is worth trying, what would be good about it.'"

   Again, give 30 seconds for people to think, then get the group's input. "What are the Yellow Hat benefits of this idea?"

7. Reset the timer for 3 minutes and announce "Black Hat." Say, "The definition of Black Hat is 'benefits, value, why this idea might NOT work.' What could go wrong? What are the risks?"

   Give 30 seconds for people to think, then get the group's input. What are the Black Hat risks of this idea?

8. Reset the timer for 3 minutes and announce "Green Hat." Say, "The definition of Green Hat is 'alternatives, possibilities, new ideas.' Green Hat is ideas for fixing the Black Hat risks. How could we lessen or prevent the risks?"

   Give a full minute for people to think, then get the group's input. "What are some Green Hat ideas for fixing the Black Hat problems?"

9. Reset the timer for 1 minute and announce "Red Hat." Say, "The definition of Red Hat is 'emotions, hunches, and intuitions.' Reasons are not given, just the feeling itself. In Quick Assessment, we are interested in your feelings *about the proposal,* after examining it. So we want to know how you feel about the idea of uniforms—are you for it, neutral, or against it?"

   Ask for a show of hands on each of the three positions.

10. Debrief by asking, "How do you see yourself using the Six Thinking Hats process?"

 nsider's Tips

- This activity is an overview of how Six Thinking Hats can be used at work. For more information, the book *Six Thinking Hats* is available at bookstores or online. Training in the use and facilitation of the system is available, as is software to manage the use of the hats and record the output.
- If the group is small enough, go around the table in a round-robin to encourage participation.

- Make sure that all stay within the hat that is currently featured; one of the biggest reasons creative problem solving does not work is that participants get off track and jump ahead or stay stuck in an earlier stage (hat).
- Make sure that all comments are about the specified FOCUS.
- Switch hats promptly when time has expired.

Source

This activity is part of my *Six Thinking Hats* (Back Bay Books, 1999) book and program. Copyright The McQuaig Group Inc., 1985. Reprinted with permission.

Edward de Bono, Ph.D., has written nearly seventy books on creativity and the direct teaching of thinking. His medical background in biological information systems inspired and enabled him to design revolutionary thinking methods. He is the inventor of the term *lateral thinking* and the designer of the CoRT Thinking Program for schools. In 1991, Dr. de Bono arranged for the incorporation of what is now de Bono Thinking Systems to publish his training materials and certify instructors to teach his thinking methods. Now more than five hundred thousand people have been trained to use the Six Thinking Hats and lateral thinking.

Edward de Bono, Ph.D.
de Bono Thinking Systems
2882 106th Street
Des Moines, IA 50322
Phone: 515.334.2687
Email: info@debonothinking.com
Website: www.debonothinking.com

Three-Stage, Successive, Rotating Group Problem Resolution

Submitted by David W. Jamieson, Ph.D.

Objectives
- To include and engage the right people in resolving difficult problems.
- To build the group's collective knowledge base and learning.
- To develop an implementable, owned solution to a difficult problem.

Audience
Ideal group size is 18–24, but larger groups could be accommodated.

The most important composition criterion is the inclusion of all stakeholders, important perspectives, needed expertise, and voices for the issue or problem, with one person from each for each rotating team. In other words, let's say that we need community representation plus engineering, customer service, human resources, finance, and operations. To create three rotating teams, we would need three different people from each of the stakeholder groups identified.

Ensure that you have participants who have authority to resolve the issue.

Creating the participant group can be more or less complex as needed for the targeted issue. However, getting the right composition is part of the intervention in this activity.

Time Required
The time will vary with complexity of issues and numbers of participants. A minimum of 3 hours and as much as a whole day should be considered. This is a powerful design and should be used for important issues that need resolution.

Materials and Equipment
- LCD projector, computer, and screen for PowerPoint.
- Four flip charts and sufficient colored markers.
- Colored adhesive dots or Post-it flags for voting.

Area Setup
Refer to the room sketch for three rotating teams and three stations.

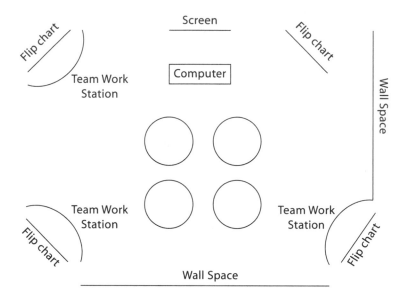

Process
Instructions provided are for three rotating teams of six members each.

Opening
1. Start in plenary with participants at round tables mixed across stakeholder groups.
2. Describe the purpose of the session and the nature of the issue being addressed.
3. Have people introduce themselves or do a warm-up exercise in which people get to know who's there.
4. Explain that the work will begin in three teams, each of which will be a microcosm of all of the stakeholders. Form the three teams and have them go to the three stations set up in different corners.

Stage One: Achieving a Common Understanding

1. Each group will develop a clear, comprehensive picture of the issue, including such things as what it looks like, when it happens, how it happens, why it happens, what forces are operating to cause or sustain it, what the consequences are, and so on. This may take 30–45 minutes.
2. After the groups are done describing the issue, one participant stays with each group's sheets, and the rest of the group rotates to the right.
3. The participant who stayed behind is now facilitator for the next step, as well as interpreter of what the group at that station developed.
4. Each group is now at another group's station and gets to add, clarify, build on, or raise objections to what's there. Any objections are noted and recorded on the team's flip chart and on the flip chart at the front of the room. This may take 20–40 minutes or more.
5. Once all groups have finished adding to the original issue descriptions, one participant (not the same one as before) again stays with the revised sheets, and the rest of the group again rotates to the right.
6. The participant who stayed behind is now facilitator for the next step, as well as interpreter of what the group at that station just discussed.
7. Each group is now at another group's station and gets to add, clarify, build on, or raise objections to what's there. Any objections are noted and again recorded on the team's flip chart as well as on the flip chart at the front of the room. (The timing of these last two rotations will depend on how much revision is taking place and how much convergence is occurring.)
8. One person from each team is selected to take and hold the now twice revised set of sheets. Everyone comes back to plenary. If there were any objections or concerns raised, these are discussed or clarified so that everyone now has the same understanding. If there were no objections raised or if they've been discussed, the group is given a break except for the three individuals holding the sheets.
9. During the break, the three participants and the facilitator either create slides or new sheets on the wall with the common understanding of the issue drawn from the collective thinking across all teams.
10. Following the break, the common understanding is shared, clarified if necessary, and left on the screen or wall for all to refer to.

Stage Two: Creating the Solution Space

1. Three new microcosm teams are formed and asked to go to the three stations.
2. Each group will now identify all the possible options and alternatives they can think of for addressing the issue as they now understand it. This will probably take 30 minutes.
3. One participant stays with each group's sheets, and the rest of the group rotates to the right.
4. The participant who stayed behind is now the facilitator for this next step, as well as interpreter of what the group at that station identified.
5. Each group is now at another group's station and gets to add, clarify, build on, or raise objections to what's there. Any objections are noted and recorded on the team's flip chart as well as on the flip chart at the front of the room.
6. One participant (not the same one as before) again stays with the revised sheets, and the rest of the group again rotates to the right.
7. The participant who stayed behind is now facilitator for this next step, as well as interpreter of what the group at that station identified.
8. Each group is now at another group's station and gets to add, clarify, build on, or raise objections to what's there. Any objections are noted and recorded on the team's flip chart as well as on the flip chart at the front of the room. (The timing of these last two rotations will depend on how much revision is taking place and how much convergence is occurring. You can expect 20–40 minutes for each rotation.)
9. One person from each team is selected to take and hold the now twice revised set of sheets. Everyone comes back to plenary. If there were any objections or concerns raised, these are discussed or clarified so that everyone now has the same understanding, and items are either left in or removed from the list. If there were no objections raised or if they've been discussed, the group is given a break except for the three individuals holding the sheets.
10. During the break, the three participants and the facilitator combine similar items and create sheets on a new wall that contain the collective set of options and alternatives in the Solution Space. Each item is written on the sheets with adequate space in front of it for up to fifty or sixty check marks or colored dots (approximately four or five options per page, side by side on a large wall space).
11. Following the break, each participant is given a marker or set of adhesive dots or Post-it flags to use to vote for priorities from the possibilities in the Solution Space. Each participant can have votes equal to approximately one-third the

number of total items available. Each person places his or her votes and sits down. (An option here is to first hold a plenary to review the consolidated Solution Space and allow for advocacy of any of the options.)

12. When all have finished voting, ask for help from some group members to total each item. Identify the top three and list them on another clean sheet or on a PowerPoint slide.

Stage Three: Developing Solutions

1. Reconfigure the teams if there is any mixing left to do (optional).
2. Each team is asked to go to one of the stations and be responsible for fleshing out one of the priority solutions. These solution plans should include who will need to be involved, any resource needs, the main action steps and key tasks to be accomplished, projected timeline, how it addresses the common understanding developed earlier, and how it will resolve the issue. Allow about 30 minutes.
3. The teams are reassembled into the plenary.
4. Each team is given a turn to present and advocate its solution plan, answer questions, and facilitate any discussion.
5. If a clear consensus begins to emerge, celebrate! If two or three alternatives are still strongly supported, then take representatives from each group and form a fishbowl in the middle of the room with a few empty chairs for others to join the discussion. Use this fishbowl group to weigh the alternatives and make a decision on what solution plan to pursue.
6. If necessary, you can form a follow-up, cross-stakeholder task group to finalize the plans or manage the implementation.

 nsider's Tips

- This is best run with two facilitators, with at least one being very experienced.
- Each time you move to a new stage, you are leaving something behind and taking something forward. Get rid of the old sheets. Clean off the walls. Create the new focus for each round of work.
- Mixing participants and rotating in stages helps everyone find room to participate, keeps everyone working, and provides numerous opportunities for people to learn something new from each other.

- With four teams, you can end up developing four solution plans. However, the number of rotations depends on how quickly people exhaust their thinking, revisions, ideas, and so on.
- Prestructure what to include in the Common Understanding and Solution Plans stages.
- The Solution Space concept is helpful in getting people to see the breadth of possibilities before focusing in on their favorites or what might be best for their situation.

David W. Jamieson, Ph.D., is president of the Jamieson Consulting Group and adjunct professor of management at Pepperdine University in the masters of science in organization development program. He has over thirty-five years of experience consulting to organizations on leadership, change, strategy, design, and HR issues. He is a past national president of the ASTD and past chair of the managerial consultation division and practice theme committee of the Academy of Management. Dave is coauthor of *Managing Workforce 2000: Gaining the Diversity Advantage* (Jossey-Bass, 1991) and coauthor of *The Complete Guide to Facilitation: Enabling Groups to Succeed* (HRD Press, 1998) and *The Facilitator's Fieldbook* (AMACOM, 1999). He also serves as editor of *Practicing,* an OD Network online journal, and on the editorial boards for the *Journal of Organization Change Management, Journal of Management Inquiry,* and *The Organization Development Practitioner.*

David W. Jamieson, Ph.D.
Jamieson Consulting Group
2265 Westwood Blvd., Suite 310
Los Angeles, CA 90064
Phone: 310.397.8502
Email: david.jamieson@pepperdine.edu

Tri-State: A Multiple Role Play

Submitted by Hank B. Karp, Ph.D.

Objectives

- To build skills in diagnosing organizational and group problems.
- To focus attention on the interrelation between content and process issues.

Audience

One 6-person group and any number of trios.

Time Required

Approximately 2½ hours.

Materials and Equipment

- One copy of the Tri-State Background Sheet for each participant.
- One copy of the appropriate Tri-State Role Instruction Sheet for each of the six role players.
- One copy of the Tri-State Consultant Worksheet for each of those in the consultant role.
- Paper and pencils for the observers.

Area Setup

One table with seating for six in the center of the room, and additional chairs forming an outer ring around the group of six.

Process

1. Present a lecturette on group and organizational dynamics, emphasizing the interaction between content and process in terms of organizational outcomes.
2. Select six volunteers to act out the role play and give each role player a Tri-State Background Sheet and a different Tri-State Role Instruction Sheet. Allow time for the players to study their roles.
3. Divide the remainder of the group members into trios and provide each trio with pencils, paper, three copies of the Tri-State Background Sheet, and three copies of the Tri-State Consultant Worksheet.

Solving Problems and Making Decisions **225**

4. Read the Tri-State Background Sheet to the group and inform the people who are not role players that they will be acting as consultants.

5. Conduct the role play in the center of the room, with the trios of consultants observing from an outer ring. Allow the role play to continue for about 30 minutes, or until a severe block occurs in the interaction.

6. When the role play is stopped, have each consultant take 5 minutes to complete an individual diagnosis and then collaborate with the two other members of the trio to present a unified diagnosis, according to the points listed on the Tri-State Consultant Worksheet.

7. Have one person from each consultant trio present the trio's diagnosis to the role players. Still role playing, the staff is allowed to question each consultant concerning the trio's diagnosis.

8. After each trio's diagnosis has been presented to the role players, have the Tri-State members choose which consultant trio they want to employ as their advisers. This is done in a group-on-group arrangement, with all consultants observing.

9. After the consultants are chosen, comment on the consultants' presentations and then lead a general discussion of approaches to the issues involved in diagnosing a group problem and planning an intervention.

Insider's Tips

- While the trios are compiling and evaluating their data, the role players may leave their roles and act as consultants to the diagnostic trios.

- Trios can prepare proposals for OD interventions (detailing budget, staff, time, and so on) that would follow from their diagnostic impressions.

- I have used this activity with great success, most recently in my graduate OD course at Hampton University. The exercise is adaptable to almost any diagnostic or group dynamic input. Participants really seem to enjoy it because it allows them to get totally involved in the process, and they can experience process observation diagnosis from start to finish.

Hank B. Karp, Ph.D., is an associate professor of management at Hampton University in Hampton, Virginia. He is also the owner of Personal Growth Systems, a management consulting firm in Chesapeake, Virginia. Hank has consulted with a variety of Fortune 500 and government organizations in the areas of leadership development, team building, conflict management, and executive coaching. He specializes in applying Gestalt theory to issues of individual growth and organizational effectiveness. He has authored many articles and written several books, including *Personal Power: An Unorthodox Guide to Success* (Gardner Press, 1994) and *The Change Leader: Using a Gestalt Approach with Work Groups* (Pfeiffer, 1995). Most recently he was lead author on *Bridging the Boomer–Xer Gap: Creating Authentic Teams for High Performance at Work* (Davies-Black, 2002), which was *Fast Forward* magazine's 2002 Gold Winner for Best Book in Business and Economics. He is currently working on a new project, *The Hubris Syndrome: Dealing with Executive Arrogance.*

Hank B. Karp, Ph.D.
Dept. of Management
Hampton University
Hampton, VA 23668
Phone: 757.488.3536
Email: pgshank@aol.com

Tri-State Background Sheet

The Tri-State Industrial Maintenance Corporation produces, and markets directly, industrial maintenance items, such as cleaners, floor finishes, industrial vacuum cleaners, and so on. The corporation services a three-state regional area. It has always put emphasis on the quality of its product and on good customer service; thus, although the company is small, it has always enjoyed a fair share of the market because of its reputation for customer satisfaction and customer loyalty.

Recently, however, Tri-State has suffered from decreased business because of an increase in competition from national corporations and the poor national economic situation. It has always been company policy that Tri-State will not cut prices.

Terry Kerr, the president and founder of Tri-State, has called in an organization development consultant to help the company cope more effectively with prevailing market conditions and to see if an analysis of the company's processes could facilitate a return to its previous level of growth.

After talking to Terry, the consultant has agreed to do some organizational diagnostic work and then to confer with the top-management team in the hope of implementing change in a positive direction.

To start the diagnosis, the consultant will observe a staff conference and then report on what he or she sees as being functional or dysfunctional in terms of how well the team works together. Attending the conference will be

Terry Kerr, founder and president

Robin Kerr, Terry's eldest child and executive vice president

Dale Tubb, sales manager

Chris Smith, head of office operations

Pat MacPherson, head of research and development

Sam Walker, head of production and shipping

Tri-State employs a total of thirty-five employees. Actual production in the small factory occurs only in late spring and summer, allowing the organization to stockpile enough reserves to last about twelve months.

Tri-State Role Instruction Sheet I

As Terry Kerr, you are the president and founder of Tri-State Industrial Maintenance Corporation. You started the business thirty-five years ago, and through hard work and diligence have built a successful operation. You attribute your success to hard work, honesty, and the quality of your service and your product. People deal with you because they respect you and what you stand for. You are convinced that what the business was built on is what will keep it successful. You feel that price cutting, fancy packaging, and slick advertising are only ways of compensating for a poor product and poor service.

You have called this staff meeting because you are aware that business is tougher to get and hold on to. You want to be open minded; however, you are not about to change just for the sake of change.

Robin suggested bringing in a consultant, and you went along with it. Robin is a hard worker, but does not have that much experience in the business.

Your basic approach to dealing with the present problem is to cut back on all unnecessary expenditures until things get better. This strategy has always been successful in the past. One thing you have been considering is to put all salespeople who are being paid a draw against commission on straight commission. That way, they either pull their weight or leave.

90 World-Class Activities by 90 World-Class Trainers. Copyright © 2007 by John Wiley & Sons, Inc.
Published by Pfeiffer, an Imprint of Wiley. www.pfeiffer.com

Tri-State Role Instruction Sheet II

As Robin Kerr, you are the executive vice president, which means that you have your hand in most phases of the business. Although you see the value of this position, you still chafe at being under Terry's thumb. All you really can do is suggest; Terry is the one who decides. Last week Terry wouldn't even listen to your ideas about a new line of vacuum cleaners.

Basically you support Terry's philosophy, but you also realize that something has got to be done to stimulate business. The old way is good, but it is just not enough to compete under prevailing conditions of competition and economic pressure.

You think that one good approach would be to invest in some good professional sales training for the sales force and to modernize the labeling for the products. You are, frankly, embarrassed by the old 1920s-type scrollwork.

At the staff meeting, you are going to try to make Terry understand that Tri-State is going to have to invest a little if it is to pull out of this successfully. You know that Dale will support this approach.

Tri-State Role Instruction Sheet III

As Dale Tubb, you are the sales manager for Tri-State's fifteen-person sales force. You and Robin have struck up a pretty close friendship over the past few years.

You honestly like and respect Terry, but feel that some of the president's views are antiquated. There is little question that quality and service are important; however, the recent infusion of competitive salespeople from nationally known organizations, coupled with the present economic situation, is putting very heavy pressure on your sales force.

Your present sales force is quite effective. You are afraid that Terry might want to cut back on it as a means of cutting costs. The president would probably do this by cutting out the draw for the newer, less experienced salespeople, making everyone go on straight commission. You think that this would be a mistake, as you have two younger sales representatives who are developing new territories and need the draw until the territories start paying for themselves. These two are good, and you would hate to lose them.

What you would like to do is to purchase local advertising, increase the commission rate by 3 percent, and run a major sales contest. The sales force has become increasingly demoralized. You are sure that your recommendations would give the organization the boost it needs to withstand the present conditions.

Tri-State Role Instruction Sheet IV

As Chris Smith, you have been with Tri-State for five years and are in charge of all office operations. You supervise the clerical workers and are responsible for maintaining the rotating inventory, filing, billing, written communications, and the like.

You know that things are tough, and it looks like they are going to get tougher. The thing that bothers you the most is that there has been an awful lot of tension and arguing in the past few months, and it is getting worse. Just last week Robin stormed out of Terry's office, and they haven't said a civil word to each other since then. Everybody has been short tempered with everyone else, and this just isn't the happy organization it used to be.

You feel that if all this bickering and tension would stop, everybody could pull together to get out of the present situation. It's just all so depressing.

Tri-State Role Instruction Sheet V

As Pat MacPherson, you are a chemist and came to Tri-State eighteen months ago to be in charge of research and development. You have known Terry and Robin for years and finally signed on with Tri-State the last time Terry made the offer.

Although things were quite good in the beginning, product improvement and new product development have taken a backseat to other organizational considerations. You and your two assistants are left with little constructive work to do.

Although Terry hired you with the best intentions, you are dissatisfied with the way things are going. You feel that if the company is going to pull out, it is going to have to spend some of its resources on product improvement. The national outfits are coming in with the latest in floor finishes, and if Tri-State cannot come up with something competitive in the same price range, it is going to lose this piece of the business regardless of economic conditions. You feel that Terry is going to have to either use you or lose you.

Tri-State Role Instruction Sheet VI

As Sam Walker, you have been with Terry Kerr as head of production and shipping since the day the business started. Back in the old days, Terry and you made the stuff and packed it, Terry sold it, and you delivered it. Terry has always been good to you and has helped you out in times of real need.

Robin is a nice kid—you even used to change Robin's diapers—but Robin will never be like Terry. You don't like the fact that Robin and Dale spend so much time together; Robin should be supporting Terry, not teaming up with that slick sales manager.

You know, from what you have overheard, that Terry Kerr is worried about the business and that there is going to be a meeting to discuss the problem. You are not sure what you can contribute to this, but you are pleased that Terry asked you to sit in. You are sure that the president knows more about what is best for the business than any of the others. You are also very concerned about the faulty master valve in the number three tank and need Terry's approval to replace it. The valve will cost about $3,500.

90 World-Class Activities by 90 World-Class Trainers. Copyright © 2007 by John Wiley & Sons, Inc.
Published by Pfeiffer, an Imprint of Wiley. www.pfeiffer.com

Tri-State Consultant Worksheet

Instructions: Observe the role play and make notes on this form for later use. After the role play is terminated, you will work with the other members of your consulting trio to develop a unified diagnosis and proposal for the Tri-State situation.

Problem Area

1. Clarity of definition of the problem

2. Causes of the problem

3. Underlying issues

4. Different views of the problem

5. Unknown data needed to understand the problem

6. How you see the problem

Group Process

1. Effectiveness of communication

2. Task effectiveness

3. Openness

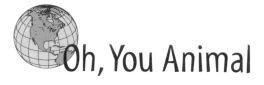

Oh, You Animal

Submitted by Richard V. Michaels, M.Ed., CDP, CCP

Objectives
- To learn to think metaphorically for the purpose of expanding perceptions and gaining new insights when problem solving.
- To provide a tool for the purpose of explaining a complex situation or problem and learning to discuss it metaphorically.

Audience
When conducted in a typical classroom of 30 or fewer, you can process the results individually. When conducted for a large auditorium audience, divide the audience into teams of 10–12 (for an audience size of about 300) and have them identify their group as an animal.

Time Required
45–60 minutes. (This includes the setup, report-back, and brief discussion of the use of metaphors in critical thinking and problem solving.)

Materials and Equipment
- Paper and pencils for the participants to capture their metaphor.

Area Setup
Any classroom or work team arrangement works.

Process
1. Tell the participants that you want them to introduce themselves as an animal. They are to think about an animal that best describes metaphorically their personality and behaviors. Have them write the name of the animal down on a piece of paper.

   Provide an example by describing yourself. For example, when I first came up with this idea for a training activity, I was explaining to my staff of writers how this activity would work. I told them that I have always thought of myself as a panther, that I can spot business opportunities and stealthily move in to close the sale, all while responding with agility to changing conditions with clients. A women named Debbie started shaking her head no, so I stopped talking and asked, "Deb, don't you understand the activity?" She replied, "Yes, of course I understand the activity, but no way are you a panther." "Well what animal am I?" I responded. She said, "You're a bear! Look at the size of you. You growl in the morning when you first come in, and watch out if someone gets in your way." I was shocked and maybe a little hurt as I thought to myself, I act like a bear? Deb could sense my feelings and smiled and said, "Do you remember Captain Kangaroo and the bear on his show?" "Of course I do," I said. "You mean the Dancing Bear?" Deb smiled and said, "Yes, you are agile, and you do move light-footedly toward new opportunities. In fact I agree with everything you said about yourself, except the animal you chose. Rich, you're a Dancing Bear, with all the qualities, good and bad, of a bear."

2. Look for individuals in the room who have written down the name of their animal and ask them to share their animal. If they don't explain why the animal fits the attributes of their personal style, behavior, and so on, probe for them to explain.

3. Proceed around the room and ask each person to present his or her animal. Each person should take only 1 to 2 minutes or less to explain.

4. Wrap up the activity by saying something to the effect that if you had asked them to generally describe their personality or behavior using normal methods, it probably wouldn't have been as deep or insightful as it now is for themselves and others in the room. Personal human behavior is a complex subject, and if someone were to ask any of us to be his or her mentor or coach, it would take us many hours of discussion to learn through traditional dialogue methods who the real person was. But in a few minutes, the participants were able to lay out a foundation of mutual understanding about themselves because they explained it metaphorically.

5. Go on to explain the advantage of using metaphors. Tell them that metaphors help us explain the unexplainable; they help us share complex problems and situations easily so that others can more quickly step in and help you problem-solve and think through various options and scenarios. State that metaphorical thinking helps us get into our right brain so that we can see the connections and the relationships among things that otherwise have been invisible to us.

6. Close the activity by asking for suggestions of how participants might use metaphors for solving problems.

Insider's Tips

- Don't give the participants much time to prepare (unless, of course, you're running it in an auditorium setting and you need to give teams time to come up with a consensus animal that describes them).

- Normally when running this in a workshop environment, after you give the participants the instructions and model what you want them to do, ask for a volunteer almost immediately (after giving the class about 20 seconds to write their answer down) or just select someone at a nearby table and ask him or her to tell you the animal that first comes into his or her head. Move on to the next person at the table and go around the room in sequence after that. If you try to do this by just calling out, "Who wants to go next?" some participants can drop out, and you won't know it; the activity will also take longer because of participants' hesitation to speak up.

Richard V. Michaels, M.Ed., CDP, CCP, is president and CEO of Great Circle Learning, which specializes in the design and development of corporate professional development programs that are grounded in the principles of critical thinking. An expert at applying critical thinking to address large-scale business challenges, Rich is responsible for the design and direction of corporate education interventions that support organizational change and growth. He is also responsible for the general operations of Great Circle Learning.

Richard V. Michaels, M.Ed., CDP, CCP
Great Circle Learning
P.O. Box 5159
Marco Island, FL 34145
Phone: 239.389.2000
Email: rvmichaels@gclearning.com

Chapter 12

Teamwork

Successful teams are an asset few organizations can afford to be without. We've been team focused in the workplace for over thirty years, yet we still need practice. I am guessing that everyone who reads this book is engaged in working with teams in one way or another. Perhaps you conduct teamwork interventions, train teams to be more efficient and effective, or work on a team yourself. Because so many of us in the training and consulting professions are intimately involved in teamwork, I was not surprised to receive a large number of submissions geared to this topic.

The truth is that almost every other activity in this book could be used to enhance teamwork. So if you are looking for something to use with a team, don't limit your search to this chapter. Check the chapters on communication, conflict and collaboration, creativity, or any of the others. The eight contributions in this chapter share one common thread: excellence in interaction. And isn't that what teamwork is all about?

Dave Arch shares an activity typical of the Bob Pike Group: creative, quick, energy promoting, hard hitting, and highly interactive. I can't wait to use this one! Building structures is always a practical team-building activity. Two contributors— Barbara Pate Glacel and Edie West—share their architectural blueprints for a successful team-building activity. Identifying similarities is a natural team activity, and Barbara Glanz and Takako Kawashima (Japan) offer their versions in this chapter. The activity I (Elaine Biech) have submitted is an opener using T-shirts that weaves its way throughout the rest of the session and becomes the theme. Jeff and Linda Russell have submitted a powerful activity that strengthens personal responsibility to a team and its goals. Mary Wacker reached back a quarter of a century to submit an activity that is still as good as the first time it was conducted. She adapted it from an activity presented at a 1981 ASTD national conference by two authorities in the field, Geoff Bellman and Forest Belcher. This oldie but goodie is a key reason for compiling this book: to ensure that the best of the past is preserved for the future.

Today's business gurus agree that teamwork is the only answer for the twenty-first century. Change is occurring too rapidly for one person to know everything about every issue, with total accuracy, in a short enough time. The only alternative is teamwork. It looks as though teamwork is here to stay.

Paper Bridge

Submitted by Dave Arch

Objectives

- To help participants compare and contrast the strengths and weaknesses of competition and cooperation.
- To draw out the more introverted participants through physical movement.

Audience

Although 14–20 has proven to be the optimal size, you can divide the participants into four groups and put them into the four corners of the room, which will accommodate twice as many people.

Time Required

15 minutes.

Materials and Equipment

- One sheet of flip-chart paper per two people on a team.
- One extra sheet of flip-chart paper per team.

Area Setup

There should be a clear area of at least two persons' width immediately next to the wall in the game area.

Process

1. Divide the group into two teams. Each team is clustered into one of the two opposite corners in the front of the room. Give them full sheets of flip-chart paper (exactly one more sheet than half the total number on their team) and tell them to stand on the paper (they will have to double up). The challenge now is for the two teams to change places by moving into the other team's corner. However, they must go around the outside of the tables—moving around the back of the room. They cannot get off their papers because the carpet has become a swamp.
2. In larger groups, you might consider dividing the group into four teams and having them stand in the four corners of the room with the two teams at each end of the room needing to exchange positions with each other.

3. Say "Go" and turn them loose. Play a little music to get the juices flowing.

4. Even though one team will win, encourage the others to continue until they also reach the corner.

5. After both teams have accomplished their goals, discuss the following questions:
   - Why did the teams make it a race? No one said it was a race.
   - What could have been accomplished through cooperation?
   - Is there a better way to accomplish the task? (Tearing the paper and sliding on the paper under the shoes of the participants? Why didn't anyone think of that?)

 ## Insider's Tips

- Give no suggestion for organization.
- Make sure not to call it a race.
- Use lively music to heighten the energy.
- Encourage the team that does not complete the task first not to quit but rather continue to completion.

Source

To my knowledge, this activity has not been published. It has not been published in any of my books.

Dave Arch is senior vice president of the Bob Pike Group and president of Dave Arch and Associates, an authorized licensee of the Sandler Sales Institute. He is a best-selling author, internationally recognized speaker, and conference presenter. He serves as the national training consultant for the Sandler Sales Institute and its 170 franchisees. Drawing on twenty-five years of training experience and a twelve-year background in personal and family counseling, Dave's sales training workshops are featured annually at national conferences. He has authored a dozen resource books currently used throughout the training industry.

Dave Arch
Sandler Sales Training
900 Buckboard Blvd.
Papillion, NE 68046
Phone: 402.873.8108
Email: dave@sandler.com
Website: www.davearch@sandler.com

T-Shirt Team

Submitted by Elaine Biech

Objectives

- To get participants' attention immediately and set the stage that this training session will be active.
- To use a creative process to introduce participants and let them know something about the trainer.
- To create a theme that can be used throughout the session to reinforce other concepts and build relationships.

Audience

Any size. Although intended for a team, this activity can be used for any seminar or training session when you want participants to get to know one another better.

Time Required

15–25 minutes as an icebreaker (depending on how many participants) and then another 5 minutes each time you assign another action throughout the session.

Materials and Equipment

- One copy of the blank T-shirt handout for each participant. (You may use a variety of paper colors.)
- Several real T-shirts that are meaningful to you—for example, an organization name, radio station, a funny saying, or a souvenir logo.
- Water-based (so they don't bleed through to the wall) markers on the tables for participants.
- Your own prepared T-shirt handout.
- Masking tape to hang the shirts.

Area Setup

Tables to accommodate all participants and wall space to hang the T-shirts.

Process

1. Tell the participants, "Some people say that you can't tell a book by its cover. I believe, however, that you can tell a person by the T-shirt he or she wears."

2. Begin to hold up the T-shirts you brought, explaining that they can tell something about you, and then briefly share where the T-shirt came from or why it is meaningful to you. For example, I always have an ASTD T-shirt and state that it is my professional organization. I also have a T-shirt that is from Hawaii, one of my favorite places.

3. Next, tell the participants that they should think about how they would like to introduce themselves. Suggest that they might consider a slogan or a picture that says who they are. Hold up your prepared T-shirt as an example. My T-shirt always has a sketch of a book, a pencil, and waves. I explain that I like books, like to write, and love to be by the water. It also has a quotation by Helen Keller, "Life is either a daring adventure or nothing," which I tell them is my life's motto.

4. Pass out the T-shirt handouts. I like to allow participants to select their own color of paper on which the T-shirt is printed.

5. State that they have about 3–5 minutes to draw a picture or write a motto that tells who they are.

6. After 3–5 minutes, ask for a volunteer to introduce himself or herself and to share his or her T-shirt with the rest of the group. Ask the volunteer to use the masking tape to hang the T-shirt on the wall. Go on to the next volunteer, continuing until all participants have introduced themselves. Encourage participants to spread their T-shirts out across the wall(s), as they will be writing on them several more times during the session.

> **Editor's Note**
>
> While participants are designing their T-shirts, I walk around and place a piece of masking tape on the table in front of each participant. This allows them to ask questions if they have any, and allows me to assist unobtrusively if someone is lost.

7. The T-shirts are now positioned to be used in many ways to build the team or relationships.

8. Periodically throughout the session, post sentence starters on a flip chart and have participants complete the statements about others. Participants will use the water-based markers, go to the wall, and write on the other participants' T-shirts. You may ask them to write on one other participant's T-shirt, or in

some cases you may want them to write on two or more T-shirts. You may use these sentence starters that have worked for me in the past, or you can develop your own based on the needs of the participants and the team.

- "Something I learned about you today . . ."
- "I like the way you . . ."
- "Thank you for . . ."
- "I wish you would . . ."
- "I am pleased that you are on our team so that we can . . ."
- Select someone with whom you need to improve communication:
    - "I'd like it if we would . . ."
    - "Our communication would improve if we . . ."
    - "I'd like you to help me . . ."

You may wish to ask participants to sign their statements. This will depend on the group and your purpose for the activity.

Editor's Note

You will most likely want to begin the session with less threatening sentence starters and require that participants take more and more risks as they get involved in the session.

9. At the end of the training session, remind participants to take their T-shirts with them and hang them on their bulletin boards at work or on their refrigerators at home.

 **Insider's Tips**

- If you print an equal number of each color for the T-shirts originally, you can use this as a way to divide the group into teams. For example, if you have twenty participants in the group and you have five T-shirts each printed on blue, yellow, green, and orange paper, the group could divide into four teams based on the color of their T-shirts.
- Ensure that you have both words and a sketch on your prepared T-shirt handout so that participants know that it is okay to do one or the other or both.
- I usually list each of the sentence starters on a flip chart (one per page) so that when I provide the instructions, the visual learners have the statement in front of them. It saves me from repeating the directions over and over.

- I usually complete Step 8 just before or after a break, though it also works well to tie the statement to an activity the group has just completed. This strengthens the meaningfulness of the activity. For example, if you just completed a trust-building activity, have participants complete a statement such as, "I'd like to build trust with you by . . ."
- I sometimes place crayons on the tables instead of markers for participants to use. This adds an element of fun, and you may hear some of your participants delight in using crayons for the first time in years.
- I've always wanted to do this activity with real fabric T-shirts, perhaps even printed with the company (or team) logo. The participants would use permanent fabric markers. Unfortunately, I have never had enough preparation time or budget to do this. Maybe next year . . .

Source

I like to create themes for the training sessions I conduct. I created this activity for a team at the U.S. Department of Navy FISC in Hawaii and have used it and versions of it many times. I also like to use a paper bag in the same way, asking, "What's your bag?"

Elaine Biech is president and managing principal of ebb associates inc, an organization development firm that helps organizations work through large-scale change. Elaine has been in the training and consulting field for over twenty-five years and is the author and editor of dozens of books and articles, including *Training for Dummies* (Wiley, 2005) and *The Business of Consulting* (Pfeiffer, 2007). A long-time volunteer for ASTD, she has served on ASTD's national board of directors and was the recipient of the 1992 ASTD Torch Award and the 2005 ASTD Volunteer Staff Partnership Award. She currently authors ASTD's "Ask a Consulting Expert" column and edits the prestigious Pfeiffer Annuals for consultants and trainers.

Elaine Biech
ebb associates inc
Box 8249
Norfolk, VA 23503
Phone: 757.588.3939
Email: ebbiech@aol.com
Website: www.ebbweb.com

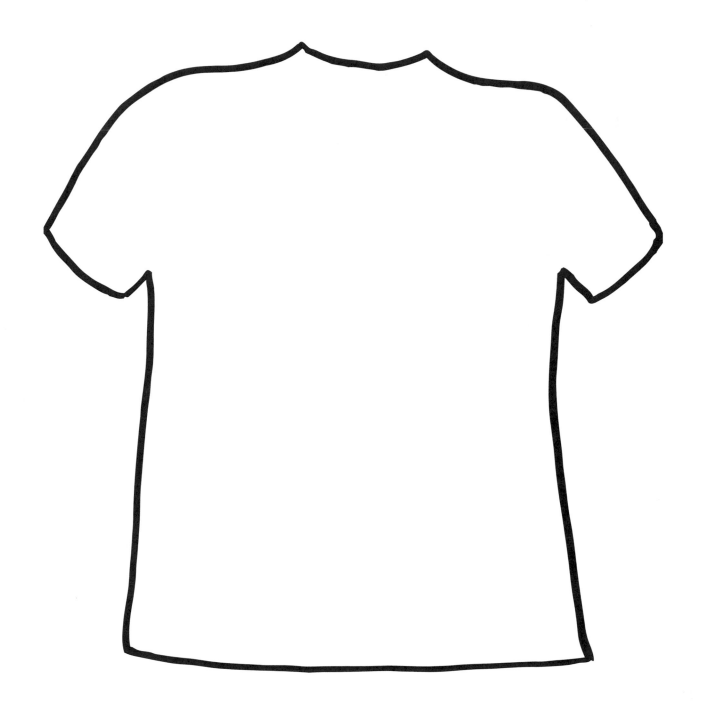

Tower Team

Submitted by Barbara Pate Glacel, Ph.D.

Objectives
- To create a situation that demonstrates the team development stages of forming, storming, norming, and performing.
- To involve a group in an exercise that resembles real life, including roles, managing differences of opinion, standards, time deadlines, and performance rewards.

Audience
Each group should have 5–8 members. This activity can be done with one team, but multiple teams that compete with one another allow a richer experience.

Time Required
2 hours (or longer depending on variations in debriefing the experience).

Materials and Equipment
- One copy of the Observer's Guidelines for each process consultant.
- One copy of the Team Observation Matrix for each participant.
- One copy of the Four-Step EIAG handout for each participant.
- One copy of the Team Learning Triangle for each participant.
- Newspapers.
- Flat cardboard or cardboard box.
- Wire coat hangers.
- Ball of twine.
- Rolls from paper towels or wrapping paper.
- Aluminum foil.
- Paper clips.
- Scissors.
- Glue.
- Markers.
- Stapler.
- Marking pens.
- Paint and paintbrushes.

- Colored construction paper.
- Other odds and ends as available.

Area Setup

Each team needs its own space where it can work without being observed by other teams. Have materials on a table in a central location.

Process

1. Tell the teams that they have one hour to assemble a tower that is aesthetically appealing, free standing, and capable of remaining standing until a predetermined time. The team creating the tallest, most aesthetically appealing tower that is still standing at the set time will receive a performance bonus.

2. Structure time for the teams to plan. Tell them that they should spend 5 minutes considering the question: How do we want to work together as a team?

3. Ask each team to select roles for team members. You may wish to post the following roles on a flip chart:
   - Supervisor/Foreman
   - Planner (architect/engineer)
   - Builders (can be more than one)
   - Suppliers (in charge of resources)
   - Process consultant (observer)
   Allow about 10 minutes for this step.

4. Tell the team members that they should spend approximately 5 minutes drawing their own individual design for the tower, which will use the provided materials and meet the requirements.

5. Have team members share their drawings with the rest of their team. Tell them they have 15 minutes to decide on a design or to combine several designs in building their towers.

6. Tell the teams that they have 30 minutes to build the towers using the materials provided, the roles selected, and the design as chosen. The completed tower will be presented to the trainers and other teams.

> **Editor's Note**
>
> The process consultant does not take part in planning or construction. The consultant will take notes on what individuals and group members do during the planning and building stages using the observer's guidelines. Provide the consultants with the Observer's Guidelines handout.

7. Give each participant a copy of the Team Observation Matrix and introduce it as a model for discussing what happened (content) and how it happened (process) in building the tower (task) and relating to others on the team (interpersonal).

8. Distribute the Four-Step EIAG handout and conduct an EIAG discussion within each team for approximately 30 minutes. Use a flip chart to document the lessons learned.

   - Experience—constructing the tower.
   - Identify—what happened?
   - Analyze—thoughts and feelings.
   - Generalize—what was learned? How is it applicable in the real organization?

Editor's Note

If there is more than one team, have the observers facilitate the discussion.

9. If there is more than one team, have teams report out their learnings using the Team Observation Matrix as a model for generalizations about content, process, task, and interpersonal behaviors. Ask the observers for additional comments.

10. Give a copy of the Team Learning Triangle to each team member and summarize the exercise by describing the Tuckman model of team development: forming, storming, norming, performing.

 nsider's Tips

- The success of this exercise comes from the richness of the debriefing process in conjunction with the overall goals of the program in which it is used. Within a two-day workshop to accompany *Light Bulbs for Leaders* (Wiley, 1996), this one exercise was used to:
  - Demonstrate the Tuckman model of team development.
  - Allow participants to give one another good feedback that was based on situation, behavior, and impact.
  - Introduce tools for planning, negotiating, implementing, and rewarding.
  - Discuss models and critique performance of meeting management and leadership effectiveness.
  - Understand a model for analyzing the content and process of any task.
  - Address the concepts of what are effective and ineffective teams.

- It is important to allow sufficient time, both for tower construction and debriefs. Don't shortchange the debriefs, as that is where all the learning takes place!
- If multiple teams compete, you can serve as judge or bring in external judges to determine the winner. If the program lasts beyond the exercise, the winner may be announced at the end of the program. The performance bonus should be a tangible reward, demonstrating that effective results bring rewards. You may want to have another reward available for a team that did not win the competition, but showed exceptional learnings from the exercise. Often the most effective learnings come from a team process that did not work well and did not produce results.
- Remember: it is really not the tower that counts! It is what lessons learned transfer back to the organizational setting.

Source

This exercise was developed in partnership with Dr. Emile "Chum" Robert as part of a two-day workshop to accompany the book we cowrote, *Light Bulbs for Leaders.* In addition, a variation of this activity was published in *A Handbook of Structured Experiences for Human Relations Training* (vol. 3), edited by J. William Pfeiffer and John E. Jones (Pfeiffer, 1974).

Barbara Pate Glacel, Ph.D., trains leaders and teams in organizations on four continents. The author of three books, including the best-seller *Light Bulbs for Leaders* (Wiley, 1996), Barbara also writes articles and speaks about the lessons of leadership and teams. As an executive coach, she works with senior leaders in the United States, Europe, South Africa, and the Pacific Rim.

Barbara Pate Glacel, Ph.D.
The Glacel Group
12103 Richland Lane
Oak Hill, VA 20171
Phone: 703.262.9120
Email: BPGlacel@glacel.com
Website: www.glacel.com

Observer's Guidelines

As you observe the activity, look at WHAT happens in terms of the task and consider HOW it happens interpersonally as process.

TASK (What) Examples	PROCESS (How) Examples
Roles are being selected.	Margaret and George both want to be the leader. George is giving in quickly.
The task is being defined and the problem understood.	Jim and Maureen are discussing with interest. Jack is not interested. Some team members are involved and some are not.
Sally is asking for a decision.	Margaret says there is not a problem, that the answer is obvious. Art tries to express a difference of opinion.
Many suggestions are being presented.	Peter and Kathy are trying to get on with the job rather than listen to different suggestions.
The job is being done.	Participation is evenly distributed. Everyone is working in some way to complete the task. For example: Peter and Kathy are … Margaret and Arthur help Peter by … Kathy's input is …

As you observe, you do not question why, nor do you try to give meaning to the actions. You simply observe the actions in both TASK (what is going on) and PROCESS (how it is being done).

Team Observation Matrix

	Task	Interpersonal
Content	• Agenda • Purpose • Goals	• Task and maintenance roles—who does what to and with whom.
Process	• How the task gets done • Problem definition • Conflict management • Leadership issues • Decision making	• How members relate—behaviors are motivated more by feelings about one another than about task concerns.

Four-Step EIAG

Experience

Do something (have an experience as a team). After the experience ends, continue with the next three steps. Reflection on the value of the experience may take place in a feedback session.

Identify

Consider the experience and describe specifically what happened. What action, activity, or behavior has been identified from the experience? What was the sequence of events? Who did what, and when?

Analyze

What were the team members thinking about during the experience? What were they feeling? Why did things happen? Make observations or draw conclusions about the nature of what happened.

Generalize

What general learnings are implied from the discussion? Generate guidelines for how to handle similar situations in the future. Document the answers as learnings from the experience.

Team Learning Triangle*

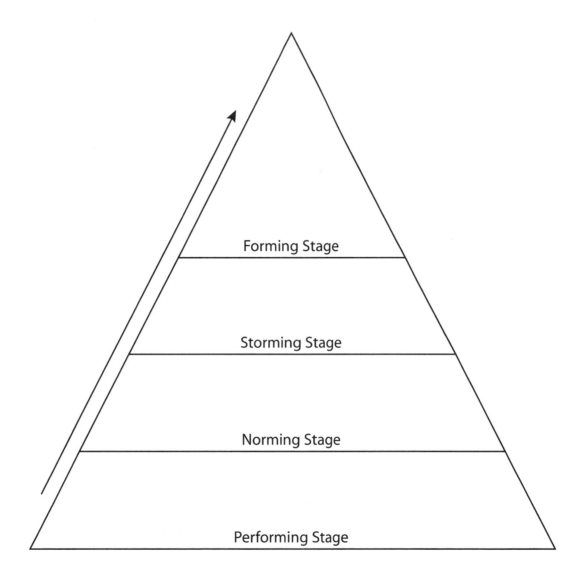

Forming Stage

Storming Stage

Norming Stage

Performing Stage

*Based on Tuckman's stages of team development.

Commonalities and Uniquenesses

Submitted by Barbara A. Glanz, CSP

Objectives
- To allow people to get to meet one another.
- To enhance team building.
- To foster creative thinking.

Audience
Any group up to 50.

Time Required
20 minutes.

Materials and Equipment
- A flip chart for the facilitator and one for each team.
- Lots of colored markers.

Area Setup
It is best to conduct this activity in a fairly large room so that the groups have space to spread out to write.

Process
1. Divide the group so that there are four people in each subgroup. I try to separate people who are sitting together, so, for example, I count off from 1 to 6 in a group of twenty-four. Then the four number 1's work together, and so on.
2. Draw a large circle in the middle of your flip chart. In the center of the circle, write "Commonalities." Then on each corner write "Uniqueness 1," "Uniqueness 2," "Uniqueness 3," and "Uniqueness 4."
3. Tell each group that you want them to spend 15 minutes with a piece of flip-chart paper and several markers. Ask them to find at least three things they have in common and write them inside a circle drawn on their flip chart. Assign each person a corner of the flip chart and have each write two things that are unique about each person but with *no names.*

Instruct them to have fun and to get their creative juices flowing, to think outside the box, and not to write obvious things like "We all wear glasses," "We all have kids," or "We all work at _____," but rather think about wild and different things like "We all broke our big toe," "We all lived in Iowa," and "We all hate broccoli."

Then, for their uniquenesses, ask them to think of something that no one knows about them, such as that someone in their family is famous. For example, I share with them my three uniquenesses, one of which is that I directed David Hasselhoff in his first high school play! This gets them laughing and thinking.

4. After they have finished their answers (you will need to remind them with minute warnings toward the end), depending on the size of the group, ask them to share what they wrote. If the group is not too large (up to about twenty-four), have each group stand together and hold up their chart with one person as the spokesperson. They read their commonalities and then the uniquenesses, one at a time. The rest of the group tries to decide which person belongs to each set of uniquenesses. If the group is larger than twenty-four, ask each group to walk around with their flip chart and share it in the same way with three other groups.

5. At the end of the exercise, ask participants to raise their hands if they learned something new about someone—and, of course, they all will. Then ask them, "What do we look for when we first meet someone?" (Commonalities.) "But what makes a great team?" (Uniquenesses.)

Insider's Tips

- Often I suggest that the training program coordinator collect the flip charts and post them in a breakout room or cafeteria and have the rest of the organization guess the person who belongs to each set of uniquenesses.
- The participants love this exercise. It is nonthreatening and a wonderful way to learn about one another. It works just as well with groups who know each other as with those who don't. The only caution is to watch the time, because if you allow it, this activity can take up to 45 minutes.
- Another way to manage larger groups is to have three or four groups of four work together and share their charts with each other.

Barbara A. Glanz, CSP, works with organizations that want to improve morale, retention, and service and with people who want to rediscover the joy in their work and in their lives. She is the author of *180 Ways to Spread Contagious Enthusiasm* (Walk the Talk, 2006); *The Simple Truths of Service* (coauthored with Ken Blanchard) (Simple Truths, 2005); *Handle with CARE—Motivating & Retaining Employees* (McGraw-Hill, 2002); *Balancing Acts* (Kaplan Business, 2003); *CARE Packages for the Workplace* (McGraw-Hill, 1996); *The Creative Communicator* (Irwin Professional Publishers, 1993); *Building Customer Loyalty* (McGraw-Hill, 1994); and *CARE Packages for the Home* (Andrew McMeel Publishing, 1998). As an internationally known speaker, trainer, and consultant with an M.S. degree in adult education, Barbara lives and breathes her personal motto—Spreading Contagious Enthusiasm™—and has presented on six continents and in all fifty states since 1995.

Barbara A. Glanz, CSP
Barbara Glanz Communications, Inc.
6140 Midnight Pass Road, #802
Sarasota, FL 34242
Phone: 941.312.9169
Email: bglanz@barbaraglanz.com
Website: www.barbaraglanz.com

Our Similarities

Submitted by Takako Kawashima, M.A.

Objectives

- To introduce participants to one another.
- To find similarities among diverse audience members.
- To demonstrate that there are many similarities among members of a team.

Audience

10–40 people. This can be used with a diversified audience of people from various countries or races or of people from various companies, or as an exercise with a team.

Time Required

10–15 minutes.

Materials and Equipment

- Paper and pens or pencils for note taking.

Area Setup

Any.

Process

1. Use this as a class opener for a diversified audience or as a team-building activity.
2. Divide the audience into several groups of four to six members each.
3. Tell the groups they have 5–8 minutes to introduce themselves to each other and to find similarities that characterize all the members in the group.
4. Call time and have each group introduce its members to the audience by telling their names and sharing their similarities with the audience. For example, a group may say to the audience, "Our members are Tina, John, Joe, Judy, and Tim. We are from South America. We have to work with various kinds of people because of mergers and acquisitions. We are sometimes frustrated by people coming from the parent company, so we all want to learn a lot from this intercultural communication course."

5. Ask each group how many similarities they have found or in what categories. The similarities may include job descriptions, preferences, races, nationalities, and present situations.

 nsider's Tips

- When volunteers tell the audience about their similarities, be sure to create a positive environment so that *everyone* feels good about sharing the information.
- When using this activity with intact teams, challenge the subgroups to list as many similarities as each group can in 5 minutes. You may reward with a prize if you like.

Takako Kawashima, M.A., received her degree in TESOL at San Francisco University. She started her career in a Japanese company as an e-learning materials developer and mentor and worked for Hitachi netBusiness as an e-learning consultant. When Hitachi netBusiness was acquired by and merged with Hitachi Information Systems, she was transferred to Hitachi Institute of Management Development, where she has worked as the HR coordinator.

Takako Kawashima, M.A.
Hitachi Institute of Management Development
Hitachi Hongou Bldg.
4-10-13, Hongou, Bunkyo-ku
Tokyo 113-0033
Japan
Phone: 813.3813.3969
Email: kawashima@hitachi-himd.com

Personal Responsibility Pledge

Submitted by Jeffrey Russell and Linda Russell

Objectives

- To build personal responsibility in each team member for both the challenges facing the team and the solutions to address these challenges.
- To engage individual team members in personal reflection on their individual role and influence on team outcomes.
- To strengthen individual team member ownership of the strategies for addressing team challenges.
- To identify personal strengths to help the team resolve a difficult challenge.
- To improve communication and build trust between team members.

Audience

This activity is designed to be used by a relatively small intact team as part of a larger organization development intervention with this team. The activity requires the team to identify a specific interpersonal or performance challenge that is limiting the team's effectiveness.

Time Required

A minimum of 40–60 minutes, depending on the size of the team.

Materials and Equipment

- Flip chart, if desired, to display instructions and to record team assets and actions for change.
- One large (4-by-6-inch) index card for each participant.
- Pens or pencils for participants.

Area Setup

No special room arrangements are required for this activity. The room, however, should be large enough for people both to work privately to complete their index card and to share their personal action plan with the team as a whole or with individual team members.

Process

1. Give each team member a blank index card and a pen or pencil.
2. Define the problem or challenge facing the team and post it on the flip chart.
3. Tell participants that on one side of the index card they are to identify what they have done or are currently doing that has contributed to this team problem or challenge. Say, "Regardless of your proximity to this problem, identify at least one thing you are doing that has made this problem worse or has enabled or sustained this problem [challenge]."

   Tell them that on the flip side of the index card they are to identify two things: first, a personal asset or strength that they can bring to solving or addressing this problem or challenge, and second, specific and personal actions that they pledge to take to help the team solve or address this problem or challenge. Say, "Be as specific as possible in identifying how you will use your personal asset or strength to take specific and personal actions or steps to help the team move forward to resolve this problem [challenge]."
4. Instruct individuals to work independently and silently to complete both sides of their personal responsibility pledge cards. Give participants about 10 minutes to complete their cards.
5. After individuals have completed their personal responsibility pledge cards, ask individual team members to pair up with another team member.
6. Direct individuals to take turns with their partner sharing their personal responsibility, personal strengths, and personal actions statements.
7. After about 5 minutes, direct participants to locate another partner from the team with whom to share their personal responsibility statements. Continue to facilitate the pairings until each team member has paired up with at least three other fellow team members.
8. At the conclusion of the team pairings, invite team members to individually share their responsibility statements with the large group if they wish.
9. Following the large group sharing of the personal responsibility statements, facilitate a discussion of the personal assets and strengths that individuals and the team as a whole bring to addressing and resolving the team problem or challenge. Record individual and team assets and strengths on a flip-chart page.
10. Complete the activity by recording the *collective* commitments and actions for change that the team and its members will take to move the team forward on its problem or challenge.

Insider's Tip

- This is a powerful activity for helping build personal responsibility and accountability by every member of the team for a shared problem or challenge. In this activity, every member of the team—even those who believe or suggest that they have no involvement in the team problem or challenge—is required to complete a personal responsibility pledge card.

Jeffrey and Linda Russell are codirectors of Russell Consulting, Inc., of Madison, Wisconsin. For more than fifteen years, they have been providing consulting and training in leadership, strategic planning, leading change, employee engagement, organization development, and performance coaching. They have authored six books, most recently *Change Management Basics* (ASTD Press, 2006).

Jeffrey and Linda Russell
Russell Consulting, Inc.
1134 Winston Drive
Madison, WI 53711
Phone: 608.274.4482
Email: RCI@RussellConsultingInc.com
Website: www.RussellConsultingInc.com

What Do We Know About Teams?

Submitted by Mary B. Wacker

Objectives

- To participate in a team-building simulation with assigned tasks and deadlines.
- To learn the stages of effective teamwork and evaluate your team experience.

Audience

This activity requires a minimum of 3 teams (4–8 participants each) and can work with up to several hundred participants. The dynamics work best with teams of 6 or 7 so that participants can fully experience the group dynamics of decision making, leadership, and carrying out team tasks.

Time Required

The activity takes 60 minutes. The overall time frame is 75–90 minutes, depending on how much time you spend debriefing the activity with the large group. I have adapted the activity for time lengths from 45 minutes to 2 hours.

Materials and Equipment

- One copy of What Do We Know About Teams? packet for each participant.
- One marker and a 1-foot length of masking tape for each team. The masking tape can be wrapped around the marker for ease of distribution.
- Two flip-chart pages for each team.

Area Setup

Tables set up for teams of four to eight participants each *or* chairs arranged in a circle for each team.

Process

This simulation can be conducted either before or after a brief discussion of effective teamwork, which might include team stages, characteristics of effective team members, and group behaviors that support trust, communication, and accomplishing goals.

Introduction (8–10 minutes)

1. Form at least three teams of four to eight participants.
2. Distribute the What Do We Know About Teams? packets, markers, and flip-chart paper. (Do not distribute the packets in advance or allow participants to read.)
3. Read through page 1 of the packet together with the group.
4. Tell the group to turn to page 2 and begin following the instructions. Tell participants they will have 12 minutes, and post the end time for each segment on a board or flip chart so all can see it.
5. Do not answer any questions about the activity. Instead direct participants back to their teams to figure out how to solve any issues or answer any questions they might have. (This is part of the team learning experience—to understand how they figure things out.)

Facilitating Task I

1. During the timed segments of the activity, stay disengaged, but notice the team dynamics, including making any notes of comments or reactions you notice. Note the group dynamics you observe and possibly ask about them during your debriefing at the end of the simulation.
2. About 8–9 minutes into Task I, ask for the group's attention and make the following observations:
   - "Notice how you are starting to work together."
   - "Notice how you are feeling about your fellow team members."
   - "Notice how you are making decisions."
3. At the end of 12 minutes, signal the group to turn to the next page and complete pages 3 and 4 (Learning Point I and Feedback Questionnaire I). Tell them they will have 8 minutes, and post the new end time.
   - One or more of the teams may not have completed Task I and will protest that they need more time. This raises the stakes in each group and becomes an issue for them to manage.
   - Your reply is to direct them to pages 3 and 4 and to restate the new end time. It is likely some of the teams may start to have issues with you as facilitator at this point. Stay calm and smiling but disengaged from any team's reactions to your directions.
4. About 6–7 minutes into the Feedback Questionnaire I time, ask the group to stop talking for a moment, and make the following observations:
   - "Consider how group input affects your opinion and your first impressions."
   - "Think about whether you changed your number scores and how that felt."

Facilitating Task II

1. At the end of 8 minutes, direct the group to turn to page 5 and begin Task II. They will have 10 minutes to complete the task. Post the end time.

    You will notice that the individual groups will become much better at time management at this point.

2. About 7–8 minutes into the time allotted for Task II, ask the group to stop talking for a moment, and make the following observations:
    - "Notice ways your team takes action."
    - "Notice the ways your team struggles for direction and how *long* everything takes."
    - "Notice how the pressure of deadlines affects the group's effectiveness (and patience!)."
    - "Notice how you are the only one who knows how it *should* be."
    - "Notice ways your group likes to find out information—by asking, reading, discussion, and so on."

Facilitating Task III

1. At the end of 10 minutes, signal the end time and ask the group to turn to the next page and continue with Learning Points II and Task III on pages 6 and 7. They will have 10 minutes. Post the end time.

2. About 7–8 minutes into the time allotted for Task III, ask the group to stop talking for a moment, and make the following observations:
    - "Notice whether you did the tasks you have been asked to do. Notice your own follow-through."
    - "Notice how satisfying it can be to use your own resources *or* notice how frustrating it is to not get something done."

3. At the end of 10 minutes, signal the group to turn to the next page and complete pages 8, 9, and 10 (Learning Point III, Feedback Questionnaire II, and Group Debrief). Tell them they will have 12 minutes. Post the new end time.

4. Ask each team to identify a spokesperson to report their responses to the debrief questions on page 10.

5. About 10 minutes into the time allotted for Feedback Questionnaire II, ask the group to stop talking for a moment, and make the following observations:
    - "Notice what is happening in your team—how much you are sharing compared with early on."
    - "Notice how you are taking responsibility."
    - "Notice how you feel when your group can talk about *how* it is working."

Debriefing the Simulation (15–30 minutes)

1. The debriefing can go in many directions related to the chosen topic: teamwork; leadership; decision making; team start-up; growth of teamwork over time; building trust; impact of tight timelines and how that mirrors their work environment; challenges of being a self-directed team; team stages of forming, storming, norming, performing; or other related topics.

2. In addition to the debrief questions on page 10, some of my favorite follow-up questions are as follows:
   - How did you handle leadership in your group? Who took the lead? All point to that person. (With groups from the same organization, you can ask how different departments or levels impacted teamwork and leadership.)
   - How did you make decisions in your group? How effective was that? What changes did you make to your decision making over time?
   - What stages of team development did you experience during this simulation (forming, storming, norming, performing)?
   - What was most memorable for you? What stood out about your team's working together?
   - What was frustrating or uncomfortable in the simulation?
   - What did this simulation remind you of in your workplace?
   - If you were to continue working together, what is one change your group could make to become even more effective?
   - What did you learn about what it takes to build good teamwork?
   - How might you apply this learning to your own teams?

3. Wrap up your discussion with a summary of key learning points from the groups and from your own team resource materials.

 ## Insider's Tips

- Inserting the facilitator observations during each portion of the activity is critical to participant learning. It helps participants step out of their immediate team dynamics and begin to make sense of that experience. Their ultimate learning about teamwork depends on their being able to apply their logic as well as their emotions to the group's experiences—whether productive, difficult, or a combination of each.

- The timelines for each segment of the activity are deliberately tight. It allows the group members to experience how they work under pressure, and it always creates interesting dynamics between those who struggle with time issues and those who manage this aspect of the task well.
- The original activity lasted about 2 hours and included another debrief conversation and a resource packet of team literature. Facilitators are welcome to provide appropriate resources to each team and to vary the length and complexity of the activity. I have adapted this activity to focus on questions (during Task I) related to teamwork, leadership, customer service, and organizational effectiveness.
- In a longer variation, you can provide three flip-chart pages to each team to use during Task I and ask each team to select and respond to two posted questions during Task II. You can also insert an additional feedback questionnaire between Tasks II and III.
- The original version included a feedback compilation form after each feedback questionnaire. One team member from each team recorded everyone's responses on the compilation form.

Source

I adapted this activity from one originally designed by Geoff Bellman and Forest Belcher. I first experienced the activity at the 1981 ASTD international conference and exposition. It was created and facilitated by Geoff and Forest with over two hundred participants in their breakout session. It was chaotic, energizing, and absolutely wonderful. In a conversation I had with Geoff recently, he mentioned the couple who approached him later in the conference, saying they had met during the activity and had been together ever since!

Mary B. Wacker focuses on life/work coaching, business performance systems, and organizational change, working both nationally and internationally. Noted for developing leaders, high-performance teams, and service systems, her work has been featured on radio and in print. Mary is coauthor of *Stories Trainers Tell: 55 Ready-to-Use Stories to Make Training Stick* (Pfeiffer, 2005).

Mary B. Wacker
M. B. Wacker Associates
3175 N. 79th Street
Milwaukee, WI 53222
Phone: 414.875.9876
Email: mary@mbwacker.com

What Do We Know About Teams?

Team-Building Simulation

You are about to participate in an exercise about working as part of a team. Throughout the course of the exercise, you may experience a wide variety of responses and feelings (possibly enthusiasm, frustration, accomplishment, anger, and so on).

It is important to be aware that the ups and downs you'll experience are *part* of understanding how teams function.

Exercise

The following pages contain a series of instructions, learning points, and feedback questionnaires. The seminar leader will guide the teams through the packet.

There will be time limits for each section of the exercise.

Each team should have the following:

- One What Do We Know About Teams? packet per team member.
- One marker with masking tape wrapped around it.
- Two flip-chart pages.

Adapted from work developed by Geoff Bellman, GMB Associates, and Forest R. Belcher, MEGA Consultants

Task I

Time: 12 minutes

1. You are a new team, starting to work together.
   You are going to learn about working in teams by doing it.

2. Meet other team members.
   Find out who they are.
   Tell them who you are.

3. Together, choose a name for your team.
   Put your team's name on the upper right corner of each flip-chart page.

4. Discuss some ground rules you'll follow to work effectively together during this exercise.

5. As a team, come to consensus on two questions about *effective teamwork* that you would like to have answers to.
   Write one question at the *top* of each page of the flip-chart paper provided, and post your questions on a nearby wall.

GOOD WORK!

(WAIT FOR THE NEXT INSTRUCTION.)

Learning Point I

Time: 8 minutes

Read the items on this page pertaining to Learning Point I and keep them in mind as you complete page 4.

Learning Point I

At the outset, major team concerns relate to getting started. Teams often ask such questions as

1. Are we a team? Do members believe they are a team?
   (Definition)

2. What do we want to accomplish? What is our purpose?
   What are our tasks?
   (Goals)

3. What resources do we have? Who is to do what?
   (Roles)

4. What procedures do we follow to accomplish tasks?
   How are we going to work together?
   (Rules)

5. What are our feelings toward one another?
   How does this affect our work efforts?
   (Relationships)

These questions may not be expressed, but many of them will be on the minds of team members.

(GO ON TO THE NEXT PAGE.)

Feedback Questionnaire I

Answer the questions by placing an X along the continuum reflecting your feelings:

1. How well did we go about establishing who we are (our team name) and what we want to know (our two questions)?

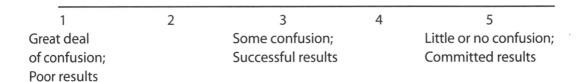

1	2	3	4	5
Great deal of confusion; Poor results		Some confusion; Successful results		Little or no confusion; Committed results

2. How did team members participate in the task?

1	2	3	4	5
A few participated. Others felt left out.		Most participated. There were mixed feelings.		All participated actively. All felt included in the work.

Briefly report your number scores and discuss your responses with your team.

(WAIT FOR THE NEXT INSTRUCTION.)

Task II

Time: 10 minutes

1. As a team, go around the room and select any ONE question from any group that you want to respond to during this time period.

2. In selecting the question, consider and feel free to use:
   - The knowledge and experience of your team
   - What your team can accomplish in the time available

3. Take the question down from the wall to your team's work area.

4. Together, develop your response and write it below the question.

5. Sign your team name at the bottom of the chart.

6. Repost the chart back on the wall where you originally found it.

(WAIT FOR THE NEXT INSTRUCTION.)

Learning Point II

Time: 10 minutes

Read the items on this page pertaining to Learning Point II and keep them in mind as you complete page 7.

Learning Point II

As teams work together, they become concerned with such questions as:

1. How are we going to assign tasks? Who is to make assignments?
   (Leadership)

2. How well do we understand each other? How good are we at clarifying? At listening to one another's suggestions and ideas?
   (Communication)

3. How are decisions made? Are decisions shared? Do a few impose on the rest? Does a "majority" govern? Do we use consensus?
   (Decision Making)

4. How do we handle differences of opinion? Are disagreements seen as constructive? Destructive? To be avoided? To be encouraged?
   (Conflict)

5. What kind of permanent working arrangements do we need to have? Should we develop a system for working together?
   (Work Systems)

(GO ON TO THE NEXT PAGE.)

Task III

1. Return to the wall to get the responses to the questions your team asked. (Both may have been worked on, or possibly neither was selected.)

2. As a team, read and discuss the responses. (If you want clarification, go to the team who responded to that question.)

3. If neither of your questions was selected, use this time for you to answer them as a team. If one was selected, review that response and then, if you have time, develop your team's response to the question that was not selected.

4. When you are through with your charts, put them back on the wall for others to read.

CONGRATULATIONS! GOOD WORK!

(WAIT HERE.)

Learning Point III

Time: 12 minutes

Read the items pertaining to Learning Point III and keep them in mind as you complete pages 9–10.

Learning Point III

As teams complete their work (or major portions of it), they have the opportunity to assess how they have worked together. A team identity often develops. Related questions are:

1. How do we feel about what we have done, our product?
   What contributes to those feelings?
   (Product)

2. How well did we plan? How well did we carry out those plans?
   How did our planning contribute to results?
   (Actions)

3. How supportive are we of one another?
   How do we help each other get our work done?
   (Support)

4. What are our feelings toward each other as a result of our work?
   How have those changed?
   (Loyalty)

5. What will we do to reinforce our success? To reconsider where we need to improve? To build on what we have?
   (Follow-up)

(GO ON TO THE NEXT PAGE.)

Feedback Questionnaire II

Now that you have finished your work together, individually consider these questions:

1. How did your team's plans and actions work out?

1	2	3	4	5
We didn't plan anything, and it showed.		We decided how we were going to work, but got off the track a lot.		We decided how we were going to work, and did it well!

2. How supportive were people of each other while the team worked?

1	2	3	4	5
No support; constantly competing		Some support, potential for much more		Very supportive; built on others' contributions

3. How much did this team learn about working together?

1	2	3	4	5
No change from the beginning; didn't learn		Some change; began to function more as a team		Significant change; got much better over time

Briefly report your number scores and discuss your responses with your team.

Group Debrief

Prepare to discuss the following questions with the entire group:

1. What did you agree on most? Where did you experience the most disagreement?

2. What did you like about how you worked together?

3. What could you do to increase your effectiveness?

The Paper Project

Submitted by Edie West, M.Ed.

Objectives

- To reinforce the importance of a team's having a plan with clearly defined mission, goals, roles, and procedures that *everyone involved understands before* taking on a project.
- To reinforce the importance of achievement—shared accomplishment—to a team or group.

Audience

This activity may be carried out with 1–5 teams of 4–6 people each.

Time Required

45–90 minutes, depending on the number of teams.

Materials and Equipment

- Five sheets per team of flip-chart paper (or other paper of similar size and thickness).
- One marker per team.
- Music CD (copyright free and appropriate for the group) and player.
- Flip chart, whiteboard, overhead, or electronic screen may be used to highlight discussion points.

Area Setup

Open floor space is required for each team to build a paper structure. (If there are moveable tables and chairs, push them toward the walls during the activity.) If available, breakout rooms may be used for the planning phase. Chairs may be used during the discussion.

Process

There are four phases to this activity: Phase 1—planning; Phase 2—building; Phase 3—presentation; and Phase 4—discussion.

Phase 1—Planning

1. Each team will have 20 minutes to choose an object and plan for the building of a three-dimensional paper structure using five sheets of flip-chart paper and one marker.
2. During Phase 2, each team will have 5 minutes to build its structure.
3. Announce that while planning, each team should make sure each member understands clearly the design of the structure, each of his or her individual roles in building the structure, and an accepted procedure for completing the structure, because there will be no talking during the building phase.
4. Before planning, each team should designate an observer for the activity. That individual will watch and take notes during the planning and the building processes. During the discussion phase, that person will report observations of the team.
5. Tell the teams to begin planning.
6. Announce when the 20 minutes are up.

Phase 2—Building

1. Provide each team with five sheets of paper, one marker, and open space for building.
2. Announce that the teams will build their structures in 5 minutes with (1) no talking; (2) music playing (appropriate to group and workshop); and (3) the observer taking notes.

Phase 3—Presentation

1. Have all teams move from one structure to the next and guess what the structure is. Team members will let them know when they guess correctly.
2. If they don't guess correctly, team members will tell them.
3. Be supportive of each team and lead a round of applause for each structure.

Phase 4—Discussion

1. Ask the total group to bring chairs into a circle for discussion.
2. Ask the following questions to stimulate discussion:
   - What did each observer note regarding plans and execution? Variances?
   - What did the teams think of their results? Did the completed structure relate sufficiently to the plan?
   - How did the team decide on a structure to build? What process—formal or informal? What did they think of the process used?

- How were role assignments made? What actually occurred? What did team members think of the process?
- Had teams clearly delineated all procedures during the planning phase? If so, what were the results? If not, what happened during execution?
- How do team members feel about the activity?
- What significant learning points come from the Paper Project?

 nsider's Tips

- This is best used as a culminating activity to a management, team, or project workshop.
- Introduce the Paper Project as an activity that is designed to reinforce what participants have discussed, and explain that they should relax and enjoy it.
- Be strict about rules. Any deviation weakens the activity.
- Keep the presentation phase celebratory (for example, by clapping for each structure), light, and moving quickly.
- Facilitate (don't lecture) during the discussion, only organizing comments or rephrasing as needed. The activity speaks for itself.
- Note significant learning points for participants to see.
- Allow as much time as the group wants for discussion.

Edie West, M.Ed., is the former executive director of the National Skills Standards Board. She is a writer and consultant. She has provided consultation, facilitation, coaching, meeting design, and speaking services to such organizations as Xerox, Ben & Jerry's, Utica National Insurance, General Electric, Corning Incorporated, the State University of New York, National Fire Academy, New York State Office of Mental Health, New York State Department of Education, the Labor Management Institute, and the Hawaii Quality Conference. Edie is the author of *201 Icebreakers* (1996) and the *Big Book of Icebreakers* (1999), both published by McGraw-Hill.

Edie West, M.Ed.
8611 Woodwren Lane
Fairfax, VA 22039
Phone: 703.927.4523
Email: ediewest@aol.com

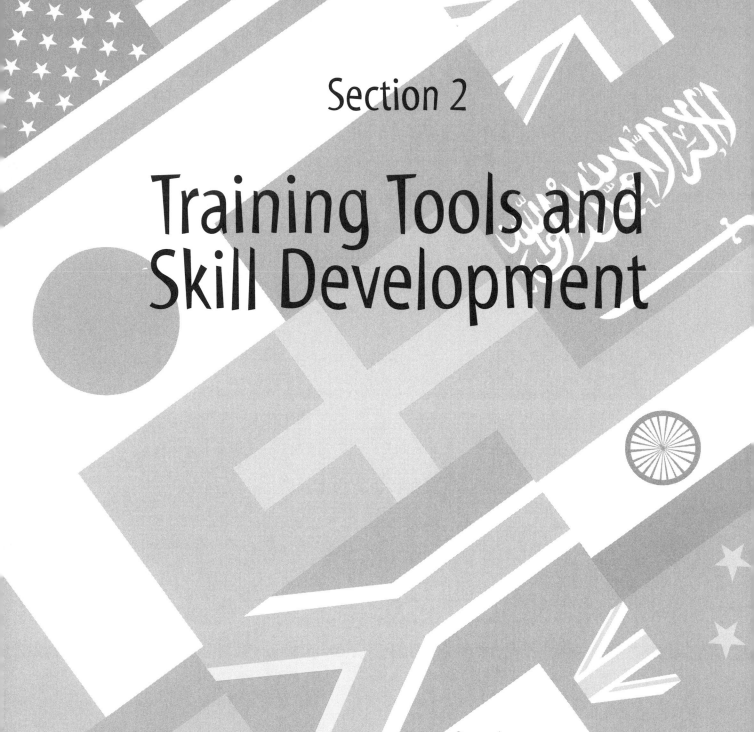

Section 2

Training Tools and Skill Development

## Chapter 13

Trainer and Speaker Skills

Conducting a train-the-trainer session or teaching speaking skills is the epitome of training for many trainers. In some ways, it says that you have made it: you are skilled enough to teach your new colleagues. So if you are reading this chapter because you will be training someone else, hats off to you! You may also be checking this chapter because you are new to the profession and are looking for some tips.

Trainers, facilitators, and speakers new to the field have so much to think about: needs assessment, the design, materials, audiovisuals, delivery, participation, and a hundred other things. The three contributors to this chapter have all been there before. (I am humbled that they have chosen to share their genius with all of us.) They know what it takes to be a great presenter—because each of them has made it!

Geoff Bellman's ingenious train-the-trainer design is one that is high on feedback and low on fussy preparation, high on participation and low on instructor control. It is a perfect event to model for new trainers. Björn Fiedler (Germany) presents a creative activity to help speakers learn to focus their attention on individuals in the audience. Don Kirkpatrick, the evaluation guru and creator of the Four Levels of Evaluation, shares a quick quiz to get discussion started about the ten requirements for an effective training program.

Enjoy this chapter; let these contributors help *you* be successful.

285

Stand-Up Skills

Submitted by Geoff Bellman

Objective
- To improve the stand-up skills of trainers.

Audience
Small group of trainer-trainees (up to 9).

Time Required
2 hours to 2 days, depending on content and depth of material.

Materials and Equipment
- Skill cards (masters provided at the end of this activity).
- Flip chart, paper, and marker.

Area Setup
Table and chairs facing the front of the classroom.

Process
1. Prior to this activity, assign content material to each trainer. If this is a generic train-the-trainer class, participants can be asked to bring presentation material with them.
2. Select enough cards so that you have one fewer than the number of trainers.
3. Identify the topic areas of cards selected and share with trainers.
4. Discuss with trainers what these areas mean and ask them to list likely indicators of skill and lack of skill in each area. Collect their responses and post them on the flip chart.
5. Distribute cards to all but one of the trainers. The one without the card will be the first presenter.
6. Ask the remaining trainers to be seated, thus becoming observers, with their skill cards folded into a tent shape, with the skill facing the presenter. This will remind the presenter which behaviors to watch closely during the session.

7. Ask the observers to read aloud the questions on the backs of their cards. This will tell the presenter in specific terms what is being reviewed. After the observers finish reading their cards, tell them that they will be asked to evaluate the presentation based on their card's questions.

8. The presenter begins presenting; the observers observe, frequently participating and taking notes. When the presenter finishes, give the observers 2–3 minutes to write comments in response to their card's questions. Ask the session presenter to critique his or her own presentation before hearing from the others. This will help the trainers become more competent and confident in self-evaluation.

9. After the presenter has finished his or her self-evaluation, have the observers answer aloud the questions on the backs of their cards. Using the specific questions helps them focus their critiques. Give the presenter a chance to ask for further clarification on comments and to add more self-evaluative statements. By now, you should have heard a fairly specific critique, which you may want to supplement.

10. Select a second presenter. Rotate the cards among the observers. This gives each observer something new to look for in the second presentation. Repeat the process until all trainers have presented once and observed from the different viewpoints. How long this takes depends on session length, depth of critique, and type of training involved.

Insider's Tips

- If you prefer not to use the tent cards provided, you can design your own. Or involve the new trainers in designing the cards. Talk with them about their needs and the kinds of behaviors they think are important for a trainer. Divide behaviors into a small number of evaluation areas and help trainers design questions in each area.
- Questionnaires are another possibility that can be useful in situations where new trainers are anxious about how others will see their initial performances. But use questionnaires carefully and only as a first step in leading to group discussion of a new trainer's performance.

- The cards also can be used by a group to evaluate another group in action. This is a fishbowl situation in which the inside group knows the kinds of actions and behaviors the outside group is considering as it observes the inside group perform. This can be especially useful in developing trainers' awareness of group processes. A group of four or five new trainers seated in the middle of a circle works together on a problem while four or five other trainers observe, using specific group process criteria. After the first group finishes its performance and critique, the outside group moves into the center, and the process is repeated.

Source

This activity was originally published in *Training HRD* (1976).

Geoff Bellman has worked in and around major corporations for forty years. His clients have included GTE, Intuit, Shell, Boeing, TRW, PacifiCorp, Booz-Allen Hamilton, and Simpson Investment, among others. He has also consulted to the public sector at the state and national levels, including work with the Governor's Council on Educational Reform for the State of Washington. In recent years, he has been focused on creating community in organizations of all kinds. Geoff is an award-winning author with several books to his credit, including *Getting Things Done When You Are Not in Charge* (Berrett-Koehler, 2001), *The Consultant's Calling* (Jossey-Bass, 2001), *Beauty of the Beast* (Berrett-Koehler, 2000), and *Your Signature Path* (Berrett-Koehler, 1996). He is a founding member of the Woodlands Group and the Community Consulting Project, as well as a longtime member of ASTD and the OD Network.

Geoff Bellman
1444 NW Woodbine Way
Seattle, WA 98177
Phone: 206.365.3212
Email: GeoffBellman@yahoo.com

ADULT LEARNINGS

1. How did the leader relate to or draw on the group's experience?
2. How did the leader relate content to the group's needs?
3. How did the leader acknowledge the variety of learning styles within the group?
4. What did the leader do to establish the learning climate?

LEADERSHIP

1. How did the leader respond to group needs?
2. What decisions were made during the session? How?
3. How much control did the leader exhibit? The group?
4. What techniques did the leader use to move the group through the design?
5. How would you describe the leader's style?

VISUALS

1. Name all the visuals used during the session. Which were most effective? Why? Which were least effective? Why?
2. What other visual techniques could have been useful in this session?
3. How did the leader use himself or herself as a visual aid?
4. What messages did this convey?

TIME

1. Keep track of the time spent on each major segment of the session.
2. Note how much time the leader talked or led.
3. Describe the pace for each major segment.
4. How did the pace feel to you?
5. How could the leader have used the available time better?

METHODS

1. Write down every training method you see used in this session.
2. Which were most effective? Why?
3. Which were least effective? Why?
4. Name three alternative methods the leader could have used.

DESIGN

1. Are the session objectives clear? Does the group share in them? How do you know?
2. How did the leader give the group a sense of direction?
3. Critique the instructions the leader gave to the group.
4. How did the leader reinforce learning?
5. What gave unity to the design of the session?

CONTENT

1. What is the primary content of this session?
2. How was this content made clear to you?
3. What does the leader do that causes you to believe he or she knows the content?
4. What does he or she do that causes you to doubt his or her knowledge of the content?

PARTICIPATION

1. How did the leader affect the group? How aware was the leader of this effect?
2. Give examples of how the group responded to the session.
3. How many in the group participated? How long? In what ways?
4. How would you describe the group's behavior?

Eyecatching

Submitted by Björn Fiedler

Objectives
- To establish direct eye contact with your audience during speeches.
- To simultaneously focus your attention on your presentation and the audience's reactions.

Audience
9–12 presentation training participants.

Time Required
20–50 minutes, depending on how many participants want to participate.

Material and Equipment
- A flip chart and marker.
- A set of eleven green cards and eleven red cards. On each set are the following audience characters printed on one side (one word per card): Nervous, Over-supportive, Bored, Tired, Self-Important, Aggressive, Sceptical, and Angel. (You can have more than one angel; depending on the number of participants, you will have from one to four Angel cards.) How many of the cards you use in the game depends on the number of participants. If you have twelve participants, you will need eleven cards. For each participant less, take one Angel card out of both sets. (For example, for nine participants you will have eight green cards and eight red cards with the following characters: Nervous, Over-supportive, Bored, Tired, Self-Important, Aggressive, Sceptical, Angel).
- A small prize (optional).

Area Setup
All participants sit around a meeting table in front of the speaker's place, which is still empty. The red cards are stacked face down in front of the speaker. The green cards are spread face down all over the table, so that the participants can grab them easily.

Role Descriptions

Process

1. Begin by describing the setup and objectives: "During a speech, it's very important to establish direct eye contact and notice reactions from your audience. At the same time, you have to deliver your presentation properly. That means you need the capacity to focus on your presentation and on your audience simultaneously. The following exercise will help you reach this goal. Unfortunately, audience participants are not always cooperative. They may play roles that are distracting." Review the eight roles and ask for ideas from participants about what they might expect to see.

   - *Nervous* is attentive and listens, but displays nervousness all the time (for example, by clicking his or her ballpoint pen).
   - *Oversupportive* praises the speaker aloud for anything during the presentation so as to get his or her attention (for example, "By the way, your slides are VERY informative").
   - *Bored* isn't interested in the speech at all. He or she is looking out the window or typing on his or her laptop.
   - *Tired* is really tired and displays it by yawning and the like.
   - *Self-Important* interrupts the speaker frequently and adds information that shows how important he or she is. If the speaker talks about Rome, Self-Important would add, "Yes, but don't forget to mention the seven hills it was built upon. I can tell you that's important because I was there in 2004 . . ."
   - *Aggressive* attacks the speaker directly by hitting him or her hard (verbally). The attacks can be aimed at the content of the speech, its delivery, or the speaker's outfit.
   - *Sceptical* doesn't hate the speaker but wants to know every detail, so he or she frequently asks sceptical questions. If the speaker talks about Rome, Sceptical would ask, "Are you sure it was built on seven hills? Which is the highest?"
   - *Angel* is a quiet supporter of the speaker. He or she smiles at the speaker, nods frequently, and is very attentive.

2. Tell the participants that when you say go, each participant will try to grab a green card from the table. Everybody reads the card silently and places it face down, so that no one else knows the character that will be acted out.

3. The participant who was not able to grab a card is the first speaker. The participant will speak for exactly 2 minutes and can choose any theme (a hobby,

a common workplace issue, and so on). The theme is not important, and the delivery quality will not be evaluated. The speaker's mission is to find out which person from the audience represents which character. Therefore, the speaker must concentrate on the audience and look at it quite often while speaking.

4. After 2 minutes, the speaker is stopped, and he or she picks up the red cards. The speaker walks around and gives the red cards to the people he or she thinks played the role on the card. The audience members still hide their green cards.

5. After every person has received a red card from the speaker, one at a time the audience members show their green card together with the red card. For every correct match the speaker gets one point, along with big applause. Write the speaker's name and points on a flip chart.

6. Prepare for the next round by shuffling the green cards and placing them face down on the table again. The red cards are stacked in front of the speaker's place once more. The first speaker sits down in the audience and takes one of the green cards. This guarantees that anyone who has spoken will not be a speaker again and that someone else will be without a green card next time.

7. Repeat Steps 2–6 until all participants have been speakers or your intended time for the game has ended.

8. Celebrate the winner and the loser with huge applause and a prize if you like.

 ## Insider's Tips

- This activity engages your participants in a competitive, action-loaded activity.
- While explaining the roles in the beginning, act them out; it's fun, and everybody will get a better understanding of the roles.
- Let one of the participants keep time so you can concentrate on the speaker.
- After the activity, turn to the question of how one should deal with the different characters while speaking. Start by asking, "Do any of you know these characters from your own experience? How did you handle them?"
- Laminate the cards to use them more than once. They are quickly torn in the wild and funny battles to grab one.
- As an alternative, you may allow speakers to present for a second round of 2 minutes to increase their scores.

Source

This activity was developed in 2002 but has never before been published.

Björn Fiedler, founder of Fiedler & Partner, Institute for Communication Consulting, is a German performance improvement consultant who has specialized in effective interpersonal communication and presentation skills since 1996. He has a master's degree in speech science and is the author of various articles about speech training and successful interpersonal communications. Fiedler & Partner supports global players in delivering their English training concepts in German, and vice versa.

Björn Fiedler
Fiedler & Partner
Institute for Communication Consulting
Verdener Str. 97
D-28205 Bremen
Germany
Phone/Fax: 0049.0421.4303990
Email: b.fiedler@fiedler-partner.com
Website: www.fiedler-partner.com

Ten Requirements for Effective Training

Submitted by Donald L. Kirkpatrick, Ph.D.

Objective

- To introduce participants to the time requirements of an effective training program.

Audience

Any size, in subgroups of 3–4.

Time Required

30 minutes.

Materials and Equipment

- One copy of the Ten Requirements for an Effective Training Program handout for each participant.
- Overhead projector or flip chart where the answers can be displayed one at a time.
- Marker.

Area Setup

Nothing special is needed.

Process

1. Have the audience break into groups of three or four.
2. Distribute a copy of the Ten Requirements for an Effective Training Program handout to each participant. Give them 10 minutes to complete it.
3. Before showing each answer, ask participants to volunteer how they have responded. Then reveal the answers one at a time.

Insider's Tips

- For a little humor, as they are working I tell them as I wander around, "I see that some of you need a little help. The answer to 3 is 'time' and 4 is 'place'!" In some groups, these are about the only ones they have!
- I start many of my sessions on evaluating training programs with this interactive list. It adds some challenge and activity to very straightforward content.

Donald L. Kirkpatrick, Ph.D., is a former national president of ASTD. Don is the training evaluation guru, known worldwide for developing the Four Levels or Evaluation, an elegant but simple approach to measure training effectiveness. He was inducted into the HRD Hall of Fame in 1997 and is the author of numerous books and articles. His most recent book is *Transferring Learning to Behavior* (Berrett-Koehler, 2005), written with his son, Jim.

Donald L. Kirkpatrick, Ph.D.
842 Kirkland Court
Pewaukee, WI 53072
Phone: 414.784.7994
Email: dleekirk@aol.com

Ten Requirements for an Effective Training Program

1. Based on _____.

2. Aimed at _____.

3. Scheduled at the right _____.

4. Held at the right _____.

5. For the right _____.

6. Conducted by an effective _____.

7. Using effective _____.

8. _____ are reached.

9. Participants are _____.

10. Program is _____.

Ten Requirements for an Effective Training Program (Answers)

1. Based on **needs.**

2. Aimed at **objectives.**

3. Scheduled at the right **time.**

4. Held at the right **place.**

5. For the right **people.**

6. Conducted by an effective **leader.**

7. Using effective **techniques.**

8. **Objectives** are reached.

9. Participants are **satisfied.**

10. Program is **evaluated.**

Chapter 14

Tools for Trainers

Training methods and the adaptations that many of us create are the meat on the bones of an otherwise (usually) boring learning event. The tools in this chapter will keep you supplied with a wide choice of new approaches to old activities. You will find a huge variety—twelve nifty ways to spice up your training sessions, from moving around in a classroom to a distance-learning online activity, from creating a contest by reviewing technical material to raising issues from different corners of the room.

Pole R. Bear (our World Class Trainer from Antarctica who contributes a bonus, 91st activity) presents a 5-minute technique to help participants be fully present for a training session. If anyone can make a game out of understanding policy manuals, Andy Beaulieu can! And he does in his submission, Are You Sure? Equally amazing is Zane Berge, who creates an online activity that is both interactive and competitive—something few of us achieve easily with our online courses. Sharon Bowman's participants are frequently caught dancing in the halls, so it is not unexpected that her activity, Birds-of-a-Feather, would have participants walking around, throwing a Koosh ball, and giving high-fives as they share what they already know. Steve Cohen uses his Four Corners exercise to bring significant issues out in the open.

Lois Hart uses People Hunt to segue into the content of her session and gives you complete directions to do the same. HRD Hall of Famer Pat McLagan presents an energizing way to discuss lots of information in a short amount of time. Beth Schimel shares a penny activity to energize a group and to learn more about other participants. Harold Stolovitch and Erica Keeps have provided their Hit or Myth activity found in a couple of their books. It was a favorite of mine the first time I saw it. You'll use it over and over. Linda Byars Swindling has created a way to form groups right from the time people walk in the door. It is a good activity for getting people who don't know each other into groups, as well as for separating those who know each other *too* well.

299

This chapter would not be complete without a contribution from Thiagi. He uses this activity to help groups identify best practices and to select the top items. As you might guess, no one is sitting still for this activity. And finally, Bill Yeomans shares his thought on getting senior managers to think creatively.

Master trainers have shared their favorite activities in this chapter. These or adaptations of them will become some of your favorites too.

Bearly There

Submitted by Pole R. Bear

Objective
- To provide a process for participants to set aside problems of the day so they can focus completely on the training session.

Audience
Any size.

Time Required
5–10 minutes.

Materials and Equipment
- One index card per person.
- One brown paper lunch bag per person.

Area Setup
Any.

Process
1. Provide each participant with an index card and state that often people attend training sessions bringing a large, even overwhelming problem with them. This prevents them from being able to participate fully. Ask participants to take a couple of minutes to write on the index card any problems or obstacles they are currently facing. Reassure them that no one will see their problems and that they will not need to reveal them to the rest of the group. Allow at least 4–5 minutes for them to write in silence. *Do not* mention the bags yet.
2. Once everyone has completed the task, state that you hope that they can "bag" these problems until after the session is over, that they will be able to relax and enjoy the session, absorbing as much knowledge and as many skills as possible.
3. Provide a paper bag for each participant. Tell them to actually "bag" their problems by placing the index card inside the brown paper bag and slipping it inside their participant manuals, out of sight.

Insider's Tips

- This activity is a perfect reminder to participants to bring their whole selves to the session.
- If appropriate, participants can pair up and share their concerns with a partner.

Source

This activity originated with Elaine Biech. She has also designed it into the ASTD Training Certificate program.

Pole R. Bear, president of True South Consulting, and his partner, I. Emma Bear, specialize in designing icebreakers and creating climates conducive to learning. In addition, they custom design training programs for residents of Antarctica in topics such as paws-ative thinking, furthering your professional career, and roar-tational assignments. Pole, with coauthor Penn Guinn, has published *Sub Zero Based Budgeting.* The book has been a glacial success. They are currently conducting research using Kurt Lewin's freezing-unfreezing theory. Pole grew up and went to school on the other side of the world and believes that creatures are wonderful and trainable no matter which side of the earth you live on.

Pole R. Bear
One Icy Way
South Pole, Antarctica

# Are You Sure?

Submitted by Andy Beaulieu

Objectives
- To reinforce critical knowledge about company policies, technical information, or other "rote" training content.
- To use a gamelike format to teach important but unexciting corporate knowledge.

Audience
15–20 participants in teams of 3–5.

Time Required
Each round of 4 questions takes about 20 minutes. A maximum of 6 rounds is recommended.

Materials and Equipment
- Policy manuals or other source material. (Instruct participants to bring them to the class.)
- One copy of each round's Question Sheet per team of three to five participants.
- One copy of the Team Response Sheet per team of three to five participants.
- Flip chart and markers.
- Pencils for all participants.
- Prizes for team performance in the game or for everyone.

Area Setup
The training room should allow participants to work in teams of three to five. A table for each team works best.

Preparation
1. Prior to the class, you must create questions from the content of whatever policy or technical manual is the subject of the training. Each round of the game should include four questions derived from one section or chapter of the material.
2. You will need to develop Question Sheets for each round. (Refer to the one included as a sample.)

3. You will also produce a Response Sheet that the teams can use to document their answers and confidence levels and to tally their points. A sample is provided. Here is the logic behind setting up the points awarded or subtracted for each confidence level:

   - The lowest confidence level provides a "safe bet" where the fewest points are gained for a right answer or lost for a wrong answer. The highest confidence level is a "big risk" where the most points could be gained for a right answer or lost for a wrong one. The middle level provides just that—a middle ground.

   - Note that the points awarded or subtracted are not always the same. For easy questions, make the penalties higher for incorrect answers than their corresponding rewards for correct answers. For hard questions, do the opposite: provide a larger positive award and smaller penalty to tempt teams to select the highest confidence level.

   - Prior to the training, participants should receive and review the policy manual or other source material. Becoming familiar with the contents prior to the class will help them succeed. Inform them that they should bring this manual to the class.

Process

1. Place participants in teams of three to five.
2. Tell participants that Are You Sure? is a series of rounds of questions. In each round, participants will work in their teams to develop a collective answer to all the questions and to identify their level of confidence in each answer. Tell them that their confidence level determines how many points they will be awarded for a correct answer or deducted for an incorrect one.
3. Ask if they are ready to begin the first round.
4. Introduce the first section by making any introductory comments about the policies, asking participants what they know about the topic. Point out the specific policies that are included in that topic area. Tell participants that they will have 4 minutes to review the material on that topic in the policy manual. At the end of these 4 minutes (or less time if all the teams agree they are ready to proceed), all policy manuals must be closed and placed on the floor.
5. Hand out the Question Sheet for just that section. Do not yet hand out the Question Sheet for any other sections. Also distribute a copy of the Team Response Sheet to each team. Have the team work together to select the answers from the choices provided or fill in the blank with the correct term.

Tell the teams to transfer their responses to the Response Sheet and also to identify their "confidence level" in each of their answers. The more confident they are, the more points they can win with a right answer or lose if they are wrong. Lower confidence levels lessen their risk and reward. This activity can end when the time has elapsed or all teams have finished.

6. Have each team send a representative to another table to "audit" that team's answers and verify their points. On arriving at the table, the representatives first verify that all answers and confidence levels are clearly marked on the Response Sheet. Once this has been completed, announce the correct answers to the questions for this topic area. The teams (with the help of their "auditor") record the number of points they are awarded or deducted for each question and compute a total for the section. For any questions where there are points deducted (meaning a team has gotten the wrong answer), you may wish to lead a short discussion of the question. The same applies if teams all got the right answer but were not sure of themselves.

7. Ask each team to report out its score; record each team's score on the flip chart.

8. Repeat Steps 1–7 for as many rounds as you wish. Each round will require about 20 minutes.

nsider's Tips

- Are You Sure? is not meant to provide a comprehensive review of company policies, technical information, or other rote content. It will cover some key points but also encourages participants to review all the source material in order to be able to answer the questions presented. Employees should supplement this activity with a comprehensive review, on their own, of any policies and standards critical to their jobs.

- Use your discretion in awarding prizes to the teams of participants. Generally providing everyone with a prize—but allowing the top-scoring team to select first from among the prizes—is better than giving prizes to only some participants and not others. This approach can diffuse rather than reinforce some of the competitiveness that may have evolved.

Andy Beaulieu's consulting and training practice, Results for a Change, achieves change using a results-first approach. His leadership development program, Extreme LD™, pits future leaders in a race against the clock to deliver a bottom-line improvement result and achieve their own development goals under a strict thirteen-week time frame.

Andy Beaulieu
Results for a Change
13036 Mimosa Farm Court
Rockville, MD 20850
Phone: 301.762.6780
Email: andy@resultsforachange.com
Website: www.resultsforachange.com

Question Sheet Sample

1. Which one of the following is NOT a category protected by EEO law:

   a. Gender

   b. Marital status

   c. Age

   d. Criminal record

   e. Veteran status

2. Which one of the following could constitute a "reasonable accommodation":

   a. Dietary restrictions

   b. Religious beliefs

   c. Single parent status

   d. Bereavement

3. Which one of the following is NOT a condition under which a person is considered disabled under the Americans with Disabilities Act:

   a. Having a physical or mental condition that substantially limits a major life activity

   b. Having a record of a physical or mental condition that substantially limits a major life activity

   c. Claiming to have a physical or mental condition that substantially limits a major life activity

   d. Being perceived as having a physical or mental condition that substantially limits a major life activity

4. Associates who report harassment or discrimination, register a complaint, or participate in an investigation of harassment or discrimination must be protected from any form of _____.

Team Response Sheet Sample

In the space provided, record your team's answers and circle to indicate your level of confidence in each answer. Your confidence level determines the number of points you are awarded for a correct answer—or are deducted for an incorrect one.

Q	Answer	Low Confidence	Medium Confidence	High Confidence
1		-2/+2	-5/+5	-10/+10
2		-3/+3	-5/+5	-10/+10
3		-4/+2	-8/+4	-15/+10
4		-1/+2	-3/+5	-8/+10
	Total for questions 1–4			
5		-3/+3	-7/+5	-15/+10
6		-3/+3	-6/+6	-12/+10
7		-2/+3	-5/+5	-10/+10
8		-2/+2	-6/+5	-13/+10
	Total for questions 5–8			
9		-1/+2	-4/+5	-8/+10
10		-2/+2	-5/+5	-12/+10
11		-3/+3	-6/+6	-12/+10
12		-2/+3	-6/+7	-13/+10
	Total for questions 9–12			
13		-1/+3	-4/+5	-11/+10
14		-2/+2	-5/+5	-10/+10
15		-2/+3	-4/+5	-8/+10
16		-2/+2	-6/+5	-12/+10
	Total for questions 13–16			
17		-1/+3	-3/+5	-12/+10
18		-2/+2	-4/+5	-8/+10
19		-2/+2	-5/+5	-10/+10
20		-2/+2	-6/+5	-9/+10
	Total for questions 17–20			
21		-1/+3	-4/+5	-8/+10
22		-2/+2	-6/+5	-12/+10
23		-2/+2	-5/+5	-10/+10
24		-3/+2	-7/+5	-13/+10
	Total for questions 21–24			
	Bonus points			
	Grand total			

Online Q & A

Submitted by Zane L. Berge, Ph.D.

Objectives
- To engage online participants in meaningful discussion about the course content.
- To provide a self-directed learning experience for participants.

Audience
Normal online classrooms from 10–50 people. This activity could also be used in a hybrid (that is, blended) classroom that meets both online and in person.

Time Required
Varies. With a group of 15–25, most discussions last a week.

Materials and Equipment
- Assigned reading(s) for content.
- Threaded discussion forum, usually part of a learning management system (LMS; for example, WebCT or Blackboard) within the online classroom.
- One copy of the Discussion Portfolio worksheet for each participant.
- Optional information on writing questions for online discussion. You could use the following:

Berge, Z. L., & Muilenburg, L. Y. (2000). Designing discussion questions for online, adult learning. *Educational Technology, 40*(5), 53–56.

Muilenburg, L. Y., & Berge, Z. L. (2000). A framework for designing questions for online learning. *DEOSNEWS, 10*(2). Retrieved February 18, 2005 from www.emoderators.com/moderators/muilenburg.html.

Area Setup
The online classroom would usually use a threaded discussion forum within the LMS of choice.

Process

1. Assign the class an article or articles to read having to do with the topic for discussion.
2. Assign each participant in the class to develop a substantive question derived from the assigned reading(s). Have them post their questions to the appropriate online forum.
3. Tell each participant in the class that he or she should respond to questions posted by at least three other participants.
4. Ask each participant to complete the Discussion Portfolio worksheet.
5. The portfolio can be self-evaluated or submitted to you for evaluation.

 **nsider's Tips**

- Occasionally a participant will state that his or her question is being ignored. The first response is to tell that person (nicely) to write better questions. That usually solves the problem.
- In the self-evaluation, or especially if the portfolio is submitted to the trainer for a grade, I weight the portfolio author's question and response more than the responses he or she receives. For example, in the grading rubric, I might say, "Give yourself two points for each of the questions you wrote and for each of the three responses you gave to your classmates (total of eight points possible). Give yourself one point for each of the responses you received to your question (total three points possible)." That way, if the participant does not receive three answers to his or her question (something out of the student's control), it does not count against the student as much. Of course, some instructors like to do the opposite, stating that they are rewarding "good questions" posed by the students that elicit responses from other participants. My experience is that the former works better.

Source

Although I may have modified it in some ways, the activity is used by many educators and trainers. For instance, Dr. Chris Swan at University of Maryland, Baltimore County (UMBC) uses this technique successfully in his environmental science courses. The portfolio layout is a modification of the one used by Dr. Swan. I have never published it, nor have I seen it published anywhere.

Zane L. Berge, Ph.D., is an associate professor and former director of the Training Systems Graduate programs at UMBC. Zane has been affiliated with the ISD-Training and Development program since 1995. He served as the director for the Training Systems Graduate programs through 2001. His chief research interests are related to distance education and online learning. He is a prolific and widely published author of texts and journal articles on this topic. His most recent publications include *Sustaining Distance Training: Integrating Learning Technologies into the Fabric of the Enterprise* (Jossey-Bass, 2000) and *Distance Training: How Innovative Organizations Are Using Technology to Maximize Learning and Meet Business Objectives* (Jossey-Bass, 1998). In 1999, Zane was honored with the Charles A. Wedemeyer Award for Distinguished Scholarship and Publication by the University Continuing Education Association.

Zane Berge, Ph.D.
UMBC
1000 Hilltop Circle
Baltimore, MD 21250
Phone: 410.455.2306
Email: berge@umbc.edu

Discussion Portfolio

Your name: _____   Date: _____

Title of article(s) you read: _____

Question you posted:

_____

Response 1 from another participant:

_____

Response 2 from another participant:

_____

Response 3 from another participant:

_____

Question 1 that you responded to:

_____

Your response:

_____

Question 2 that you responded to:

_____

Your response:

_____

Question 3 that you responded to:

_____

Your response:

_____

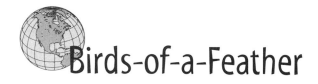

Birds-of-a-Feather

Submitted by Sharon L. Bowman, M.A.

Objectives

- To form a psychologically safe, productive learning community by getting learners connected to each other early.
- To connect the training participants to the training topic so that learners become aware of the knowledge they bring to the training.
- To connect learners to what they hope to learn from the training.

Audience

12 or more, up to 100.

Time Required

3–15 minutes.

Materials and Equipment

- Flip chart, flip-chart paper, and markers (or overhead projector, transparency, and marker).
- Koosh ball or other soft throwable object.
- Index cards (optional).

Area Setup

Participants need to have room to move around, so a breakout space at the back of the room or large aisles and space in front and in back are necessary. The amount of space needed depends on the size of the group: the larger the group, the more space required. Furniture can remain in place as long as there is room to walk around tables and chairs.

Process

1. Print in large bright print on one page (or on a transparency):
   - What three things do you already know about the training topic?
   - Why are you attending this training, and what do you hope to learn?
   - What is one question you want answered by the end of the training?

2. Tell the participants that there are some people in the room who are absolutely crucial to their learning success. In order to find these people and begin a dialogue with them, they will take part in a Birds-of-a-Feather people hunt.

3. Explain that they need to think of the first word or phrase that comes to their minds when they think of the training topic.

4. Tell them to stand and walk around the room repeating their word or phrase out loud to others until they find two or three other participants who thought of the same or a similar word or phrase as theirs. Allow about 1 minute for them to form standing groups of three to five people with others who have words or phrases similar to theirs. If someone is left out, invite that person to join any group or to make a group with others who don't yet have a group.

5. Direct their attention to the flip chart or overhead transparency. Tell them they will have about 30 seconds each to answer the first question. Give them about 2 minutes total time, then signal for silence.

6. To process the answers, use a Random Response Device (the Koosh ball) and let them know that when the Koosh ball is thrown to their group, one person needs to repeat what someone in their group said (which helps build more psychological safety than if they had to repeat what they themselves said).

7. That group then tosses the Koosh ball to another group and so on until all or most groups have had a chance to share one response.

8. Tell them to say farewell (or give a high-five to their new friends) and now think of a sport that could represent the topic. Provide them with an example. For instance, in a communication skills training, the sports mentioned might be team sports like football or baseball. Or the sport may be a metaphor for the topic—for example, racquetball for an accounting training because you have to know all the angles. After a couple of seconds, tell them to find new standing partners who thought of the same or similar sport.

9. Have them introduce themselves to their new group partners.

10. Ask them to answer the second question. Give them about 2 minutes, then process with the Random Response Device in the same way that you did the first time. If time permits, you might ask them to name the sport and why they thought of it as a representation of the training topic.

11. Tell participants to say farewell to their group and now think of a word that describes how they are feeling about being at the training. Have them find two or three others with the same or similar words.

12. In their final standing group, have them share their answers to the third question.

13. Ask them to come up with a group question—something that would represent a composite of the questions they shared. Ask them to state the question while you write it on a chart. Alternatively, they can write it on an index card and hand it to you.

14. When that task is completed, invite them to give high-fives once again to their new friends and then sit down.

    You now have a group of training participants who:

    - Feel psychologically safer with each other because they have connected with a number of others in the room.
    - Have begun the process of forming a productive learning community.
    - Have focused on the prior knowledge they have and will later connect it to the new information they will learn.
    - Have become aware of their own learning goals and questions—in effect, their own "Why?" for being there.

Insider's Tips

- Depending on the size of your whole group, the time you choose to spend doing the activity, the amount of processing you choose to do (not all groups have to answer if time is an issue), and the richness of the dialogue, the activity can be a short one (3–5 minutes) or a longer one (5–15 minutes).
- You can tailor the questions to be more specific to the topic, or phrase them as review questions if you choose to do the activity after you have presented new information. Or the questions can summarize the learning for a closing activity, for example:
  - What are the three most important things you learned during this training?
  - What do you plan to do with what you learned?
  - How will this information change your behavior?
  - Who are three people you can share this information with?

- Besides having participants form standing birds-of-a-feather groups with similar words or phrases or metaphors like sports, you can also have them form groups according to any trait or characteristic you can imagine. The following are just a few examples. Tell participants to find two to three other people who:
    Like the same junk food that they do.
    Like the same genre of movie or book that they do.
    Like the same hobby.
    Like the same fantasy vacation.
    Are wearing the same color of shoe.
    Are wearing the same jewelry item.
    Were born in the same season.
    Have the same first or last name initial.
    Have the same kind of pet.
    Hate the same sport.
    Enjoy the same free-time activity.
    Were born in the same state.
    Have visited the same historical site.
- Instead of using the metaphor of a sport to represent the topic, you can ask the participants to think of an animal that represents the topic, or something in nature, a kitchen item, a color, a food, a famous person, or a TV show or movie.

Source

This is one of my favorite activities; it has been published in *Training and Performance 2001* (McGraw-Hill, 2000), edited by M. Silberman and P. Phillips. Reproduced here with permission from McGraw-Hill.

Sharon L. Bowman, M.A., author and traveling teacher, helps educators and businesspeople "teach it quick and make it stick." She fine-tunes their information-delivery skills and turns their passive listeners into active learners. Sharon is the author of seven popular teaching, training, and motivation books, including her newest title, *The Ten-Minute Trainer! 150 Ways to Teach It Quick and Make It Stick* (Pfeiffer, 2005). Over fifty thousand of her books are in print. Sharon is a professional member of the National Speakers Association, the director of the Lake Tahoe Trainers Group, and the owner of Bowperson Publishing & Training, Inc.

Sharon L. Bowman, M.A.
P.O. Box 564
Glenbrook, NV 89413
Phone: 775.749.5247
Fax: 775.749.1891
Email: Sbowperson@aol.com
Website: www.Bowperson.com

Four Corners Exercise

Submitted by Stephen L. Cohen, Ph.D., CPT

Objectives
- To bring to light significant issues related to the topic at hand.
- To openly discuss and share challenges presented by the topic.

Audience
18–28 participants.

Time Required
30–45 minutes (could be longer).

Materials and Equipment
- Four flip charts and markers.
- Overhead projector and transparencies, computer with LCD projector, or extra flip chart.

Area Setup
Four flip charts should be positioned in the four corners of the room with one of the following written on each: Strongly Agree, Agree, Disagree, and Strongly Disagree.

Process
1. First create three to four provocative statements about the topic—for example, "Our managers show favoritism when promoting people."
2. Flash these on a screen, one at a time. (Alternatively, you can post these on a flip chart.)
3. For each statement, have participants go to the corner of the room with the flip-chart label that most accurately represents their level of agreement or disagreement.
4. Have those in each corner discuss among themselves why they chose that corner (as opposed to others) for 5–10 minutes.
5. Ask each group to select a spokesperson to summarize for the rest of the class why they chose that corner.

6. Proceed similarly for the next statement, having participants move, as they desire, to the corner most accurately representing their feelings about each statement.

7. After all statements have been discussed, conduct a large group debrief using these questions:
   - How would you summarize what occurred?
   - What surprised you the most?
   - What surprised you the least?
   - What issues arose that we need to address in this session? (List the issues on a flip chart.)

 nsider's Tips

- This activity is particularly good to use as an introductory "icebreaker with content" at the beginning of a program.
- The exercise surfaces many issues right up front that facilitate subsequent discussions. Be prepared to address them in your session.
- When soliciting participant responses, choose with care which corner you start and end with. You may (or may not) want to begin with the most controversial corner.

Source

I am unaware of this activity's having being published anywhere. It's about time that it is!

Steven L. Cohen, Ph.D., CPT, was named as one of the industry's "thought leaders" by ASTD. He has earned worldwide recognition for his accomplishments in the field of HRD, with more than 150 articles, chapters, and presentations to his credit. For over thirty years, Steve has advanced the strategies of major corporations and leading training suppliers around the globe by creating groundbreaking learning solutions. As one of the learning industry's experts on the "art, science, and business" of program development, Steve has strategically directed the creation of nearly one hundred off-the-shelf training products as well as over a thousand custom learning programs. Formerly CEO and founder of the Learning Design Group, Steve currently is vice president for Carlson Marketing's Learning Solutions Group.

Stephen L. Cohen, Ph.D., CPT
Carlson Marketing Group
1405 Xenium Lane
Plymouth, MN 55441
Phone: 763.212.6948
Email: Steve.cohen@carlson.com

People Hunt

Submitted by Lois B. Hart, Ed.D.

Objectives

- To provide an opportunity for participants to become better acquainted.
- To discover interesting facts about or experiences of other participants.
- To segue into the content of a workshop with a large number of people.

Audience

This activity works best with lots of people—a minimum of 20.

Time Required

30 minutes for instructions and milling time; more if followed up with small or large group discussion.

Materials and Equipment

- Pens or pencils.
- One copy of the People Hunt handout for each participant. Please note that the photocopy master includes thirty examples; before printing, you will need to select fifteen to twenty key items. Print the handout on card stock so that the participants can write more easily while milling.
- Prizes.

Area Setup

Large open space for milling about during the activity; seating areas for the beginning and end of the activity.

Process

1. There are two ways to introduce this activity: either distribute the People Hunt handout as people enter and have them start to mingle immediately, or wait until everyone has arrived to begin.
2. Introduce this get-acquainted game by first relating how much fun the game of Scavenger Hunt was in our childhood. Explain that this game is a "people hunt." Cite the purpose of the activity—to get better acquainted and to learn some interesting things about the people they will be spending time with in this workshop or program.

3. Make sure the entire group is standing before you begin. If you haven't done so already, pass out the People Hunt handout. Let participants read the directions and skim the items.

4. Announce that there will be prizes for the first three people completing their People Hunt handout.

5. Every few minutes, remind participants that they should be moving around to meet new people. You could suggest a minimum number of people with whom they should talk.

6. When the time is up, either have them return to their seats or form groups of four to six.

7. Process the experience with the participants. If you have formed small groups, have them discuss the following questions in their groups first, and later summarize with the total group.

    • What was the most interesting bit of information you learned about another person?

    • Which information was easiest and which was hardest to give out to others?

    • Which information was easiest and hardest to ask others?

    • How can we help ourselves and others become comfortable more quickly when we are in new groups of people?

8. Suggest that participants keep the names of people they met during the activity and make arrangements to continue developing these relationships during breaks or after the session.

Variation

You may wish to personalize People Hunt to meet your needs. This is a favorite activity of participants when the items are adapted to fit their interests and background. You can personalize it with specific information about the participants. You can also introduce the content while getting acquainted. Here are examples of each of these two ideas.

1. Use information you know about participants to adapt the People Hunt handout. For example, participants can be asked to find someone who . . .

    Won a prize in a bake-off contest.

    Was recently Employee of the Month.

    Has worked at the company for thirty-two years.

    Was featured in the company newsletter.

    Once worked for *Fast Company* magazine.

2. Adapt items to fit the content of the workshop. Here are some examples that were used for a workshop on decision making. Find someone who . . .

Recently made a last-minute decision he or she now regrets.

Recently made a last-minute decision that worked.

Likes to make decisions alone.

Prefers to involve others in his or her decision making.

Makes decisions better in the morning.

Makes decisions better in the afternoon.

Can define the word *consensus*.

Has a favorite saying that guides his or her decision making.

Source

I published this activity in *Connections! 125 Activities for Faultless Training* (HRD Press, 1995), which is currently out of print.

Lois B. Hart, Ed.D., is the founder of the Women's Leadership Institute, a yearlong program of mentoring, coaching, and training executive women. She also heads the Courageous Leadership Consortium, which develops and disseminates innovative designs and materials to advance women leaders. She has thirty years of experience in conducting workshops, facilitating groups, and consulting to organizations. Lois is the author of *50 Activities for Developing Leaders,* vol. I (HRD Press, 1994) and vol. II (American Management Association, 2004), *Faultless Facilitation: A Resource Guide and Instructor's Manual* (HRD Press, 1996), *Dealing with Conflict* (Jaico Publishing House, 2005), *Training Methods That Work* (Crisp Learning, 1991), and *A Conference and Workshop Planner's Manual* (AMACOM, 1979).

Lois B. Hart, Ed.D.
Leadership Dynamics
11256 County Road 23
Fort Lupton, CO 80621
Phone: 303.587.6444
Email: lhart@seqnet.net

People Hunt

The purpose of this activity is to get acquainted with the other people in this workshop or, if you already know some, to find out something new. As you mingle, match up a person with each of the items listed below. You must actually speak to people; you cannot just rely on prior knowledge. Put the name or initials of each person next to the appropriate category. You have 30 minutes to do this. Let the facilitator know when you have names for all of the items.

[Sample items: select fifteen to twenty before photocopying]

Find someone who . . .

_____ Can name a hero or heroine who has been a model for him or her

_____ Has heard a joke recently and is willing to share it

_____ Took a risk this past week

_____ Traveled the farthest to get here

_____ Enjoys leadership

_____ Has a tip on managing stress

_____ Carries at least eight membership cards

_____ Aspires to move to the top of his or her organization

_____ Is not sure why he or she is here today

_____ Is sure why he or she is here today

_____ Feels great

_____ Needs a shot in the arm

_____ Has blue eyes

_____ Has the same astrological sign as you do

_____ Traveled to another country for vacation

_____ Has the same hobby as you do

_____ Has given up a habit recently

_____ Had a "first" this year

_____ Had a child born or adopted into his or her family this last year

_____ Had a child move out this year

_____ Got married or divorced this year

_____ Was born in the same city or town as you were

_____ Knows where the bathrooms are

_____ Had a success recently

_____ Has written a book

_____ Wants to write a book

_____ Needs a backrub

_____ Recently fought a consumer battle

_____ Talks to his or her houseplants

_____ Had a conflict today

Question Queue

Submitted by Patricia A. McLagan, M.A.

Objectives
- To get full participation in sharing information.
- To provide an opportunity to consolidate views and themes.

Audience
Any group that is exploring a topic.

Time Required
About 60 minutes, but it depends on the number of questions.

Materials and Equipment
- One set of five questions for each participant.
- Paper and pencils for all participants.
- Flip charts and markers.

Area Setup
Set up chairs facing each other—one facing pair per question. Create as many rows as needed to ensure that all participants have a seat. For example, if you have twenty participants and five questions, the seating would be arranged as follows:

1	2	3	4	5		1	2	3	4	5

1	2	3	4	5		1	2	3	4	5

Process
1. In preparation for this exercise, create a list of five thought-provoking questions related to the topic you will address.
2. Have participants select a chair and assign numbers to each pair. Pass out a set of questions to each person. If the number of participants does not divide evenly, then pair people—in other words, a team of two stays together.
3. Assign all 1's question 1, all 2's question 2, and so on. For the entire exercise, individuals will always ask the assigned question.

4. Start the questioning process. At the beginning, individuals will be sitting across from others who have the same question. Start the process by having each pair ask each other the assigned question. For this first round, the individuals in each pair will be asking the same question. Give them 2–3 minutes for one of the pair to ask the question. Have them write the responses on notepaper. Then ask the second member of the pair to ask the question.

5. After each facing pair has asked and answered their assigned questions, ask people in one facing row to move to the chair to their right. The person on the end switches to the beginning of the row.

6. Continue rotations until all questions have been asked of all participants.

7. Consolidate responses. All participants with question 1 will meet to create a flip-chart summary of what they heard. Participants with question 2 meet to do the same. Participants with question 3, those with question 4, and those with question 5 will also create flip-chart summaries of what they heard. Allow about 5–10 minutes for this step.

8. Each question group will report their consolidated remarks to the entire group.

> ### Editor's Note
>
> Only one row moves. The other row will remain stationary for the entire exercise. By Step 5, person 1 in the stationary row will be facing the person with question 5 from the moving row. Person 2 in the stationary row will be facing person 1 from the moving row, and so on. Allow 2–3 minutes for each member of the pair to again ask and answer his or her assigned question. Remember, the question a person asks never changes.

Insider's Tips

- This exercise works well to get everyone involved and contributing on all issues. It is high energy and fast paced, and it gets a huge amount of information on the table very quickly. The activity is a bit difficult to choreograph, but worth the effort.
- You may use more than five questions and reconfigure the setup.

Source

This is a great exercise that I learned from my former partner, Richard Hallstein.

Patricia A. McLagan, M.A., is chairman of McLagan International, Inc. Author, speaker, and consultant on a broad range of HR management and strategy implementation issues, she is the fifteenth person and second woman inducted into the HRD Hall of Fame and a member of the International Adult and Continuing Education Hall of Fame; she has also been honored with many leadership awards. Pat has been a member of ASTD's national board of directors and board of governors. She has been honored with ASTD's highest award for service to the profession, clients, and community. She is on the editorial board of many research-to-practice journals and is the author of eleven books and reports and thirty-nine articles and chapters.

Patricia McLagan, M.A.
McLagan International, Inc.
3136 O Street NW
Washington, DC 20007
Phone: 202.944.3992
Email: patmclagan@mclaganint.com
Website: www.mclaganint.com

Penny for Your Thoughts

Submitted by Beth A. Schimel, Pharm.D.

Objective
- To energize the group by having them learn something unique about the other participants.

Audience
Can be used in a small group (3 or 4) or a larger one (approximately 10).

Time Required
5–20 minutes.

Materials and Equipment
- Enough pennies for the group to grab one each.
- Overhead with directions (optional).

Area Setup
Any; this activity has been done around a dinner table and in a meeting room (round tables work best).

Process
1. Display overhead or PowerPoint with directions (optional).
2. Have each person grab a penny. Tell participants to look at the year on the penny and to determine something significant that happened to them that year—for example, graduated, got married, passed the boards.
3. Allow 30–60 seconds for participants to decide what to share of significance from that year. Then begin to go around the room and ask each participant to briefly explain his or her significant event.
4. Optional: To transition back to the topic, ask participants to suggest something that occurred during the year on their pennies that is significant to the topic you are discussing.

Insider's Tips

- Keep it fun and lighthearted; you should start out so that no one feels that he or she is in the spotlight.
- We use this in new-hire orientation as well as to help new team members become acquainted with each other.

Source

I received this activity from a colleague, Susan "Sam" Brandes. I have never seen it published.

Beth A. Schimel, Pharm.D., is a pharmacist by training. For seven years, she trained the pharmacy staff at a local hospital on clinical programs. Currently she trains other doctoral colleagues regarding how to perform the field-based medical professional job at Novartis. Beth works with a training team of five other medical professionals.

Beth A. Schimel, Pharm.D.
Novartis Pharmaceuticals
3270 S. Highpointe
New Berlin, WI 53151
Phone: 262.814.1713
Email: beth.schimel@novartis.com

Penny for Your Thoughts

- Select a penny and identify the year it was minted.

- Identify something significant that happened to you that year.

- Share your event with the group.

Hit or Myth

Submitted by Harold D. Stolovitch, Ph.D., CPT, and Erica J. Keeps, M.Ed., CPT

Objectives
- To create a learning session leveraging provocative statements to introduce new material.
- To encourage discussion to dismiss commonly held beliefs.

Audience
Any size.

Time Required
45–60 minutes.

Materials and Equipment
- Projected visuals.
- LCD projector (or overhead). With a small group, a flip chart may substitute for projection.
- One Hit or Myth handout for each participant.
- One handout with details and/or explanations about each statement (including references if relevant) for each participant.

Area Setup
Large screen visible to all (if you are using an LCD projector or overhead); any room setup that permits a clear view of the screen or flip chart

Process
1. Gather common misperceptions, or research an area where there are enthusiastic but false beliefs about a subject.
2. Create five to ten unambiguous statements, each dealing with a commonly held false belief.
3. Create a projection visual (or several visuals) that contain the statements and the ⊙ hit and ⊙ myth symbols. Prepare additional visuals, one

per statement. Each should contain a statement separately with relevant supporting information.

4. Prepare Hit or Myth handouts, one with all the statements and two columns, each headed by hit and myth symbols as shown in the example with this activity. Prepare a second handout with the statements and all relevant information supporting the statement as a hit or a myth.

5. At the start of the session, distribute the handout with the five to ten statements and hit and myth symbols. Have participants individually decide whether each statement is a hit (true) or a myth (false). Project or display on a flip chart the statements as well.

6. Once participants have made their decisions for all statements, project or display each statement individually, and successively disclose the correct answer with supporting information.

7. If you so desire, you can have participants score themselves to determine the best myth-busters.

8. Debrief the entire activity focusing on how myths lead to misconceptions and ineffective or even counterproductive practices.

Hit or Myth Example

	🎯	🎯
1. Immediate and instant feedback is always the preferred mode for improving performance.		
2. Action plans prepared during training increase transfer of training to the job.		
3. Experts are the best persons to train novices.		

nsider's Tips

- Hit or Myth works best when all statements are myths.
- If you decide to score the activity, here are two ways to increase the fun:
  - For each statement, count those who got it right and those who got it wrong. To those who got it right, give one point plus one additional point for each participant who got it wrong.
  - For each incorrect statement, have participants subtract one point from their total score of correct answers.
- Hold a general debriefing to discuss how acting on myths affects our decisions and actions. Determine the consequences of operating by myth. Draw out examples from participants.
- Draw from the group other myths that circulate. List them on a flip-chart sheet and determine ways to combat these.

Source

We have used this concept in our books to present specific content. See, for example, *Training Ain't Performance* or *Telling Ain't Training,* both published by ASTD.

Harold D. Stolovitch, Ph.D., CPT, and **Erica J. Keeps,** M.Ed., CPT, have devoted a combined total of over seventy years to making workplace learning and performance both enjoyable and effective. They are coauthors of the award-winning best-sellers *Telling Ain't Training* (2002), *Training Ain't Performance* (2004), and *Beyond Telling Ain't Training Fieldbook* (2005), all published by ASTD.

Harold D. Stolovitch, Ph.D., CPT
Erica J. Keeps, M.Ed., CPT
HSA Learning & Performance Solutions LLC
1520 S. Beverly Glen Blvd., #305
Los Angeles, CA 90024
Phone: 310.286.2722
Email: info@hsa-lps.com
Website: www.hsa-lps.com

We're All a Piece of the Puzzle

Submitted by Linda Byars Swindling, J.D., CSP

Objective
- To increase networking and "mixing" of participants.

Audience
Best when group is at least 25 but under 300.

Time Required
15 minutes.

Materials and Equipment
- Children's cardboard puzzles.
- Fishbowl.

Area Setup
Any area with tables where groups can get together.

Process
1. Prior to the session, partially assemble each of the puzzles on separate tables, and put all remaining puzzle pieces into the fishbowl.
2. Have participants select their puzzle piece out of the fishbowl.
3. Tell participants to find the puzzle where their piece fits.
4. When they find their puzzle, they sit at the table with the new team members.

 nsider's Tip

- We place numbers on the puzzles and also on the pieces that are handed out to give hints.

Source

Lorri Allen of Good News and I used this with the theme "We're all a piece of the puzzle."

Linda Byars Swindling, J.D., CSP, is called by *American Airways* magazine "a bargaining expert" for her ability to help people get results through negotiation. A recognized authority on negotiation, workplace issues, and persuasive communication, this "recovering" attorney is an author, consultant, and award-winning presenter. She works with chief executives and sales professionals to harness the power of positive influence, persuasion, and negotiation.

Linda Byars Swindling, J.D., CSP
Passports to Success
3509 Cimarron Drive
Carrollton, TX 75007
Phone: 972.416.3652
Email: Linda@lindaswindling.com
Website: www.passportstosuccess.com

# Thirty-Five

Submitted by Sivasailam "Thiagi" Thiagarajan, Ph.D.

Objectives
- To identify best practices from a group of participants.
- To select the top items from a list of best practices.

Audience
Any number. The best size for this activity is 16–100.

Time Required
20–30 minutes.

Materials and Equipment
- Index cards or pieces of paper.
- Pens or pencils.
- Whistle.

Area Setup
Provide plenty of space for participants to walk around.

Process
1. Explain that people learn best when they create the content and share their best ideas with each other. Present an open question related to the training topic (examples: *How can we delight our customers?* or *What can we do to increase the productivity of our work teams?*). Ask each participant to come up with a practical idea that provides a response to this question and write it on an index card. Instruct participants to keep the idea short, specific, clear, and legible. Announce a 2-minute time limit.
2. After about 2 minutes, blow the whistle and ask each participant to review his or her idea and bask in its brilliance. Then ask participants to emotionally detach themselves from their ideas and get ready to launch them into the world for comparative evaluation.

3. Ask participants to hold their cards with the written side down. Tell them to walk around and exchange the cards with each other. Ask them not to read the ideas on the cards at this time but immediately keep exchanging the cards. After about 20 seconds, blow the whistle to stop the exchange process. Ask participants to pair up with any other nearby participant.

4. Ask each pair of participants to review the ideas on the two cards they have. Instruct them to distribute seven points between these two ideas to reflect their relative usefulness. Request that the participants avoid using fractions or negative numbers. Direct them to write their scores on the back of each index card.

5. After waiting to make sure that everyone has completed the scoring process, ask participants to repeat the process of moving around and exchanging cards. Then blow the whistle after 20 seconds or so, and ask participants to find a new partner, compare the two ideas on their cards, and distribute seven points. Instruct them to write the new score points on the back of the card, below the previous number.

6. Announce that you will be conducting three more rounds of the activity. Ask participants to maintain high levels of objectivity by disregarding earlier score points and by keeping a poker face if they receive their own card.

7. At the end of the fifth round, ask participants to return to their seats with the card they currently have. Ask them to add the five scores and write the total on the card.

8. After pausing for the totals to be computed, explain that you are going to count down from thirty-five. When a participant hears the total on the card, he or she should stand up and read the idea from the card. Begin counting down to identify the card with the highest score. After the participant reads the idea on the card, lead a round of applause. Repeat the countdown process until you have identified the top five to ten ideas.

9. Thank participants for generating and evaluating useful ideas. Ask them to select a few ideas for immediate implementation. Also encourage them to keep exchanging their best practices with each other.

Sivasailam "Thiagi" Thiagarajan, Ph.D., is the president of Workshops by Thiagi, Inc., an organization with the mission of helping people improve their performance effectively, enjoyably, and ethically. He has lived in three different countries and has consulted in twenty-one others, while publishing forty books, 120 games and simulations, and more than two hundred articles in the area of interactive experiential approaches to training. Thiagi wrote the definitive chapters on simulations and games for the International Society for Performance Improvement's *Handbook of Human Performance Technology,* ASTD's *Training & Development Handbook,* and the American Management Association's *Human Resources Management and Development Handbook.* He currently edits the simulation/game section in the journal *Simulations & Gaming* and publishes a monthly electronic magazine *Play for Performance: Seriously Fun Activities for Trainers, Facilitators, Performance Consultants, and Managers.*

Sivasailam "Thaigi" Thiagarajan, Ph.D.
Workshops by Thiagi, Inc.
4423 East Trailridge Road
Bloomington, IN 47428
Phone: 812.332.1478
Email: thiagi@thiagi.com
Website: www.thiagi.com

Getting Senior Managers to Think Creatively

Submitted by William N. Yeomans

Objective
- To develop strategic plans or to work on specific problems management wants to resolve.

Audience
Usually the CEO and senior managers, a group of 5–10.

Time Required
1–3 days.

Materials and Equipment
- Flip charts and markers.

Area Setup
Preferably U-shaped.

Process
1. Introduce an exercise that has nothing to do with the business or the problem at hand. Have participants solve the problem. Allow them to work on it without much guidance from you. This is tough because managers are used to going right for the solution without generating new ideas. Allow about 20 minutes. Use these questions to process what happened:
   - How did it go?
   - What helped solve the problem?
   - What hindered the process?
   - What could you do better?
2. State that using new techniques is often helpful to solve problems. Lead the group through a creative problem-solving session. Allow about 30–40 minutes to introduce new techniques.

3. Finally, turn them loose to address the problem they are there to solve. Ensure that they use the new techniques you have introduced.
4. Bring it all together near the end of the session so that new, yet practical, approaches are agreed on. This was the best part for me, after hours of struggling to get the group to relax and have some fun with ideas: to see them excited about what we had accomplished.

Insider's Tip

- I found wishing and word association were helpful in generating new ideas, but I never felt comfortable getting too goofy with senior managers. You should take as many risks as you feel comfortable with to encourage creative thinking. There are many great ideas to do this. Remember that senior executives often need a little boost to do their best.

Source

The description of this activity has been published in several of my books, including *1000 Things You Never Learned in Business School* (Signet Books, 1990) and *7 Survival Skills for a Reengineered World* (Plume Books, 1998).

William N. Yeomans held senior executive positions with JCPenney, including corporate director of HRD, responsible for the training and development of two hundred thousand employees. He was the national president of ASTD in 1988. JCPenney moved to Dallas and Bill opened his own consulting firm, working with several major corporate and nonprofit clients in management development, strategic planning, customer service, and sales training. He has served as president of his local library board, president of the Hamilton College alumni association, president of a JCPenney retiree group, and president of his local historical society. He has written eight career and management books and numerous articles and has appeared on TV and radio news and talk shows.

William N. Yeomans
Retired Executive and Consultant
7 Old Stone Church Road
Upper Saddle River, NJ 07458
Phone: 201.934.6932
Email: wyeoman@rcn.com

Chapter 15

Icebreakers and Energizers

Icebreakers and energizers are brief activities that are usually related to a session's topic, but on a rare occasion may not be. Icebreakers, sometimes called warm-ups or openers, occur at the beginning of a session to establish the climate of the session, introduce the topic, and acquaint participants with one another and the trainer. Well-designed icebreakers create immediate participation, provide an initial assessment, establish session norms, identify something about all participants, and put participants at ease.

Energizers, sometimes called motivators, are used when the group's energy is ebbing. They may be used as a relaxer after a tense discussion, to get the cobwebs out following an extended period of information absorption, or during the "post-lunch blahs." Try some of these favorite activities for creative ways to introduce and revitalize your sessions.

Kim Barnes shares an icebreaker that has people up moving around and meeting lots of people. Pat Cataldo, Peter Garber, and Michal Settles have contributed icebreakers that encourage participants to share something that most people probably do not know about them. This leads to interesting conversation during the breaks and continued relationship building throughout the rest of the session. Karen Lawson uses movie posters to organize participants in different groups. The posters not only serve a purpose but also add color and interest to the room.

Sometimes people are concerned that energizers "use up time." Dana and Jim Robinson contribute an energizer that saves time! You won't want to miss this one. I immediately went out to buy the book that they reference in their energizer, *The Top Ten of Everything*. Dana and Jim credit Bob Pike for this creative energizer. Max Rodrigues (India) shares an energizer that is a bit on the risky side; proceed with caution! Ed Scannell, coauthor of the well-known *Games Trainers Play* series, invented the now famous Bingo icebreaker that is a staple in every trainer's tool kit. Here's your copy directly from one of the most prolific authorities in the profession.

An icebreaker is a vessel designed to clear an opening in frozen water that allows the flow of other ships. This is a good metaphor for what you are trying to accomplish with an icebreaker in your sessions: to clear an opening in a cool atmosphere that allows the flow of communication and relationship building.

Incorporation

Submitted by B. Kim Barnes

Objectives
- To provide an opportunity for large groups of people to meet one another as individuals and begin to develop connections.
- To demonstrate both diversity and commonality within the group.

Audience
Should be at least 30 people, most of whom are not known to one another. There is no upper limit as long as there is enough space.

Time Required
Flexible, but should be at least 20 minutes.

Materials and Equipment
- A microphone for the facilitator is helpful; otherwise a chime or other means of getting the group's attention.

Area Setup
There should be a large open space. Any tables and chairs should be pushed against the walls during the activity.

Process
1. Tell participants that they will be forming groups according to the categories named. They are to get into the groups quickly and then, when another category is called, they must regroup. While they are in the groups, they are free to chat with others and introduce themselves unless they are given a specific assignment.
2. You may select any categories you like, but they should meet the following criteria:
   - Use no categories that include rank.
   - Use no categories that create division along political or religious lines.
   - Ideally, categories should be selected that are either neutral or relevant to the topic of the meeting or conference.

- Select some categories that can be used to start conversations (see examples below).
- In general, it's best to use categories based on history, circumstances, interests, or characteristics rather than opinion.
- Following are some examples of categories:
  - Country or state where participant was born. (You can indicate an imaginary map on the floor—north, south, east, west—and let people place themselves accordingly.)
  - Job title.
  - Years in the job.
  - Favorite leisure-time activity.
  - Favorite type of music.
  - Eye color. (Do this one nonverbally so people have to look at each other.)
  - Position in family (oldest, middle, youngest, only). Ask people to discuss what it was like to be in each of those positions. After a few minutes have them call out two or three words or phrases that summarize what they discussed.
3. Call out the first category. Let the groups form and then give them 5 minutes or so to chat, then move on to the next category. End with a category that is relevant to the meeting.
4. If possible, use the final grouping to segue to the content of the meeting. For example, ask people to form groups of eight with people they did not know before the session and proceed to a table for the first activity.

 nsider's Tips

- Keep the groups moving and changing. The smaller the group, the more frequently participants should move.
- If you see that there are "isolates" who are not part of a group during a round, suggest that they get together and discuss why they put themselves where they did and what it feels like to be "different" from the rest of the group.
- Aim for enough variety so that the group makeup will be different each time and everyone will have the experience of being both "same" and "different" and have a basis for conversation later with many others.
- Use at least one category that is surprising or funny. Keep it light.

Source

I learned this activity at the Institute for Humanistic Education about forty years ago, though I do not know whether it has ever been published.

B. Kim Barnes, CEO of Barnes & Conti Associates, Inc., in Berkeley, California, is the primary developer of Exercising Influence, Constructive Negotiation, Strategic Thinking, Constructive Debate, Inspirational Leadership, and other Barnes & Conti programs. She is the author of *Exercising Influence: A Guide for Making Things Happen at Work, at Home, and in Your Community*. Kim has been in the profession for over thirty years, and her work has been translated into Spanish, French, Japanese, Hungarian, Polish, Danish, Hebrew, Thai, Korean, and Chinese.

B. Kim Barnes
Barnes & Conti Associates, Inc.
940 Dwight Way, Suite 15
Berkeley, CA 94710
Phone: 800.835.0911
Email: bcinfo@barnesconti.com
Website: www.barnesconti.com

Little-Known Fact

Submitted by Pat Cataldo, M.B.A.

Objectives
- To get a group to begin to bond.
- To personalize standard introductions.

Audience
Any size.

Time Required
About 30–45 seconds to 1 minute per person.

Materials and Equipment
- None.

Area Setup
Classroom style—nothing special.

Process
1. Ask each participant to introduce himself or herself with name, title, division, or company and to give a "little-known fact" about himself or herself. Give a little-known fact about yourself first—for example, "My little-known fact is that I have a published recipe . . . New England Shellfish Kabobs."
2. Continue around the group until each participant has shared a little-known fact. This introduction always opens up the class and gets people more relaxed.

 nsider's Tip

- Some very interesting facts have been shared—for example, one participant had qualified for the Olympics; another was a member of a well-known music group.

Source

This is a staple of the training world.

Pat Cataldo, M.B.A., is the associate dean for executive education for Penn State Executive Programs, where he is responsible for the design, development, and delivery of executive education programs supporting the needs of customers worldwide. Pat received his M.B.A. from Boston College and an honorary Ph.D. from Grand Valley State University. He has written numerous articles and chapters in the field of training and development. Throughout his career, Pat has done business in fifteen countries and has been active in ASTD, including serving on the national board of directors. ASTD has recognized him for Distinguished Contribution to an Employer and as the International Trainer of the Year.

Pat Cataldo, M.B.A.
Associate Dean for Executive Education
Pennsylvania State University
University Park, PA 16802
Phone: 814.863.9715
Email: pcataldo@psu.edu

What's My Line?

Submitted by Peter R. Garber

Objectives
- To introduce an interactive communication session.
- To introduce participants.

Audience
Any group size could work, but ideally fewer than 20 participants. Can be an intact work group or new faces.

Time Required
10–20 minutes, depending on group size.

Materials and Equipment
- Printed instructions (optional).

Area Setup
Any setup could work; ideally, tables.

Process
1. Introduce the activity by telling group members that the purpose is to get to know one another better.
2. Tell them that each participant will describe his or her ideal job or vocation. It is acceptable for participants to state their current job, but preferably they should talk about something other than their current job. Each participant will also add why he or she would like to have the job or vocation described.
3. One executive, for example, said that his ideal job would be growing vegetables and selling them at a roadside stand. Probe why the stated vocation would be appealing to the person. Ask, "What aspects of this job are interesting to you?" or "Why would this occupation be meaningful to you?"
4. A variation of this exercise could be to have each participant write down his or her ideal occupation. You could then read each one and ask participants to guess to whom each occupation belongs.

Insider's Tips

- This is one of the best icebreakers I use for meetings or conferences.
- If the group is larger than twenty, form two or more smaller groups.

Peter R. Garber is the manager of employee relations for PPG Industries, Inc., headquartered in Pittsburgh. He is the author of a number of HR- and business-related books and articles, including his recently published *Leadership Lessons from Life* series.

Peter R. Garber
PPG Industries, Inc.
One PPG Place
Pittsburgh, PA 15272
Phone: 412.434.2009
Email: Garber@PPG.com

At the Movies

Submitted by Karen Lawson, Ph.D., CSP

Objective
- To help participants get to know each other at the beginning of the session in a nonthreatening way.

Audience
Any size; subgroups should consist of no more than 7 people.

Time Required
45 minutes.

Materials and Equipment
- One copy of the Participant Instructions handout for each participant.
- Seven to ten movie posters (more if there are over fifty people in the session).

Area Setup
Room can be arranged in any way, but there needs to be enough room for participants to move about easily to form subgroups. Prior to the activity, hang or display movie posters on the wall or on easels around the room.

Process
1. Distribute the Participant Instructions handout to each person.
2. Tell participants that they are to look around the room at the movie posters and select their three favorite movies. Explain that there will be three rounds of groupings or gatherings. During Round 1, they are to go to the designated area for their first movie choice; Round 2, their second choice; Round 3, their third choice.
3. Say, "We are ready to begin Round 1. Go to your first movie choice. Note that there should be no more than seven people in a group, so if the group you choose is full, please move to another group."

4. Once the subgroups are formed, ask the participants to discuss the questions or topics that appear on their instruction sheet for the round.
5. After 7 minutes, call time and process the activity by selecting participants at random to respond to the following questions:
   - When was the last time you went to a movie theater? What did you see?
   - Why did you like the movie you selected?
6. Next, direct participants to gather at their second-choice poster. Have them respond to the questions or topics on the instruction sheet for the round.
7. After 7 minutes, call time and process the activity by asking the following question: What did you find you have in common?
8. Conduct Round 3 as you did the other two rounds. Use the following questions to process the activity:
   - What were the major concerns or expectations in your group?
   - What relationships did you find between the movies and this session's topic?
9. Have all participants return to their places.
10. For the final debrief, discuss the activity by asking the following questions:
    - What did you experience during the activity?
    - What was the value of this activity?
    - How can your experience in this activity benefit you as you interact with people in the session or on the job?

Variations

- Instead of using movies, you may choose other ways to form groups, such as:
  Favorite activity or sport.
  Famous person they would like to meet.
  Country they would like to visit.
  Favorite animal.
- You can also use this activity at any time during the session by making the questions content-specific. For example, in a change management program, you might ask the following:
  Round 1: What changes are you experiencing in your organization?
  Round 2: What is the impact of change on employees?
  Round 3: What is the impact of change on you as a manager?

Insider's Tips

- Be sure to adhere to the suggested time frames and move people quickly from one round to the next.
- Choose movies that people can easily identify with or relate to. Also choose movies from different genres: action, comedy, drama, and so on.
- You may need to give a brief summary or synopsis of each one in case people are not familiar with one or more of the selections.

Source

This activity was published in my book *New Employee Orientation Training* (ASTD, 2002).

Karen Lawson, Ph.D., CSP, is an international consultant, speaker, executive coach, and author. She has held many key leadership positions in professional organizations, including ASTD and the National Speakers Association (NSA). She has also received numerous professional awards for her contributions to the training profession. She is the author of nine books on the subjects of training, coaching, and communications.

Karen Lawson, Ph.D., CSP
Lawson Consulting Group, Inc.
1365 Gwynedale Way
Lansdale, PA 19446
Phone: 215.368.9465
Email: KLawson@LawsonCG.com
Website: www.LawsonCG.com

At the Movies
Participant Instructions

1. Look around the room at the movie posters and select your three favorite movies. This activity will consist of three rounds of groupings or gatherings. During each round, you will go to the designated area for one of your movie choices.

2. There should be no more than seven (7) people in a group; therefore, if the group you choose is full, please move to your next choice.

3. Once your groups are formed, please discuss the topics listed here for each respective round:

   - Round 1
     - Please introduce yourself to your group members by stating your name, where you live, and your position and location with the organization.
     - Explain briefly why you selected this movie as your favorite.

   - Round 2
     - Identify something you have in common with the other members in your group. Some possible topics might include hobbies, sports activities, family, pets, or job.
     - Explain what you liked most about this movie choice.

   - Round 3
     - Discuss what you hope to learn during this session.
     - Identify something in this movie that is related to the session topic.

4. Each round will be 7 minutes long. Your facilitator will give you a signal to move to the next group.

On Time Top Ten Trivia

Submitted by Dana Gaines Robinson and James C. Robinson

Objectives
- To encourage participants to return from break on time.
- To energize the group.
- To save precious training time.

Audience
Any number (whatever the size of your training session). Participants need to be in the same teams for this activity that they are in throughout the entire session. If participants are not working in teams but are sitting at separate tables, each table can form a team.

Time Required
About 5 minutes after every break.

Materials and Equipment
- You will need a copy of *Top Ten of Everything* (DK Adult, 2005), by Russell Ash. This book lists the top ten of, well, everything! Lists include the last ten Academy Awards, the top ten golfers, the top ten race horses, and the top ten richest people in the world.
- Flip chart and marker.
- Prize(s) for winning team (optional).

Area Setup
Nothing special, but you'll need a place near the front of the room to track team points.

Process

1. Prior to the session, select several top ten lists from the *Top Ten of Everything* book; you will use these to challenge the teams.
2. Prior to the first break, introduce the event and state that the competition will begin at the announced time that participants are to return from break. Establish the rules:
   - The event will begin on time after every break, including lunch.
   - You will identify a category, and each team will create a maximum list of ten, with the goal being to match the list in the *Top Ten* book.
   - Teams will be allowed 2 minutes to create their list of ten.
   - Teams will receive one point for every correct item on their lists. They are not penalized for guessing. The items do not need to be in the correct order.

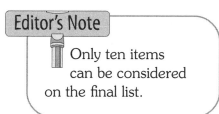

Editor's Note

Only ten items can be considered on the final list.

3. Announce that the last top ten challenge will be worth double points. This helps everyone feel as if they are still in the game, even if they have the fewest points.
4. Also announce that points will be totaled and a prize given to the winning team. We like to give a CD to each of the winning team members.
5. You may wish to conduct a practice run before the first break.
6. When teams are to return from the break, announce the first category and tell teams to compile their lists.
7. After 2 minutes, ask the teams to stop. Read the list of correct answers.
8. Ask each team for the number of correct responses and begin to tally scores on a flip-chart page in the front of the room.
9. Each time the teams return from a break, provide a new category and have teams compile and then score their lists.
10. At the end of the session, announce the winning team and present the prize(s).

# Insider's Tips

- This is an excellent activity for longer training sessions. It energizes participants and most definitely gets them back from break on time, every time—even after a three- or four-day session when it is easy for participants to begin to drift. It becomes self-governing.
- A one-day session probably does not have enough breaks to make the exercise worthwhile. Besides, if the trainer sets the standard and starts on time, participants tend to return on time the first day.
- We like to select activities that are related to the organizations with which we work. For example, when working with the Coca-Cola Company, we might ask for the top ten countries that consume Coca-Cola.
- You may wish to ask each of your teams to select a team name.

Source

We do not believe that this activity has ever been published, but we would like to share the credit with Bob Pike, from whom we learned this activity.

Dana Gaines Robinson and James C. Robinson founded Partners in Change, Inc., in 1981, as a research-based consulting firm. The Robinsons are renowned leaders in the area of aligning people strategies with business goals. They were the first people to author a "how-to" book in the area of performance consulting, a process through which workplace performance is enhanced in support of business goals. These foremost leaders in the human performance movement are recognized worldwide. Their most recent publications include two books, *Performance Consulting* (Berrett-Koehler, 2000) and *Strategic Business Partner* (Berrett-Koehler, 2005).

Dana Gaines Robinson and James C. Robinson
Partners in Change, Inc.
105 Trenton Circle
McMurray, PA 15317
Phone: 724.942.7768
Email: jrobinson@partners-in-change.com
Website: www.partners-in-change.com

Alphabet Adjectives

Submitted by Max Rodrigues, M.Sc., LL.B, Dip Ind'l Mgt.

Objectives
- To allow participants to feel comfortable with one another.
- To lighten the environment and to have fun.

Audience
20–25 people.

Time Required
About 20–25 minutes, depending on group size.

Materials and Equipment
- None.

Area Setup
Preferably U-shaped.

Process
1. Tell the participants that all our names begin with one letter of the alphabet. Have them introduce themselves to the individuals on their right and left to learn with what letter of the alphabet their colleagues' names begin. Continue by saying that this will take some coordination, as they may be in demand by individuals on their left and their right at the same time.
2. After a minute or two, ask participants to assign an adjective that begins with the same letter as the first letter of their neighbors' names (both the right and the left).
3. Give them some time to meet the person and to think of some crazy, wacky adjective that begins with the first letter of their neighbors' names.
4. Have them introduce both of their neighbors—for example, "My friends are Mysterious Max and Astounding Alison." Note that each person will be introduced twice.

Insider's Tips

- The activity works equally well with a known group or a new group. It is best conducted as an energizer any time during the workshop.
- Allow the participants the freedom to use a maximum of three adjectives. You will find some participants asking to use more adjectives—use your discretion.

Max Rodrigues, M.Sc., LL.B, Dip Ind'l Mgt., is a master trainer with NIS Sparta Ltd., a performance enhancement solutions company. Max specializes in training and certifying trainers. His areas of interest include behavioral training, team building, and self-development.

Max Rodrigues, M.Sc., LL.B, Dip Ind'l Mgt.
NIS Sparta Ltd.
G Block, 2nd floor, DAKC Khopar
Khairne, Navi Mumbai
India
Phone: 0932.4604712
Email: maxr.nissparta@relianceinfo.com

Bingo

Submitted by Edward E. Scannell, CMP, CSP

Objective

- To enable participants to meet new friends in a fun way.

Audience

Best used with groups of fewer than 50.

Time Required

8–10 minutes.

Materials and Equipment

- A Bingo game sheet for each person. (See Preparation section and sample at end of activity.)
- Prize for winner.

Area Setup

Any type of room setup is okay, as participants will be moving around the room.

Preparation

1. Before the session, email or phone people who you know will be attending the event and ask them for some little-known "secret" or interesting fact about themselves.
2. Using the information you've gathered, construct a Bingo sheet similar to the one shown in the example.

Process

1. Use this activity at the beginning of a session as an icebreaker.
2. Distribute a copy of the Bingo sheet to each participant.
3. Have participants mingle and talk to one another in an effort to find someone to "fill in the blanks" on their Bingo cards. Note that each person can sign a Bingo card only once, even if more than one item applies to that person.
4. End the game after the allotted time or when someone gets Bingo.
5. Award a prize to the winner.

nsider's Tip

- This can be used for groups that do—or do not—know one another. You'll be amazed at some of the responses you get!

Source

I originated this now famous Bingo icebreaker. It is a staple in every trainer's tool kit. The activity was originally published in *Games Trainers Play* (McGraw-Hill, 1980).

Edward E. Scannell, CMP, CSP, is actively involved in ASTD. He has presented programs for over one thousand audiences around the world. The books in his *Games Trainers Play* series are used by speakers, trainers, and facilitators worldwide. Ed served as national president of ASTD, MPI (Meeting Professionals International), and NSA, and formerly taught at Arizona State University and the University of Northern Iowa.

Edward E. Scannell, CMP, CSP
Center for Professional Development and Training
4234 N. Winfield Scott Plaza
Scottsdale, AZ 85251
Phone: 480.970.0101
Email: EESAZ@aol.com

Bingo

Directions: Each blank space identifies something about the people here. Meet and greet your colleagues, and if one of these items pertains to them, ask them to sign their name in the appropriate space on your sheet. Each person can sign your sheet only once, even if more than one space applies to them.

GOOD LUCK! HAVE FUN!

Drives a sports car _____	Went to college with Tom Cruise _____	Has two children _____	Worked in Malaysia _____	Was born on New Year's Eve _____
Raised in Nebraska; lived in Iowa _____	Raised baby chicks _____	Is a gourmet cook _____	Is a professional artist _____	Almost became a nun _____
Was a classical Russian ballet dancer _____	Has season tickets _____	Raised on an Indian reservation _____	Raised rabbits for a living _____	Swam with barracudas _____
Plays golf _____	Was born on farm outside USA _____	Is an accomplished wood-worker _____	Rode a camel in Africa _____	Was captain of HS pom-pom team _____
Is a Texas two-stepper _____	Was a long-haul truck driver _____	Is a white-water rafter _____	Was born in Lucille Ball's hometown _____	Has run a marathon _____

Penny Toss

Submitted by Michal Foriest Settles, Ed.D.

Objective
- To promote the sharing of information in an icebreaker.

Audience
6–50 participants.

Time Required
10–90 minutes.

Materials and Equipment
- Glass mason jar.
- Pennies (with dates from the last twenty years), at least one per person.

Area Setup
Circle (best) or U shape.

Process
1. Have participants select one penny from the jar.
2. Tell participants to share something of significance in their life that corresponds to the date on the penny.
3. Have the participant flip his or her coin to any person who has yet to participate and ask that individual to share something significant that occurred in the same year.
4. After the first penny has been flipped to a specified number of people (generally three to six works well), have another participant start a new round by announcing his or her date and sharing something of significance. Have the participant flip his or her coin to someone who has not yet participated.
5. Continue this process until all participants have announced the dates on their pennies.

Insider's Tip

- This icebreaker can get very long, so you may wish to establish a rule that participants may use only one sentence to describe the event.

Michal Foriest Settles, Ed.D., is the HR department manager at the San Francisco Bay Area Rapid Transit (BART) District. In addition to serving as an adjunct business faculty member at the University of San Francisco and San Francisco City College, she is currently on the ICMA-RC advisory board and was selected as the 2001 Outstanding Business Woman of the Year by the Iota Phi Lambda sorority. She has provided consulting and training for such clients as the U.S. Navy, Bechtel, USDA, Pacific Bell, and San Francisco Veterans Hospital.

Michal Foriest Settles, Ed.D.
BART
500 Cayuga Avenue
San Francisco, CA 94112
Phone: 510.464.6239
Email: msettle@bart.gov

Chapter 16

Closure

Reviewing Content and Transferring Knowledge

Bringing closure to a training session is a lost art. Too often training sessions draw to a close with no ending exercise to bring closure. An evaluation may be completed, but there is no shared experience, no review, no checking on expectations, no saying good-bye. Blame this on a lack of time or a lack of understanding, but I believe it is important to close the loop.

The purpose of training is to provide participants something that they can apply, in the form of skills or knowledge, back at the workplace. Therefore, one of the critical requirements of a closing activity should be to review the content and transfer the knowledge to the workplace. That is exactly what our seven contributors have shared with you.

Brooke Broadbent (Canada) shares an exhilarating, fun-filled race to test that learning occurred during the session. Fanny Caballero (Peru) lets the participants create their own review. No advance planning required; all you need is a stack of index cards. If you've ever attended one of Bob Lucas's presentations at ASTD, you would expect to find a rowdy activity as his contribution. He does not let you down. Toni Lucia creates a test for reviewing what was learned, and she makes it fun! Jack Phillips, the master of ROI, explains a powerful process for overcoming barriers to transferring what was learned to the workplace. Bill Sewell (South Africa) introduces an adapted fishbowl method that gives participants ample

365

practice time with a verbal skill. We wouldn't expect anything but action from Mel Silberman, and that's exactly what he gives us. Mel contributes a lively activity that gets participants up and moving around for a very practical purpose. As with all of Mel's activities, be sure to have plenty of room to move about. There is no better trainer in the world than Mel to end this book. He is best in class!

I have enjoyed editing this book more than almost anything else I have written. The contact with the contributors, the excitement when yet one more of the gurus said yes, the satisfaction of locating excellent contributors from every continent—each step along the way was thrilling. And now, as with every good closure, I have a sense of completion and accomplishment. I turn *90 World-Class Activities by 90 World-Class Trainers* over to you to savor, enjoy, and put to good use. Never before has so much training talent been put together between two covers. Thank you all for your contribution.

Race to Remember

Submitted by Brooke Broadbent, M.A.

Objective

- To energize participants while conducting a review of critical-to-know information.

Audience

Up to 30 total participants in teams of 4–5.

Time Required

20–30 minutes.

Materials and Equipment

- One set of concepts and one set of content for each team. Each team's set should be on a different colour of card stock. (An example of one concept is Gremlin. That would be on one card. On another card of the same colour would be the content for Gremlin: negative thoughts that hold us back in our personal growth.)
- Roll of masking tape for each team.
- Prizes (optional).

Area Setup

Separate tables for each team; wall space for taping card pairs; a room that has enough open space for running to the wall.

Process

1. Prior to the session, select a list of concepts (terms, policies, or other knowledge) that are critical for participants to remember following the training session. Also make a list of content (accompanying definitions, key policy points, or other critical information) that is related to each of the concepts. Create sets of equal-size (approximately 3-by-8-inch) cards with the concept on one card and the content on the other card. Create several sets on different colours of card stock or construction paper. Have at least ten pairs in each set.

Closure

2. Deliver a lecturette regarding the concepts and content that participants must know. Ask what questions any of the participants have about the information they just heard.

3. Once you have answered any questions, tell participants that they are about to participate in a "Race to Remember." The goal of the race is to be the first team to correctly match a set of concepts and content and to hang the matched cards on the wall.

4. Assign a specific amount of wall space to each team. The walls should be approximately the same distance from each team's table. You may wish to assign walls that are on the opposite side from each team's table to create a longer racing distance for each team.

5. Place a set of concepts and content (not in order) face down on each table. Tell participants that once you say go, the team members are to work together to match the concept on one card with the definition found on another card. One person will run to the team's wall space and use the masking tape at each table to tape the pair to the wall. Only one person with one matched pair can leave the table at any given time. If a team discovers an error, one team member must go to the wall to retrieve the mismatched pair before the correct pairing can be taped up.

6. Tell participants that a prize will be given to the first team that has correctly matched and hung all its concept and content cards (optional).

7. Illustrate how to match the cards by selecting one set from the pile. Match them and place them on the wall the way the rest are to be placed. Have each team do this.

8. Allow all the teams to finish, but note the order in which teams complete the activity.

9. Once everyone has completed the task, have the group walk with you from one team's wall space to another, checking for accuracy. If one of the pairs is incorrect, allow the team to make the correction.

10. If you award prizes, you may wish to use bags of individually wrapped candy and reward everyone for a great job.

11. Ask if any concepts need to be explained; if they do, provide the explanations.

Insider's Tips

- Be sure to deliver the directions energetically so that the participants are excited about winning the race.
- Print the cards from your computer using a very large font, such as 30 or 40 point.
- Remember that the purpose of this game is learning. Monitor learning and ensure that it occurs.
- You may wish to use different colours of index cards and hand-print the card sets.

Brooke Broadbent, M.A., is a learning expert, writer, and certified business coach. He is the author of four popular international books and over eighty articles. He holds a master's degree in adult education. His latest book is *Living from the Heart, Learning to Live Without Struggle* (Trafford, 2005).

Brooke Broadbent, M.A.
177-207 Bank Street
Ottawa, ON K2P 2N2
Canada
Phone: 613.862.4459
Email: coach@www.brookebroadbent.com
Website: www.brookebroadbent.com

I Got It

Submitted by Fanny Caballero

Objectives
- To provide a review of the key points of a training session.
- To make sure participants clearly understand the concepts.

Audience
Any size.

Time Required
15–25 minutes.

Materials and Equipment
- Index cards.
- Pens.
- Small prizes (optional).

Area Setup
It doesn't really matter; however, if the group is large, place participants into smaller subgroups.

Process
1. Give each participant an index card and ask them to write a question about something that was learned in the class. Collect the cards. Shuffle them and ask for several volunteers.
2. Ask each volunteer to choose a question card. Read the card and have the volunteer answer the question.
3. Lead an applause for each volunteer. You may optionally recognize each person with a small prize.
4. Go through as many cards as you have volunteers.

# Insider's Tips

- Keep the activity moving quickly so that you can give as many volunteers a chance as possible.
- Don't force anyone to answer a question, unless you are going to require everyone to answer a question. Use prizes and applause to motivate participants to volunteer.
- If there are many participants, you may wish to have smaller groups and assign one person in each group the leader role. The leader will facilitate the use of the question cards.

Fanny Caballero has been a trainer for Minera Yanacocha SRL in Cajamarca, Peru, for six years. She delivers human management training for supervisors and managers. In her free time, she is a partner with her two sisters in a private school, C.E.P. Acuarela. She is passionate about training, teaching, and learning from people of other cultures.

Fanny Caballero
Minera Yanacocha SRL
Vía Camino Real 348
Terre El Pilar Piso 10
Lima 27
Peru
Phone: 511.2152600
Email: fanny.caballero@newmont.com

Reviewing and Reinforcing with a Beat

Submitted by Robert "Bob" W. Lucas, B.S., M.A., CPLP

Objectives

- To provide participants an opportunity to reflect on key concepts learned.
- To identify any primary elements of key points that learners missed and that need further emphasis by the session leader.

Audience

Any size group, subdivided into smaller groups of 6–8 learners each.

Time Required

Approximately 10–20 minutes, depending on overall group size and review options selected.

Materials and Equipment

- A Musical Pickle for each subgroup.
- Flip chart (if option two is chosen).
- Masking tape (if option two is chosen).
- Assorted colored markers (if option two is chosen).

Area Setup

Open space large enough for all small groups to form into circles.

> **Editor's Note**
>
> This activity is a takeoff on the children's game Musical Chairs, except chairs are not used or taken away. It is designed to enhance the learning experience by adding fun and novelty while causing learners to reflect on what they have learned. It reinforces the learning through verbalization of key concepts.

Process

1. Form small groups of six to eight learners and ask each subgroup to stand in a circle.
2. Give each group a Musical Pickle.
3. Explain that when told to begin, the person holding the pickle will start the music by pressing the button on the bottom. He or she will then shout out a key concept, idea, strategy, or technique learned or experienced during the session and pass the pickle to the person on his or her right.

4. Each person in turn continues this process until the music stops. Participants cannot repeat anything said by someone else in the group.
5. The person holding the pickle when the music stops will shout out a concept, give the pickle to the person on his or her right, and have a seat.
6. The review continues until there is only one person per group left standing. Have everyone give a round of applause for their efforts and reward the remaining participants left standing from each group with a small prize or toy related to the program theme or topic.

Option One

Instead of ending the review as outlined, follow these steps:

1. Form a group made up of the remaining standing participants and have them continue until there is only one remaining participant.
2. Have everyone give a round of applause to the winner.
3. Reward him or her with a small prize or toy (for example, smiley-face squeeze balls for a customer service or interpersonal communication class, a small whistle or clicker attention-getter for a train-the-trainer class, or something related to money for a session on financial matters).

Option Two

To add a bit of competition to the review:

1. Form small groups of six to eight participants.
2. Give each group a flip chart, markers, and masking tape.
3. Randomly select a group recorder using some novel and interesting method (for example, choose the person who traveled farthest to get to the program or the person with the most jewelry on) and instruct him or her to capture each key concept or idea shouted by team members during the review.
4. When there is only one member of the group still standing at the end, have the recorder count the total responses from the group (making sure none are repeats). Have everyone give a round of applause.
5. Reward the individuals still standing for their efforts and also reward the team with the most responses.

Closure

# Insider's Tips

- You can purchase a Musical Pickle from Trainers Warehouse, www.trainers warehouse.com.
- Research has found that including such elements as color, sound, movement, motivational stimulus, novelty, and fun in a learning event can enhance acquisition, retention, recall, and successful application of knowledge and skills. This review activity incorporates all those elements and more. For example, by simply having learners give a round of applause, you provide instant recognition for performance and add sound, movement, fun, and novelty to the learning environment. If you do not want to use the Musical Pickle, you can simply start and stop a CD with music; however, the pickle adds color, levity, and laughter to the event. It is well worth the trouble of bringing pickles to your session!

Robert "Bob" W. Lucas, B.S., M.A., CPLP, is president of Creative Presentation Resources, a Web-based company marketing over a thousand creative toys, games, and other products for the learning environment. He has been training since 1972 and is a popular conference presenter. He has written and contributed to eighteen books, including *The Creative Training Idea Book* (American Management Association, 2003), *The Big Book of Flip Charts* (McGraw-Hill, 1999), and *People Strategies for Trainers* (AMACOM, 2005).

Robert "Bob" W. Lucas, B.S., M.A., CPLP
Creative Presentation Resources, Inc.
P.O. Box 180487
Casselberry, FL 32718
Phone: 407.695.5535
Email: blucas@presentationresources.net
Website: www.presentationresources.net

Quick Content Quiz

Submitted by Anntoinette "Toni" Lucia

Objectives
- To assist participants, who need a refresher to be reacquainted with content.
- To review program content in an interactive format.

Audience
There is no limit to the overall group size; participants will work in teams of 5–7 for part of the activity.

Time Required
30–45 minutes.

Materials and Equipment
- Quiz for each participant.
- Slides for content review with large group (optional).
- Prize for the winning team (optional).

Area Setup
Table groups or a setup that is convenient for groups of five to seven to have a brief discussion.

Process
1. Prior to the session, compose a twelve-question multiple-choice quiz based on key program content.
2. Hand out the quiz and have individuals complete it. Allow about 5–7 minutes for completion.
3. Have participants form groups of five to seven to discuss their answers and reach consensus. Allow about 10 minutes.
4. Have them return to the large group to review the questions and answers. As you go through the quiz, you can review content, ask and answer questions, give examples, and elicit applications from participants. This will take about 15 minutes.

5. Either during or after the discussion, you can use slides to highlight and review content, models, or concepts (optional).

6. Award a prize to the group with the most correct answers (optional).

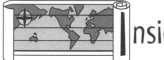 nsider's Tips

- The setup should get participants ready for some fun. On the agenda for the day, the topic might be "review content from previous session," but when you begin the review, you could say that a review by one person in the front of the room isn't terribly fun and could even be boring. Therefore, the review will give everyone a chance to participate. Participation will be in the form of a quiz. You might even hear a groan or two, but if participants know they will not be judged individually and that they will ultimately work to reach team consensus, they will jump in.

- If you opt to award prizes, you can let participants know that up front. If the group enjoys competition, or if there is a way to give several quizzes throughout the session, teams can accumulate points and the winners be determined at the end of the session.

Anntoinette "Toni" Lucia is president of West End Consulting, Inc. Toni's consulting work includes facilitating strategic organizational change, team building for senior management teams, and designing, conducting, and evaluating executive and management development programs. Toni's publications include two books, *The Art & Science of 360 Feedback* (Pfeiffer, 1997) and *The Art & Science of Competency Models* (Pfeiffer, 1999). She is a member of the Instructional Systems Association and on the advisory board of Better Communications, Inc.

Anntoinette "Toni" Lucia
West End Consulting, Inc.
191 D Main Street
New Canaan, CT 06840
Phone: 203.801.0733
Fax: 203.801.0736
Email: toni@tonilucia.com

Overcoming Barriers

Submitted by Jack J. Phillips, Ph.D.

Objectives

- To understand the barriers to implementing skills and knowledge learned in a formal learning and development program.
- To develop a plan of action to utilize the new skills and knowledge, effectively overcoming the barriers.

Audience

Any audience of 16–24 participants, working in groups of 3–5.

Time Required

30–60 minutes, depending on the size of the group and the number of barriers identified.

Materials and Equipment

- Flip charts for each team.
- Flip-chart markers in three or four colors for each team.

Area Setup

The group should be arranged at tables with three to five people per team at each table.

Process

1. Tell participants,

    Transferring the skills and knowledge to the job is a challenging and perplexing problem for workplace learning and performance professionals. Research continues to show that 60 to 90 percent of what has been learned is not utilized on the job, even though learners should be using these skills and knowledge in the workplace. There are many barriers to utilization. If the barriers can be minimized or removed, or if the learners can go around the barriers, the newly acquired skills and knowledge can be transferred to the job. A plan to overcome the barriers becomes a plan of implementation.

2. Have participants work in their small teams of three to five. Ask each team to discuss the barriers to the implementation of what they have learned. Tell them to itemize all the factors that will inhibit the actual use of the skills and

Closure

knowledge taught in the program. There are no restrictions on the types of barriers or areas to consider.

Request that the teams list all the barriers on their flip chart so that everyone can read them. Allow about 10 minutes.

3. When time is up, have each team identify a person to report to the entire group. The report should include enough information about each barrier that the entire group can understand it.

4. Have each team tackle each barrier, one at a time, indicating what can be done to eliminate, minimize, or go around the barrier. If duplicate barriers are announced, teams can decide which one will address it, keeping the number of barriers approximately equal among the teams.

5. Have each team report the steps to overcoming the barriers.

6. Have each individual develop a personal action plan that follows the ideas generated by all the teams, selecting those actions that the learner can accomplish to ensure that he or she utilizes the skills and knowledge on the job.

7. Have learners state one or two of their planned actions with a commitment to follow up in two to four months to check on the status of the actions outlined in the plan.

8. Following the session, compile all the teams' lists into a composite list for the group and, if feasible, provide copies of it to them in some convenient form.

 nsider's Tips

- This exercise provides a powerful way to gain ownership and commitment to implement new skills following a learning and development program. It is particularly useful with individuals who have learned valuable skills and information but see barriers to use because of so many organizational issues. For individuals or teams who are responsible for implementing new skills and knowledge, this activity results in the development of the implementation plan for major learning and development efforts. Because learners have identified both the barriers to implementation and ways to overcome the barriers, they have ownership of the implementation and are willing to make progress in the workplace.

- Many "ah-ha" moments occur during this activity as learners see a road map to success. When participants are listing the barriers, they often generate an extensive list as they recognize the multitude of obstacles that can get in the way of successful implementation. They often become cynical or dogmatic about the barriers. The second part of the exercise, identifying ways to overcome the barriers, makes them examine what they can do—positive steps they can take—in the face of that barrier. The "ah-ha" moments happen here.

- This activity is not positioned as an action planning exercise. Although action plans come out of the process, the activity itself is presented as an implementation exercise or simply as a barriers exercise.

Jack J. Phillips, Ph.D., is a world-renowned expert on measurement and evaluation. He is chair of the ROI Institute, providing consulting services for Fortune 500 companies and workshops for major conference providers throughout the world. He developed the ROI Methodology™ used worldwide by corporations, governmental entities, and nonprofit organizations. Jack is the author or editor of more than thirty books and more than one hundred articles.

Jack Phillips, Ph.D.
ROI Institute, Inc.
350 Crossbrook Drive
Chelsea, AL 35043
Phone: 205.678.8101
Email: jack@roiinstitute.net
Website: www.roiinstitute.net

Word Wheel

Submitted by Bill Sewell, M.P.A.

Objectives
- To practice skills in verbal communications and interaction.
- To reinforce conceptual issues through peer group role plays.

Audience
12–30 people from diverse cultures or backgrounds but with enough in common to interact (including language and past experiences).

Time Required
30–45 minutes.

Materials and Equipment
- No equipment is essential, but realism and fun can be enhanced by the use of:
  - A flip chart for posting the questions or topics.
  - Coloured caps or scarves to denote roles or affiliate groups.
  - A whistle.

Area Setup
Space for large concentric circles of participants (depends on the number of people).

Process
1. After a learning input, say, "Now we are going to have some fun practising how to tell someone in our family or neighbourhood about what we have been discussing today."
2. Group participants into two concentric circles (for example, count off and ask the people with even numbers to form the inner circle, facing partners in the outer circle).

3. Clarify the roles you want participants to play. For example, tell the participants in the inner circle that they are each to be a neighbour or fellow passenger on the bus, who asks the question; tell the members of the outer circle that they are each to be a community development worker who is knowledgeable and able to give the advice or information.

4. Show or tell the question and allow 2 minutes for the partners to conduct the role play (blow a whistle, if you have one, when time is up). Topics could include the following:
   - "How to apply for a child care grant."
   - "How to prepare for a job interview."
   - "Why I like to belong to (my church, political party, or civic group)."
   - "How to conduct a performance review."
   - "What do you expect from your town councillor?"
   - "How to increase diversity in your organisation."
   - "How to avoid being infected with HIV-AIDS."

5. Ensure that participants are engaged in a meaningful experience by listening and checking for understanding (ask for feedback).

6. Tell one circle to step to the right, changing partners. Repeat, as often as required, while interest is maintained.

 **Insider's Tips**

- Use caps or scarves to identify roles.
- Get feedback on answers and issues that may need more clarity.
- As an alternative, you can use this before a learning or information input session, telling people, "We are going to have some fun first, to see how you feel about (name the topic or question)." You may wish to post the question or topic on a flip chart.

Source

This activity has been frequently used in South Africa by a community development group, the Education & Training Unit (www.etu.org.za). To my knowledge, this activity has never been published.

Bill Sewell, M.P.A., is a Master HR Practitioner and a Certified Performance Technologist (ISPI). His consulting experience for the past twenty years has included performance evaluation and performance improvement for public and private sector organizations throughout southern Africa.

Bill Sewell, M.P.A.
Anchor International/Partners in Change
Anchor House, Greenford Office Estate, Punters Way
Kenilworth, Cape Town
South Africa
Phone: 27.21.6833258
Email: bill@anchor-international.com

Index Card Match

Submitted by Mel Silberman, Ph.D.

Objective

- To review course material through a lively game.

Audience

This activity is adaptable to a group of 10–40 participants.

Time Required

10–20 minutes.

Materials and Equipment

- Index cards.

Area Setup

An open space for participants to mill around.

Process

1. Write on separate index cards the names of techniques and concepts examined in the training session. (For example, one card might say "fishbowl discussion" or "supply chain management.") Create enough cards to equal half the number of participants.

2. On separate cards, write clear, reader-friendly definitions of each of the techniques or concepts you have chosen. For example, a fishbowl discussion is "a way to have a small-group discussion in a large-group setting." Supply chain management can be defined as "improving the way a company finds the raw components it needs to make a product or service, manufactures it, and delivers it to customers." In a session on quality management, you might develop the following list of analytical tools and their definitions for a group of eighteen participants:

   - *Affinity diagram*—Organizes ideas into natural groupings; categories and new ideas are generated by team members working silently.
   - *Cause-and-effect diagram*—Used to identify root causes of the effect being analyzed.

- *Pareto diagram*—Organizes causes by frequency; also known as 80/20 rule.
- *Histogram*—Shows frequency of occurrence of different measurements for a given quality attribute; used to depict variation in an observed measurement.
- *Scatter diagram*—Depicts the relationship between variables, thereby helping to substantiate whether root cause is related to effect.
- *Control chart*—Used to determine whether or not variation is due to common or special causes.
- *Flow chart*—Used to understand a process by depicting its various activities and decision points.
- *Relations diagram*—Display of the cause-and-effect relationship between factors in a complex situation.
- *Tree diagram*—Displays range of subtasks needed to achieve objective.

3. Combine the two sets of cards and shuffle them several times so that they are well mixed.

4. Give out one card to each participant. Explain that this is a matching activity in which some participants have the names of techniques or concepts examined in the training session and others have definitions.

5. Direct participants to find their matching cards. When a match is formed, ask each pair of participants to find seats together. (Tell them not to reveal to other participants what is contained on their cards.)

6. When all the matching pairs have been seated, have pair members quiz the rest of the group on their technique or concept by reading aloud its definition or example.

7. You can vary the game by:
   - Developing cards containing a sentence with a missing word to be matched to cards showing the missing word. For example, one card might say "Many salespeople fail to _____ after a sale" and its matching card would say "follow up."
   - Developing cards containing questions with several possible answers. For example, one question might be "What are ways to defuse a conflict?" Match each card to a corresponding card that contains an assortment of answers. When pair members quiz the group, have them present the question and obtain several answers from the participants.

Insider's Tip

- Keep handy a large enough set of cards to be matched for a topic you teach often so that you can quickly use the activity each time you need it. For example, if you have twenty sets of matching cards and a class has ten participants, select five sets. (You can play the game again with another set drawn from the same "deck.")

Source

This activity has been adapted from another activity in *101 Ways to Make Training Active* (2nd ed.) (Pfeiffer, 2005).

Mel Silberman, Ph.D., is president of Active Training, a provider of train-the-trainer programs, most notably the Active Training Institute. He is the author of *Active Training* (Pfeiffer, 2006), *Training the Active Training Way* (Pfeiffer, 2006), *101 Ways to Make Training Active* (2nd ed.), (Pfeiffer, 2005), *The Best of Active Training* (Pfeiffer, 2004), and *The 60-Minute Active Training* series (Pfeiffer, 2004). Mel is Professor Emeritus of Adult and Organizational Development at Temple University, where he won its Great Teacher Award.

Mel Silberman, Ph.D.
Active Training
303 Sayre Drive
Princeton, NJ 08540
Phone: 609.987.8157
Email: mel@activetraining.com
Website: www.activetraining.com

About the Editor

Elaine Biech is president and managing principal of ebb associates inc, an organization development firm that helps organizations work through large-scale change. Elaine has been in the training and consulting field for over twenty-five years, working with business, government, and nonprofit organizations.

Elaine specializes in helping people work as teams to maximize their effectiveness. Customizing all of her work for individual clients, she conducts strategic planning sessions and implements corporation-wide systems, such as quality improvement, reengineering of business processes, and mentoring programs. She facilitates such topics as coaching today's employee, fostering creativity, customer service, time management, stress management, speaking skills, training competence, conducting productive meetings, managing change, handling the difficult employee, organizational communication, conflict resolution, and effective listening.

Elaine has developed media presentations and training materials and has presented at dozens of national and international conferences. Known as the trainer's trainer, she custom designs training programs for managers, leaders, trainers, and consultants. Elaine has been featured in dozens of publications, including the *Wall Street Journal, Harvard Management Update, Fortune Magazine,* and the *Washington Post.*

As a management and executive consultant, trainer, and designer, Elaine has provided services to Land O' Lakes, McDonald's, Lands' End, General Casualty Insurance, the IRS, PricewaterhouseCoopers, American Family Insurance, Marathon Oil, Hershey Chocolate, Johnson Wax, the Federal Reserve Bank, the U.S. Navy, NASA, Newport News Shipbuilding, the Kohler Company, ASTD, the American Red Cross, the Association of Independent Certified Public Accountants, the University of Wisconsin, the College of William and Mary, ODU, and numerous other public and private sector organizations to help them prepare for the challenges of the new millennium.

Elaine is the author and editor of dozens of books and articles, published by Jossey-Bass/Pfeiffer except as otherwise noted. Her publications include *12 Habits of Successful Trainers Infoline* (ASTD, 2005); *Training for Dummies* (Wiley, 2005); *Marketing Your Consulting Services* (2003); *The Consultant's Quick Start Guide* (2001); *Successful Team-Building Tools* (2001); *The Business of Consulting* (1999); *The Consultant's Legal Guide* (2000); *Interpersonal Skills: Understanding Your Impact on Others* (Kendall-Hunt, 1996); *The Pfeiffer Annual, Training* (1998–2007); *The Pfeiffer Annual, Consulting* (1998–2007); *The ASTD Sourcebook: Creativity and Innovation—Widen Your Spectrum* (McGraw-Hill, 1996); *The HR Handbook* (1996); *TQM for Training* (McGraw-Hill, 1994); *Diagnostic Tools for Total Quality Infoline* (ASTD, 1991); *Managing Teamwork* (Kendall-Hunt, 1994); *Process Improvement: Achieving Quality Together* (Kendall-Hunt, 1994); *Business Communications* (Kendall-Hunt, 1992); *Delegating for Results* (Kendall-Hunt, 1992); *Increased Productivity Through Effective Meetings* (Kendall-Hunt, 1987); and *Stress Management, Building Healthy Families* (CESA-12, 1984). Her books have been translated into Chinese, German, and Dutch.

Elaine received her B.S. from the University of Wisconsin-Superior in business and education consulting and her M.S. in human resource development. She is active at the national level of ASTD and served on the 1990 national conference design committee, on the national board of directors, and as the society's secretary from 1991 to 1994; she initiated and chaired Consultant's Day for eight years and was the chair of the international conference design committee in 2000. In addition to her work with ASTD, she has served on the advisory committee of the Independent Consultants Association (ICA) and on the board of directors of the Instructional Systems Association (ISA).

Elaine is the recipient of the 1992 National ASTD Torch Award and the 2004 ASTD Volunteer-Staff Partnership Award. She was selected for the 1995 Wisconsin Women Entrepreneurs' Mentor Award. In 2001 she received ISA's highest award, the ISA Spirit Award. She has been the consulting editor for the prestigious training and consulting annuals published by Pfeiffer for the past ten years.

Pfeiffer Publications Guide

This guide is designed to familiarize you with the various types of Pfeiffer publications. The formats section describes the various types of products that we publish; the methodologies section describes the many different ways that content might be provided within a product. We also provide a list of the topic areas in which we publish.

FORMATS

In addition to its extensive book-publishing program, Pfeiffer offers content in an array of formats, from fieldbooks for the practitioner to complete, ready-to-use training packages that support group learning.

FIELDBOOK Designed to provide information and guidance to practitioners in the midst of action. Most fieldbooks are companions to another, sometimes earlier, work, from which its ideas are derived; the fieldbook makes practical what was theoretical in the original text. Fieldbooks can certainly be read from cover to cover. More likely, though, you'll find yourself bouncing around following a particular theme, or dipping in as the mood, and the situation, dictate.

HANDBOOK A contributed volume of work on a single topic, comprising an eclectic mix of ideas, case studies, and best practices sourced by practitioners and experts in the field.

An editor or team of editors usually is appointed to seek out contributors and to evaluate content for relevance to the topic. Think of a handbook not as a ready-to-eat meal, but as a cookbook of ingredients that enables you to create the most fitting experience for the occasion.

RESOURCE Materials designed to support group learning. They come in many forms: a complete, ready-to-use exercise (such as a game); a comprehensive resource on one topic (such as conflict management) containing a variety of methods and approaches; or a collection of like-minded activities (such as icebreakers) on multiple subjects and situations.

TRAINING PACKAGE An entire, ready-to-use learning program that focuses on a particular topic or skill. All packages comprise a guide for the facilitator/trainer and a workbook for the participants. Some packages are supported with additional media—such as video—or learning aids, instruments, or other devices to help participants understand concepts or practice and develop skills.

- *Facilitator/trainer's guide* Contains an introduction to the program, advice on how to organize and facilitate the learning event, and step-by-step instructor notes. The guide also contains copies of presentation materials—handouts, presentations, and overhead designs, for example—used in the program.

- *Participant's workbook* Contains exercises and reading materials that support the learning goal and serves as a valuable reference and support guide for participants in the weeks and months that follow the learning event. Typically, each participant will require his or her own workbook.

ELECTRONIC CD-ROMs and web-based products transform static Pfeiffer content into dynamic, interactive experiences. Designed to take advantage of the searchability, automation, and ease-of-use that technology provides, our e-products bring convenience and immediate accessibility to your workspace.

METHODOLOGIES

CASE STUDY A presentation, in narrative form, of an actual event that has occurred inside an organization. Case studies are not prescriptive, nor are they used to prove a point; they are designed to develop critical analysis and decision-making skills. A case study has a specific time frame, specifies a sequence of events, is narrative in structure, and contains a plot structure—an issue (what should be/have been done?). Use case studies when the goal is to enable participants to apply previously learned theories to the circumstances in the case, decide what is pertinent, identify the real issues, decide what should have been done, and develop a plan of action.

ENERGIZER A short activity that develops readiness for the next session or learning event. Energizers are most commonly used after a break or lunch to stimulate or refocus the group. Many involve some form of physical activity, so they are a useful way to counter post-lunch lethargy. Other uses include transitioning from one topic to another, where "mental" distancing is important.

EXPERIENTIAL LEARNING ACTIVITY (ELA) A facilitator-led intervention that moves participants through the learning cycle from experience to application (also known as a Structured Experience). ELAs are carefully thought-out designs in which there is a definite learning purpose and intended outcome. Each step—everything that participants do during the activity—facilitates the accomplishment of the stated goal. Each ELA includes complete instructions for facilitating the intervention and a clear statement of goals, suggested group size and timing, materials required, an explanation of the process, and, where appropriate, possible variations to the activity. (For more detail on Experiential Learning Activities, see the Introduction to the *Reference Guide to Handbooks and Annuals*, 1999 edition, Pfeiffer, San Francisco.)

GAME A group activity that has the purpose of fostering team spirit and togetherness in addition to the achievement of a pre-stated goal. Usually contrived—undertaking a desert expedition, for example—this type of learning method offers an engaging means for participants to demonstrate and practice business and interpersonal skills. Games are effective for team building and personal development mainly because the goal is subordinate to the process—the means through which participants reach decisions, collaborate, communicate, and generate trust and understanding. Games often engage teams in "friendly" competition.

ICEBREAKER A (usually) short activity designed to help participants overcome initial anxiety in a training session and/or to acquaint the participants with one another. An icebreaker can be a fun activity or can be tied to specific topics or training goals. While a useful tool in itself, the icebreaker comes into its own in situations where tension or resistance exists within a group.

INSTRUMENT A device used to assess, appraise, evaluate, describe, classify, and summarize various aspects of human behavior. The term used to describe an instrument depends primarily on its format and purpose. These terms include survey, questionnaire, inventory, diagnostic, survey, and poll. Some uses of instruments include providing instrumental feedback to group members, studying here-and-now processes or functioning within a group, manipulating group composition, and evaluating outcomes of training and other interventions.

Instruments are popular in the training and HR field because, in general, more growth can occur if an individual is provided with a method for focusing specifically on his or her behavior. Instruments also are used to obtain information that will serve as a basis for change and to assist in workforce planning efforts.

Paper-and-pencil tests still dominate the instrument landscape with a typical package comprising a facilitator's guide, which offers advice on administering the instrument and interpreting the collected data, and an initial set of instruments. Additional instruments are available separately. Pfeiffer, though, is investing heavily in e-instruments. Electronic instrumentation provides effortless distribution and, for larger groups particularly, offers advantages over paper-and-pencil tests in the time it takes to analyze data and provide feedback.

LECTURETTE A short talk that provides an explanation of a principle, model, or process that is pertinent to the participants' current learning needs. A lecturette is intended to establish a common language bond between the trainer and the participants by providing a mutual frame of reference. Use a lecturette as an introduction to a group activity or event, as an interjection during an event, or as a handout.

MODEL A graphic depiction of a system or process and the relationship among its elements. Models provide a frame of reference and something more tangible, and more easily remembered, than a verbal explanation. They also give participants something to "go on," enabling them to track their own progress as they experience the dynamics, processes, and relationships being depicted in the model.

ROLE PLAY A technique in which people assume a role in a situation/scenario: a customer service rep in an angry-customer exchange, for example. The way in which the role is approached is then discussed and feedback is offered. The role play is often repeated using a different approach and/or incorporating changes made based on feedback received. In other words, role playing is a spontaneous interaction involving realistic behavior under artificial (and safe) conditions.

SIMULATION A methodology for understanding the interrelationships among components of a system or process. Simulations differ from games in that they test or use a model that depicts or mirrors some aspect of reality in form, if not necessarily in content. Learning occurs by studying the effects of change on one or more factors of the model. Simulations are commonly used to test hypotheses about what happens in a system—often referred to as "what if?" analysis—or to examine best-case/worst-case scenarios.

THEORY A presentation of an idea from a conjectural perspective. Theories are useful because they encourage us to examine behavior and phenomena through a different lens.

TOPICS

The twin goals of providing effective and practical solutions for workforce training and organization development and meeting the educational needs of training and human resource professionals shape Pfeiffer's publishing program. Core topics include the following:

Leadership & Management

Communication & Presentation

Coaching & Mentoring

Training & Development

E-Learning

Teams & Collaboration

OD & Strategic Planning

Human Resources

Consulting

What will you find on pfeiffer.com?

- The best in workplace performance solutions for training and HR professionals

- Downloadable training tools, exercises, and content

- Web-exclusive offers

- Training tips, articles, and news

- Seamless on-line ordering

- Author guidelines, information on becoming a Pfeiffer Affiliate, and much more

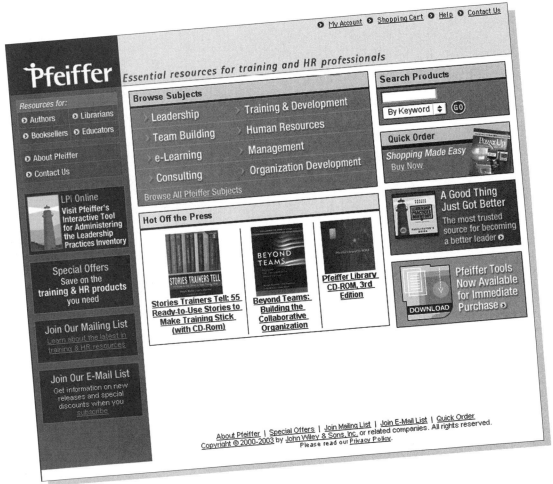

Discover more at www.pfeiffer.com